John Harrison's award-winning trav~~el writing~~ *ad, Where the Earth Ends* and *Forg~~~~* ~~~~ ourneys in South America and Antar~~~~  er Cordell Travel Writing Prize twice ~~~~ ard twice (the outright English lang~~~~ Creative Non-fiction category in 2~~~~ ~~~~ recent book *Forgotten Footprints* won the narrative book of the year award from the British Guild of Travel Writers. When not guiding and driving powerboats in polar regions, or traveling for his own interests, he lives in London and is a Fellow of the Royal Geographical Society.

PARTHIAN

1519

A JOURNEY TO THE END OF TIME

John Harrison

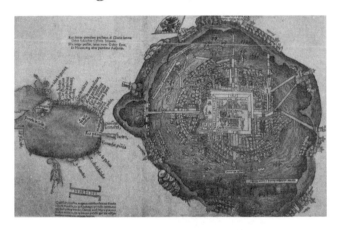

The more you try to describe the minute detail, the more confused the reader will become, and the more the reality of the thing itself recedes.
LEONARDO DA VINCI

PARTHIAN

Parthian, Cardigan SA43 1ED
www.parthianbooks.com
First published in 2015
© John Harrison 2015
© Illustrations John Harrison
© Maps Rob Harries
ISBN 9781910409800
Editor: Francesca Rhydderch
Cover design by www.theundercard.co.uk
Typeset by Elaine Sharples
Printed and bound by Dinefwr Press, Llandybie, Wales
Published with the financial support of the Welsh Books Council
British Library Cataloguing in Publication Data
A cataloguing record for this book is available from the British Library.

Celia: For Being There

In the sky, a moon
on your face, a mouth.
In the sky, many stars
on your face, only two eyes.

POEM, OTOMÍ CULTURE

Contents

The Maya Creation Story

Popol Vuh, the *Book of the People*

This is the account of when all is still, silent and placid. The face of the earth has not yet appeared. Alone lies the expanse of the sea, along with the womb of all the sky. There is not yet anything gathered together. All is at rest. Nothing stirs. All is languid, at rest in the sky. There is not yet anything standing erect. Only the expanse of the water, only the tranquil sea lies alone. There is not yet anything that might exist. All lies placid and silent in the darkness, in the night.

Journal of Christopher Columbus
13 and 14 October 1492, the first two days after landfall in the Americas

The people are also very gentle. Since they long to possess something of ours, when they have nothing, all that they do possess, they give.

They can all be carried off to Castile or held captive in the island itself, since with fifty men they could all be held in subjection and forced to do whatever may be wished.

Part 1

The Anvil in the Sea

1. General Map of Central and Southern Mexico

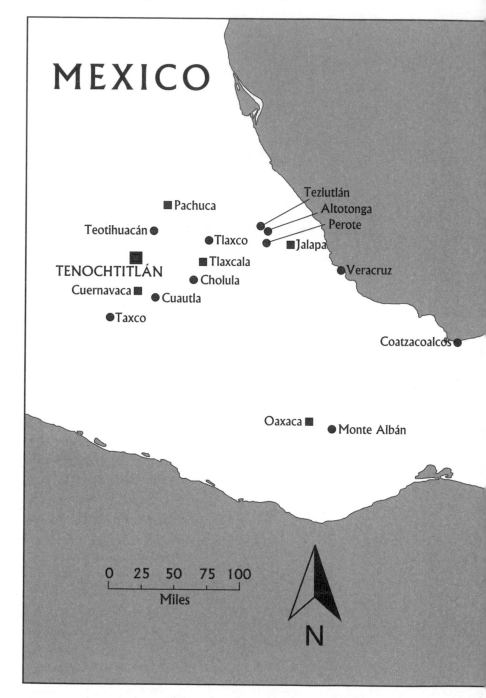

MEXICO

■ Pachuca

Teotihuacán ●

Teziutlán
Altotonga
Perote

● Tlaxco

■ Jalapa

TENOCHTITLÁN

■ Tlaxcala

● Cholula

● Veracruz

Cuernavaca ■

● Cuautla

● Taxco

Coatzacoalcos ●

Oaxaca ■ ● Monte Albán

0   25   50   75   100

Miles

N

1

To Begin at the End

Time is about to end. Again.

I woke in my room above the lagoon of Río Lagartos, on top of the Yucatán peninsula, with a sharp wind whistling at the windows. Sixty-five million years ago, a large meteorite struck the sea beyond the lagoon and exploded, throwing our planet into twilight, killing the dinosaurs, and creating opportunities for puny creatures called mammals to prosper. The disaster opened the door for the evolution of humans.

Magnificent frigatebirds posted unmistakable silhouettes: a long, deeply-forked tail, and angular wings, longer than those of all but the greatest albatrosses, which jut forward at the central joint on the leading edge of the each wing. They streaked past at eye-level, pterosaur shapes slipping through time cracks to cast Jurassic shadows on the earth. Below me boats were bumping each other and the stocky wooden piers, but when I went onto the terrace the wind was warm, and chinks of sun were wedging open the low clouds and prising them apart, lighting up stripes of ripples on the lagoon.

This is Mexico, where time runs in cycles. Because time is cyclic, beginnings are also endings, and endings are beginnings. Aztec and Maya historians looked at unfolding events, which had all happened before, and studiously corrected errors in ancient accounts, to better understand them the next time they came round.

I was planning my last excursion after four months' travelling through Mexico in the footsteps not just of the Conquistadors, but of the first Americans, who ruled sophisticated cities and empires dating back to the time of Homer. I tried to rein in my excitement because today was chancy. I had tried to reach Cabo Catoche four months ago. On my maps, every road coming from the east petered out. The sea was no easier. Currents, coral and limestone reefs maze the shallows: tinglingly beautiful but able to tear a hull apart. I wanted to get there because the first real contact between people of the continental New World and the Old took place along this coast, at the north-east corner of the Yucatán Peninsula, the anvil on which the Caribbean beats. Cabo Catoche is the name that Spanish ears heard when they came ashore here, and listened to the Maya saying *Cones catoche*: that is 'Come to our houses.' The hand that wrote down those words for us belonged to twenty-four-year-old Bernal Díaz, and without this literate soldier, our picture of the human contact between these two worlds would usually remain monochrome. He can make it blaze into colour; he can touch your heart not just for the grandeur that was destroyed, but also for the working soldiers, racked by wounds and fevers, who tore the riches to the ground, and trampled on them in patched-up sandals.

In 1517, three ships under Díaz's commander, Francisco de Córdoba, were probing westwards along the Yucatán Peninsula. By 4 March they were twenty-five days into the voyage. One of the ships had been bought on credit from the Governor of Cuba, Diego Velázquez, accompanied by his illegal demand that they take slaves from other islands to pay him. They refused. A contemporary of Velázquez with no grudge against him defined him as 'covetous of honour, but even more so of wealth.' Velázquez became the sponsor, then the persecutor of Hernàn Cortés, who would force his way across Mexico with Velázquez's hirelings snarling at his heels.

Cabo Catoche seemed impossible to get to. I looked again at satellite images on my iPad. There was a road from the west heading twenty miles to Cabo Catoche, but it was a sand track, crossed by rivers and cut by the necks of lagoons. Zooming in on the satellite imaging, I saw that if I could get to Holbox Island, I might reach Cabo Catoche from the sea.

In a packed *colectivo,* a stop-on-demand minibus, patient locals made room for my backpack among sacks and a second-hand microwave. Someone hailed the man in the front seat as *Pachoyo!*, Maya for driver. In fifty minutes I was behind *Willy's* supermarket in the little town of Tizimin, looking for the bus to Chaquilá, the ferry port for Holbox Island.

Holbox is a chill-out and dive centre whose selling point is the chance to swim with whale sharks, but it was not the season for the world's largest fish, and things were quiet. It had been raining hard, and water filled the sandy streets which, four or five town blocks to the north, meet the opposite shore. Two months before, a high tide, fuelled by a storm surge driven before a cold front, had poured through the streets of the island's only village, from shore to shore.

Local fisherman Pablo captained a fibreglass boat with new twin sixty horse-power Yamaha engines. He knew Cabo Catoche and could take me there. I mentioned another place, Bahía Iglesia, or Church Bay.

There was a change in his eye. He said, 'No one ever goes there.' 'Have you been there?' I asked.

'Yes, but it was,' he paused and frowned, as if surprised by his own recollection, 'over twenty years ago.'

'Is the church still there?'

'Who knows?'

A Spanish Colonial church from the early 1500s was buried in the mangrove swamps.' I want to go to Catoche and the church.'

He said, 'Yes, but not today.' Hope shrivelled.

'East wind. In Holbox we have some lee, but the channels leading to the church are on the other side of Cabo Catoche.'

I drive small craft myself. Conditions did not look tough for a twenty-foot boat. Was he trying to avoid going?

I had two further days left. He didn't like the next day either, but late in the afternoon, the wind fell, and squadrons of brown pelicans, flying in lines offshore, passed by lower and slower. Tomorrow would be my last chance.

At dawn I swam. A great egret on an offshore rock let me glide closely by, the yellow eye-ring circling the dark pupil. It was calm.

Pablo was fifty-five, wiry, with neat hair, a striped polo shirt, and cut-off denim shorts. We planed east along the seaward side of Isla Holbox. The sky was ultramarine, and the sea pale jade. Neo-tropic cormorants squibbed underwater, and burst back into the light, cowls of water sheering from their olive plumage.

7

I pictured how the shore would look if, like the Spanish, I had been nearly a month at sea, out of Cuba: mute. The land seen from the sea gives away nothing about the interior. The edge of the limestone plateau which forms the body of the Yucatán is low, but Holbox is two-dimensionally flat. It forms a slender island a mile wide, extended west like a cricket's leg from the peninsula's north-east corner, enclosing a shallow lagoon five miles north to south. The beach is white sand the width of a dirt road. No land rises over thirty feet, so the hinterland was invisible. Outside the village, the skyline is not the tropical signature of palm fronds lazing on slender grey trunks. All that presents itself to any stranger, seeking explanations, or at least clues, is a soft fuzz of feathery cypress branches whisking the air. But from their ships' masts, perhaps fifty feet up, the Spanish spied a town bigger than any encountered in twenty-five years' exploration of the Caribbean. 'This land was as yet undiscovered,' said Díaz, but they would hear cries they did not heed, telling them they were not the first.

The Spanish model for alien culture was the Moors, so they called this town 'the Great Cairo.' On the morning of 4 March, ten large dugout canoes, left the shore with up to forty men in them, and approached under sail and oar, displaying no fear. More than thirty men boarded the Spanish flagship, where they showed great interest in its construction. The Spanish offered each a string of green beads: a fortunate choice, since green stones enjoyed high status among the Maya.

Whatever was communicated was done by sign language. The Maya chief would return next day with enough canoes to ferry them ashore, which he did 'with a smiling face and every appearance of friendliness'. The Spanish would not have known they had landed on an island, or that they were not walking to the Great Cairo, which was on the other side of the lagoon.

They took all the arms they could carry, including steel swords, crossbows and muskets: all unknown in the New World. They followed a road until it reached some low hillocks, where the chief yelled an order. The first flight of arrows wounded thirteen Spanish. The Maya followed up with lances, and slings, which at close quarters were as effective as muskets. The Spanish unleashed a counter-attack and drove off their attackers, leaving fifteen of them dead. They also seized two Natives both cross-eyed which the Maya considered a sign of beauty. The Spaniards' treatment of them set the tone for the next three hundred years. They were not treated as citizens of sovereign states, or prisoners of war. They were baptised and re-named, like pets or livestock: Julian and Melchior. We do not now know their real names.

There is no doubting Spanish courage. They marched on, into enemy territory, reaching a small square with masonry temples, containing gold and copper items which they stole, along with ceramic figures 'which seemed to represent Indians committing sodomy.' Detecting sodomy would become an obsession, because it was a hallmark stamping the practitioners with heresy, and heretics had no rights.

Cabo Catoche was marked by a lighthouse until the storm of November 2013 smashed the tower into the sea, where it measures its length in broken masonry. As we moored at the short pier, made from bags of sand and cement laid in the water, brown pelicans shuffled from one paddle-sized foot to another.

Behind the pier stood the ground-floor offices of the lighthouse and alongside it the twisted pylon of its radio tower. A homemade ladder gave access to the roof. When I straightened it to climb, it hinged into a line of lozenges. Pablo reminded me where the nearest hospital was, and I settled for visiting the offices. The seaward doors had held firm and the interior was orderly. I was leafing through the keeper's maintenance record for 1912, when the door opened and a muscular man entered, bare-chested because his shirt was tied across his face. He was holding a long knife and a piece of steel. He growled, then dropped his shirt to reveal grinning teeth in a black beard.

'Pablo!'

'Luis!'

Pablo embraced him. 'Luis is a fisherman; they make camp here to cook and sleep.' We shook hands. I saw that the length of steel was a long pair of barbecue tongs. I picked round their camp, the floor strewn with coconuts, delivered by gravity, and piles of empty bottles of vodka, gin and *Sol* beer.

After this skirmish, the Spanish sailed on. It was a reconnaissance mission, and their chief pilot was convinced the Yucatán Peninsula was an island, plausible given its very low relief and swift coastal currents.

Pablo and I continued east to the more remote inlet of Bahía Iglesia. The cypresses thinned, and the mangrove trees crowded closer to the sea, compressing the beach. Here and there a Maya-style hut appeared with an oval plan and thatched roof. Pablo edged up to a homemade buoy topped by a ballroom mirror ball, and marking the entrance to two broad channels. The mangroves stepped out on their angular roots into the brackish water, slowing the current, causing more mud to be deposited. It was colonising the sea, abetting the land to creep out and smother it.

Pablo nosed slowly in; forked choices opened up. I crouched in the bow watching for sandbanks, observing the current comb the head-sized clumps of weed; small fish wove through gorgon hair. The channel narrowed, but he kept on; branches on either side began to touch, then interlace. A dislodged lizard fell in my lap. The channel entered a pool with no outlet. We tracked every channel. They all closed on us. Pablo slid from quiet confidence to head-shaking. 'The church is over there,' he waved an arm towards the heart of the labyrinth. 'But, twenty years, it's grown so much. Everything is narrower.'

He went up the coast a mile before heading into an even remoter channel. We were soon pushing mangrove branches off our heads again. Each probe ended with us wedged tight, and the boat was a pig to reverse. Pablo was one of those rare people who can be taciturn without seeming unfriendly, but I could see what he was thinking, and wasn't surprised when he said, 'The tide has started to fall. There is one more place, but it is very shallow.' We backtracked two miles into the main lagoon through a channel so shallow that an egret fifty yards out from the mangrove was standing only ankle deep. There was a faint stippling on the surface of lagoon, because every few yards a single shoot stood like a thin whip with a bud at the tip. The mangrove had seeded across the entire lagoon; it would soon be land, and the church a folk-tale. In the middle of the lagoon, he slowed to a crawl and I heard the stems of the engines rasping through the sediments, before we returned to deeper water. With four o'clock approaching, our deadline if we were to return in daylight, I saw something rising above the vegetation. There was a slight ridge running along the mainland shore, and at its high point a small block of masonry: my binoculars showed me a church tower.

We anchored in a shallow bay, took off our shoes, and I tried not to think about the soft things my toes felt in the glue-like sediments. The shore was a two-yard wide band of stinking black mud, then some stinking brown mud, then a narrow trail. In ten yards it was dry and we were gently climbing through woodland when, through the underbrush, I glimpsed ruins.

I was walking back five hundred years into free-floating time, to the brief years in which the only the fringes of the Americas were known to Europeans. A pile of stones and a huddle of men were left here with the task of completing the conversion of the heathens of two continents.

The friars, with their subject Natives, laboured in the hardest of conditions to build something that mattered to them, that would stop their own souls from disappearing into the maw of malevolent time. As the Spanish arrived in the New World, eight hundred years of Arab rule in Spain had just ended. On 6 January 1492, four days after the surrender of Grenada, the young Caliph Boabdil gave the keys of the Alhambra Palace to Queen Isabela of Castile and King Ferdinand of Aragon. The heretic Moors were driven out or forced to convert, and Moorish tolerance was also expelled; before the end of year, the Jews were given the same option. Spanish armies had triumphed in Italy, and their ships were opening up West Africa, and colonising the Canaries. In the Americas, a new hemisphere of creation had been revealed to them by God. The world was approaching its culmination, the last work was to convert all those Natives who would listen to his word. Columbus had pored endlessly over religious works to calculate

11

the timing of the last days, and concluded they were coming in 1650. Many agreed.

God would draw the ages of the world to a close. There could be no further use for the earth, and the physical universe would be destroyed. Experiment over; close the laboratory. Mesoamerican time, in the lands from Central Mexico down to Costa Rica, would revolve through its final cycle until the end of the fifth sun. Four have already passed. So Spanish time and Aztec time were ending; two cultures were acting out the last days.

This religious duty was all the more remarkable because few came to help. There were often more churches than friars. I would like to summarise the history of Bahía Iglesia, but I found none, except it seems to have been abandoned after 1650: that date again. Ahead, on the right, was a half-clearing with rough stone masonry. I stepped over a low wall and into a yard. I first took the ruins to be a church, but I soon realised there was no tower; this was not the building I had seen from the lagoon. Ducking under a stone lintel, I entered another yard which led into two dark strong-rooms, with small windows still barred by crude wooden poles. This block was their store and dormitory.

The trail passed by the side of these, veered left, and continued up the gentle slope. Two zebra-winged butterflies circled me before disappearing into the forest on stuttering wing-beats. Caterpillars for so long, they revelled in the miracle of flight, briefly given. I felt a deeper silence waiting. Sunlight on the path ahead signalled a clearing. In a moment I was staring at the massive tower of a church. The nave was roofless and, with knee-high vegetation, had the air of a neglected vegetable garden. The altar and transepts were almost intact, though dilapidated; no one lived near enough to rob the stone, precious in this region. My boots disturbed the ground and, recognising the sharp smell, I looked up. Needle eyes stared down from a ceiling carpeted with brown velvet knuckles: bats, symbols of death and darkness. Because in flight they pluck fruits from a tree, fruit bats were associated in Native cultures with decapitation and sacrifice.

The church was a dream strangled by the relentless gods of

vegetation, of the cycle of death and rebirth, of time that seemed to pass, but just went round and round, going nowhere: a victory for the older gods.

Pablo kept looking at his watch. The tide was still falling over the sandbanks we had barely scraped over an hour before.

Contemplating the ruins at Bahía Iglesia, I wondered whether their confidence in setting up in this green wilderness was a touching sign of unshakeable faith, a project of the highest hubris, or just plain mad. 1650 has come and gone, and domesday is always approaching but never arrives.

The Maya creation myth, the *Popol Vuh* describes the creation as if it is happening in real time in front of the author and the reader, which is as it should be. A myth is something that happened before time, something that never happened and something that is always happening. It is truer than the things that happen in secular life and time, so it does not fall away into the past with them, it lodges in time, in us.

But time is not real. From Immanuel Kant to Albert Einstein, philosophers and physicists have argued that time is a frame we put on reality, not a property that exists outside us. Quantum mechanics is the physics of the nano-world where the properties of atoms give way to the properties of their parts. There are theories in quantum mechanics which set out to describe the universe, but have no need of time in their equations to do so. The universe does not need it.

The tower is a testament to the strength of purpose of the Spanish. It endures, over 350 years after they thought the universe would end. The tower speaks of both their will and their hubris, but it was not mad. Pablo and I were speaking Spanish; the people are mostly Catholic. They succeeded, but like most ventures, not in the way either party intended.

In the middle of the lagoon, I stepped out of the boat and walked alongside for twenty yards while Pablo winced as his expensive outboards scraped over the sand. I took one last look back at the circle of green trees stretching as far as the eye could see to east and west, broken only by the single stone tower's serrated top. Perhaps just a little mad.

When the boat came alongside the low pier at Holbox, the sun had gone and the last light silhouetted the palms along the soft sand. I stripped off and went for my final swim; the warm air and the silk stroke of the water rising up and over my skin were especially delicious, because I was, on the best medical opinion, supposed to be dead.

2

A Shadow on My Mind

On the Saturday of the Notting Hill Carnival I was alone in the London heat, my partner Celia out of town. I left Hyde Park where, propped against a tree, I had been reading something as stuffy as the day, and crossed the Bayswater Road. In Clarendon Place I passed the beige brick house built for himself by the architect Giles Gilbert Scott, designer of the classic K2 London phone box. It was so hot the pavement began to sag beneath my feet.

I stopped. It was firm again. I walked on a few strides and reached another patch where I felt I was crossing a slack trampoline. I went into the Kendal pub thinking that if I already had a drunken walk, a beer would do me no harm, knowing in perfect parallel this was nonsense, but I was rattled. I drank two pints of Greene King IPA and began the short walk home. The pavement remained solid. In two days Celia returned. I did not tell her.

Over the following weeks, parts of the pavement sagged again; I blamed Westminster Council. When the grass in the park could not always support my weight, I blamed the Royal Parks. When it began happening nearly every day, I told Celia, then my GP.

Two questions get you through year one of medical school. 'Do you smoke?' asked the locum.

'Never smoked.'

'How much alcohol do you drink?' I gave an answer which satisfied him, thanks to my ability to divide by three. Eyes, ears and mouth were opened, and a small flashlight delved.

Blood tests showed raised prolactin levels. 'Have you noticed any discharge from your nipples?' He was a fresh-faced Chinese

Australian in his early thirties, chubby in an asexual way. He could shave in a minute.

'No,' I said.

I was sent to the Chelsea and Westminster Hospital for tests on my muscles. I envisaged soft pads and minute currents which would make my skin tingle. He produced a long needle which he slid into my flesh in many places. He said, 'Very good.' But he was holding the blunt end of the needle.

It wasn't the muscles.

X-rays were taken of my head. The consultant, James Audley, who talked me through them, was slim and well over six foot tall, suave in a natural, low-key way, who spoke in a received English accent with a warm nasal resonance. I looked at the pictures of my skull, the sharp bones of the nose and sinus, the smooth sweeping lines of the cranium and the tight meanders of the suture lines joining its plates: rivers on the moon. If it had been an X-ray of my foot or my arms I would not have thought of mortality, but it was my skull, so I became Hamlet. In that cavity, the size of my two fists, my brain stored all my experience of the universe: harm this tissue, and my universe disappears. Doctor Audley pointed to an area slightly to the front of the centre of my brain. 'That is the pituitary gland, it releases hormones that control your other hormone glands. Below it is a shadow. That's not normal. That's what we are interested in. It doesn't belong.'

A shadow. No. I am not ready. Never will be.

'We need a better look at it. X-rays show bones very well. For soft tissue we need an MRI scan, and we have a brand new machine, the best.'

I lay in a mobile scanner unit outside St Mary's Hospital, Paddington, beneath the second-storey corner room where Alexander Fleming discovered penicillin. A nearby pub where he drank after work is named after him, dating from the days when doctors could admit to going to pubs. It is a gentle downhill slope to Sussex Gardens, to rooms by the hour, and women who are the subject of regular liaison meetings between the Hyde Park Residents' Association and local police. I lay still, as instructed, for fear of having to repeat it, while the moving tube of the scanner banged above me, as close to my face as the lid of a coffin. For thirty minutes there was nothing to do but think about the shadow.

On 12 August I was back in Doctor Audley's consulting room. Looking back at my diary there is no mention of the shadow in the weeks preceding. I was blanking it. Outside, jack-hammers were breaking up concrete slabs on the vast building site at the side of Paddington Station.

'I have your results.' He would now tell me in his warm voice how long my life might run. He leaned forward towards the screen. 'Today is our first morning with a new improved computer system, and of course it is much slower than the old one.' We waited. My skull appeared. The MRI scan showed very clearly the pea-sized pituitary, half a gram determining whether I have testosterone and virility, or a discharge from my nipples. Below it, and larger, lay the shadow. He clicked on zoom and the shadow grew. 'About the size of a walnut. It's impossible to say how long it's been there: at least a few years; maybe all your adult life. You may have been born with it.'

Is the shadow my excuse for me sometimes finding life difficult, my impatience – this presence that might be pressing on my brain?

He consoled me with: 'There is much good news.'

(No need to worry about my three years' missing National Insurance contributions? Or maybe shorter term: no need to waste money on new winter socks.)

'The image is soft. It's not firm tissue; it's definitely benign ...' Benign is a beautiful word.

'It's probably a cyst filled with fluid. But it is in a good position; if it should turn malignant we can get at it from the front without disturbing the brain. We used to do terrible things, such as lift the brain to one side to have a look. Wonderful thing, MRI.'

A benign shadow accompanying me through life for sixty years. 'We'll keep an eye on it.'

I'll buy warm socks.

But I was not done with scans.

17

2. Routes of Córdoba and Grijalva

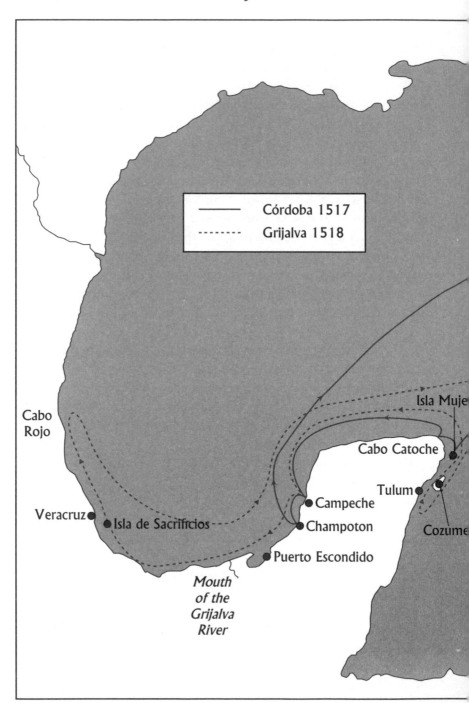

Córdoba 1517
Grijalva 1518

Cabo
Rojo

Isla Muje[res]

Cabo Catoche

Tulum

Veracruz ● Isla de Sacrifcios ● Campeche

Cozume[l]

● Champoton

● Puerto Escondido

*Mouth
of the
Grijalva
River*

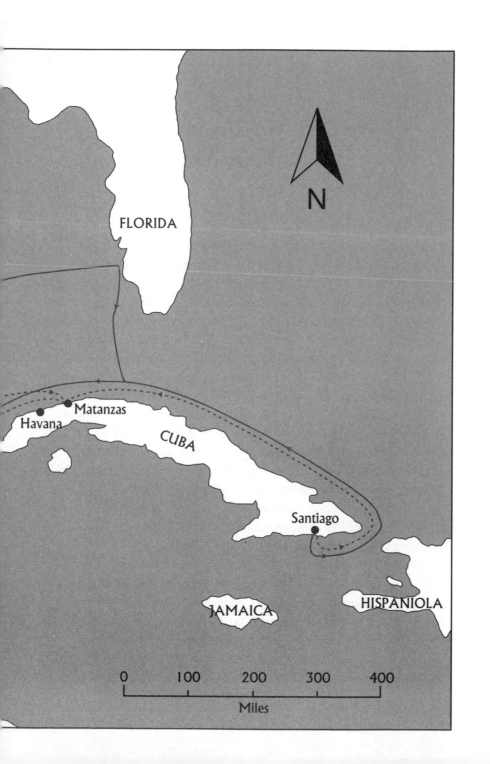

3

We Did Not Understand
What They Meant

After the ambush at Cabo Catoche, the Spanish, on Díaz's admission, 'went forward very cautiously, sailing by day and anchoring by night'. I followed them overland, to see the land as they had seen it, to look at the places they had come ashore, to build a mental stage and lead the actors onto the boards. In the closing pages of *The Great Gatsby*, Scott Fitzgerald wrote of European sailors first seeing the New World: '[F]or a transitory enchanted moment man must have held his breath in the presence of this continent, compelled into an aesthetic contemplation he neither understood nor desired, face to face for the last time in history with something commensurate to his capacity for wonder.' The key words are 'nor desired'. The Spanish did not know what they had found, either in terms of the limitless land, almost as large as Asia, or of peoples. Land is simpler. New people bring disturbing questions. First the explorer asks, *What are you?* Then *What are we?* Questions breed other questions. Nothing will be the same again. In this journey, I wanted to explore this rupture in human thought, forced on humankind by the discovery of the Americas.

There was another question which each generation answers differently. How could a few hundred Spanish conquer millions of Native Americans? I did not buy the story I was told at school, which many popular histories still present as true: superior civilisations progress more rapidly and conquer inferior ones.

Columbus's great voyage of 1492 was not a dramatic leap, before which everyone crept timidly along the coast. Of course most voyages were as commercial and routine as a modern container ship's, but there had long been exploratory forays looking for new business opportunities. By 1341, Europeans had reached the Canary Islands. Less than a century later they were in the Azores, whose western outpost, Flores, is 1200 miles from both Newfoundland and Lisbon: they were halfway to America.

Díaz's boss, Córdoba, hoped to expand west from their base in Cuba, plodding along the Mexican coast at walking pace, averaging about twenty miles a day, anchoring each night. They were desperately low on water. Short of funds, they had economised on cheap barrels which leaked. After fifteen more days, they saw a large town located in an open bay. The town is once again known by its Native name: Campeche.

After the plains of Yucatán, there was a shock as my bus neared Campeche: hills, not big, just enough to anchor the rudderless eye. Small quarries, sliced into their flanks, exposed fresh, bright limestone. Glimpses of steely sea cooled the gaze.

The modern city is home to 210,000 people, so I was not expecting the same view as Córdoba's lookout, but it has a historic centre where the old has been well renovated and the new located elsewhere. Pastel colours dominate, with architectural details picked out in white. The guidebook called it a Colonial fairyland: you will, it said, 'wonder if it's a real city', which made me concerned that if the writer visited Oxford he might expire from an attack of the vapours. One reason it is unspoiled is the problem faced by its first tourists in 1517: 'On these bays or inlets the water drops very considerably at low tide. So we had to leave our ships anchored more than three miles offshore.' It is far too shallow for modern ships, so the old port area, around my hotel, is unspoiled and, due to reclamation, dry. The Hotel Campeche's facade had undergone a heritage makeover in white and Wedgwood blue, but its reception was reassuringly Mexican. Three women whose bodies were tributes to the constraining power of Lycra pants sat at reception devouring a takeaway. The desk was strewn with tortilla crumbs and drops of sweet and sour sauce. A man as thin as a photograph brought a cooked chicken, which he put in the middle of the table. Without pausing to look at him the women tore the bird to pieces and went on feeding.

'I would like a room,' I said, to give them a hint as to why a stranger with luggage stood before them. One slid a sticky key across the desk. 'Try number fifteen.' It fell on the floor. She left it for me to pick up.

Inside the seventeenth-century city walls, built after a particularly fierce pirate raid, the Colonial era customs house on the corner of the plaza was being excavated by archaeologists. Two large sections of the city wall survive as do seven of the eight forts that once commanded it. Until the 1950s, each high tide lapped at the other side of the walls, then a promenade was built out on reclaimed land. A short taxi ride took me to the northerly of Campeche's two satellite forts, San José del Alto, on Bellavista Hill. The low fort with pepper-pot turrets corbelled out at each corner sits behind a stone-lined moat. From this hill, I could see the kind of landscape which Córdoba might have seen. Marshes stretched north along the curve of a flat coast with irregular, featureless bays fringed with mangroves that gave way inland to true forest wherever the ground rose a few feet. It offered no encouragement to man to land or linger.

It rained hard in the afternoon, but being rinsed by the rain was a pleasant feeling after being clammy with sweat in the jungles of the interior. When evening came, I realised that until now it had not been rain at all, just a little mist, for now the rain doubled and then stepped up to full cloudburst. The spouts from the gutters spattered onto the hotel courtyard like wet feet slapping. I was the first customer in a restaurant with a stone arcade in dressed limestone, whose proprietor, Leo, sported a Ramon Navarro moustache. Above the bar was a collage of Mexican film stars from the forties and fifties, and he struck a pose against the counter, inviting favourable comparisons. Patrolling the floor in a faintly camp manner, half stage-gaucho, half chorus-hoofer, he tried to drum up trade among the well-to-do locals returning from shopping, running hunched through the downpour to their four-wheel drives. Unlike the shoppers, he would not hurry his graceful walk, and he always arrived just after they had dived into the smoked-glass interiors. As

I ate, he leaned against a pillar of the arcade, the street light behind creating a corona round his profile. 'The rain must be done by the end of October.' He sounded like Rex Harrison decreeing the climate for Camelot.

When Córdoba and Díaz landed here, torn between caution and brute thirst, they landed using their boats and the smallest ship, carrying all the arms they could muster. They found a pool of clear water and began filling the barrels. Before they could finish, a party of fifty local people from the nearby town came peacefully, dressed in graceful cotton cloaks which impressed the Spanish, who were used to Caribbean islands where near-naked people lived in huts. Lack of clothing was, like sodomy, another sign of being uncivilised, even if it did not quite make you a heretic.

Spanish curiosity had been blunted by the treachery at Cape Catoche, but after an exchange in sign language, the Natives spoke a single word to them, repeating it.

'Castilan! Castilan!'

They were asking if they came from Castile, even though the shore party had never uttered that word.

The locals invited them to their town, and after discussion, the Spanish agreed. 'They led us to some very large buildings of fine masonry which were the prayer-houses of their idols, the walls of which were painted with the figures of serpents and evil-looking gods. In the middle was something like an altar, covered in clotted blood, and on the other side of the idols were symbols like crosses, and all were coloured. It appeared that they had just sacrificed some Indians to their idols, so as to ensure victory over us.'

Díaz was no stylist as a writer – modern translations smooth out his rough sentences – but he knew how to tell a story, because he then added, 'Many Indian women were strolling about most peacefully, laughing and amusing themselves.' Human sacrifice was normal, humdrum. Now priests appeared, their hair matted with blood from sacrifices, 'so it would have needed cutting before it could be combed and parted'. Some priests lit a small fire while others burned copal incense over the visitors, and signed that if the Spanish were still there when the fire burned out, they would be

23

killed. The Spanish had just thrown overboard the bodies of two men who had died of wounds sustained at Catoche. They 'decided to retire to the coast in good order'. Their hearts sank when they saw their landing area and boats surrounded by warriors, but they were allowed to board and leave. Oddly, all Díaz has to say about the extraordinary cry, *Castilan*, is that 'we did not understand what they meant'. The answer would be vital to their expedition' success.

The next town was Champoton, and it had a river, and a semblance of shelter in the estuary. They were concerned about the tides, and anchored three miles out.

The bus from Campeche to Champoton runs inland before returning to the coast for the last ten miles. The rain finally stopped, and the fields came to life as horses and cattle left the shelter of trees to graze. Great egrets, elegant art nouveaux assassins, fished the pools and lagoons. The shadows of turkey vultures passed over them, the black chic of their primary feathers extended in flares, seeking the thermals' up-draughts. The bus entered Champoton on a riverside road, followed it onto the coast, and turned left into a dark bus station. I found what seemed to be the town's only policeman, a kindly man who not only gave me directions to the *Hostal Emanuel,* but escorted me there. House rules were on the wall. Number five read: In the interests of hygiene please do not spit on the walls. Most of the others were about spitting too. To summarise, they were against it.

When Córdoba and Díaz arrived, no one had had the skill to repair the barrels, and water was again short. There followed a more grievous repetition of the encounter at Campeche. Drums beat. The Maya surrounded them, and attacked with arrows, darts and stones, quickly killing fifty Spanish. Córdoba suffered ten arrow wounds, and Díaz three, one of which pierced his ribs. The Spanish bravely drove through their attackers to the shore, but discipline had gone, and everyone tried to climb in the first boats, and they began to sink. Some men were towed back to the ships without ever getting in a boat. They abandoned all their barrels on the shore. There were no longer enough men to man all the ships, so one was burned.

They sailed on, parched, their tongues and mouths dried and

cracked. It was hard to know whether the injured were dying from wounds or thirst. After three days, a hasty shore party returned with full water barrels, which were found to hold undrinkable brine. They continued north, and on to Florida, arriving just in time to save most of their lives, though not that of Córdoba. Histories promoting the inevitable victory of the superior civilisation do not dwell on such episodes.

The survivors made their way back to Cuba, with their captive translators, Julian and Melchior, and the gold and copper work from Catoche's temple, which aroused Governor Velázquez's cupidity enough to finance another expedition under Juan de Grijalva, this time with three ships, a brigantine and 240 men. Díaz did not want to go, but as soon as he was back in Cuba he put all his money into a trading enterprise which went spectacularly wrong, and he had no choice.

They sailed from Cuba on 8 April 1518, with Julian and Melchior as translators. The officers included some names that would become famous, and others that would become infamous. The latter included Alonso de Ávila, Francisco de Montejo and Pedro de Alvarado, whom we will meet again with Cortés. Alvarado was a brave and tenacious soldier, from a family of impoverished nobles, who later became governor of Guatemala, but he was also a violent butcher and slaver. Very few surviving objects can be traced to individual conquistadors: characteristically, one fine piece of workmanship that belonged to Alvarado is four pounds of iron, possibly Italian, in the form of an engraved breastplate. I had stood before it in the British Museum, shuddering to imagine what gore had been spilled on it. An aura of danger plays around him. He was the same age as Cortés, who knew his worth and his limitations. He was the one man Cortés would not face out. Cortés liked to hunt with falcons; he named one Alvarado.

Drifting off course on the current, they made landfall near the north-east corner of the Yucatán, discovering the low, almost featureless island of Cozumel, meaning Island of Swallows, now a shopping town for passengers on behemoth cruise ships. Blue-collar Americans troop ashore in Hawaiian shirts, and hire golf carts to tour the island. When I visited, I took the forty-five minute ferry from the mainland resort of Playa del Carmen. My efforts to imagine the early Spanish there were helped by a replica sixteenth-century caravel moored next to two 80,000 ton cruise liners: a mouse posing in front of a pair of elephants.

I was met by tourist touts, friendly and unaggressive in the Mexican way. In 1518 the population hid. Grijalva found two old men hiding in a field because they were too infirm to run to the woods like everyone else. Díaz met a Jamaican woman who had been there two years after a fishing boat she was in drifted ashore on the same current. Her male companions had suffered an enforced career change, becoming human sacrifices. Grijalva abandoned ideas of contact and took the woman with them.

They cruised a short way south and discovered, on blinding white limestone cliffs, a remarkable town that was a late throwback to the Classic Maya culture of six centuries before: Tulum. If you have seen a poster of cliff-top Maya ruins above a white beach, that is Tulum. I visited in broiling humid heat, walking through modest temples and apartments. It was just a country town compared with the great Mayan cities of Tikal, Palenque and Copán, but most of the Spanish hailed from towns no greater. I lunched on bread and bananas on the picture-book beach, stalked by a beefy iguana who knew there was food in the sea, but found it a great deal more agreeable to mug picnickers.

For an era, the Maya culture had been interrupted by an influx of people who had interacted with the culture of the Mexico City area. They were the Itzá who built the staggering complex of Chichén Itzá in the heart of the Yucatán, now painstakingly recovered from the jungle. They were despised by the old Maya, suffering nicknames like 'the lewd ones' and 'people without fathers or mothers,' while their leader was 'he who butchers our language'.

This was not the high flowering of Maya culture that built the complexes of palaces, offices, temples and ball-game courts that draw visitors from all over the world. This was a late reversion to pride half-forgotten. But the Spanish saw a city with enclosing walls, and white-washed stone temples with gaudy murals. It was plainly a sophisticated culture, perhaps powerful. They did not make contact with the people of Tulum.

The appearance offshore of ships, to people who knew only rafts and canoes, must have been a disturbing sight that gnawed at memory. It was as though spacecraft were to hover above Hastings for an hour, then disappear. There would be time for everyone to hear of the apparition, and stare at things never seen before that refused to resolve themselves into any meaning.

The fleet sailed round the Yucatán, reaching Champoton, where Díaz would have remembered the fifty killed ashore on his previous voyage, and the six further corpses which followed, flung overboard as they died. The Spanish had learned that the Native 'armour', quilted jackets stuffed hard with cotton, was lighter and cooler than iron armour, and better at stopping arrows. Many Spanish now wore it, and when, as expected, they were attacked, sixty were injured but few died. The fields where they fought were full of small locusts, Díaz wrote, which the armies startled into flight. Soldiers ignored new volleys of arrows, mistaking them for more locusts. Grijalva had teeth broken by arrows, but with swords and crossbows they drove the attackers into a swamp. After the skirmish, the Spanish stayed three days, making gifts and trying to reassure them of their good intentions.

Champoton seemed a harmless place today, until I tried to get anything done. The ATM would not read my card, restaurants seemed as rare as hotels, so when I found a bar with comfortable seats and no one in it, I ordered an early evening beer from a tall, stout man around seventy years old, with a slow, grand manner about him. He asked for the money, which was odd, as everywhere ran tabs. I paid and put on my iPod to learn the lyrics to a Warren Zeavon song about Veracruz and Zapata. I had two verses, when the stout party wiped a finger across his military moustache, pointed at me, and said 'Come on, get out, I am closing.'

I said 'Fine, I'll just finish this and go.'

He said 'I am closing now.' Mexican bars keep strange hours, but I could not imagine any law required him to serve me a drink at 6:15 and throw me out at 6:20.

I won't say I had never been thrown out of a pub before, but I have usually been allowed time to drink and cause trouble first, and the last time was forty years ago. I looked round the room for clues as to why this might be happening. The walls were papered with handwritten notices, lamenting, dear customer that, times being what they were, this thing had to be brought to your attention. A little way along another screed pointed out a lapse in his customers' standards. They recorded all those matters of behaviour that require only a friendly hand on the shoulder and the words: 'Knock it off, Sunbeam.' This was not the proprietor's way; he wrote an editorial. He was what ethnographers call a prat.

Another man came in, also tall, but thin and greasy. They conferred and approached my table. He was about my age. I thought about three men with a combined age of two hundred, in a bar fight over the speed at which one bottle of beer should be drunk.

'Out!'

I thought I would keep it simple. 'No.' I could obviously play safe and go, but early training made it difficult to leave a drink I had paid for.

'I'll call the police,' said the stout party.

I thought of the kindly and small policeman who would remember me as the Gringo he had escorted to his hostel. He would find a sober tourist drinking what he had paid for. 'Go on then.'

The stout party's agricultural eyebrows shot up his face, 'Aren't you bothered?'

'No.' I put the earphones back in. I do not know how to say Mexican stand-off in Spanish, but I suppose we had one. I drank the fizzy beer as fast as I could without giving him the impression I was rushing because of him. I left, smiling at him, while quietly calling him names in English, something I am sure he guessed. I still have no idea what this was about.

Continuing west, Grijalva at last reached a fine harbour running deep into the land. They called it Puerto Escondido, or Hidden Port. Everywhere there were signs of abandoned homes. They took a greyhound bitch ashore and with her help hunted down ten deer and many rabbits. She became over-excited, and when it was time to sail could not be found. She was left to found her own colony. Around this time, a distant prince received a report of strangers on the coast and sent servants with gifts and a very disturbing order. 'If, by any chance, he does not like the food that you gave him, and is desirous of devouring human beings, and wishes to eat you, allow yourselves to be eaten.' The prince would look after their widows and orphans. He received reports of the Spaniards' every move.

The coast they now sailed is more hospitable with its harbours, but none is easy. All over Champoton's estuary I could pick out changes in the texture of the water surface caused by sand bars and shoals. At their next landing the locals had seen them in time to call in reinforcements from all over the region, and negotiated from a position of strength. They exchanged gifts, including small items of gold jewellery; the Natives did not overlook the way in which the Spaniards' eyes lit up at the sight of gold. Through Julian and Melchior, they explained it was all they had, but in the direction of the sunset there was much more. They pointed west and repeated '*Colua, Colua,*' and '*Mexico, Mexico.*'

They continued along the coast. At one point Alvarado was a little ahead and entered a large estuary, and traded for food. When Grijalva caught up, he tore a strip off him for his irresponsibility in going alone. Alvarado was showing himself once again to be a loose cannon.

Soon they were invited ashore, but Julian and Melchior could not understand the language because they had left Maya lands and were among speakers of Nahuatl, the language of the Aztecs. Grijalva took possession of the country in the name of his majesty Emperor Charles V. The Natives carried on with their daily lives. The Spaniards' own world was being challenged each day, seeing new animals, some, like armadillos, unlike any they'd ever seen. Questions would form in their minds. How, after Noah's ark landed on Mount Sinai, did these animals get here, across 4000 miles of ocean, and why were there none like them on the other continents?

Grijalva's modest fleet made its way up the coast until they were near modern Veracruz, having sailed about 900 miles from their first landfall at Cozumel. Five miles offshore, they saw an island, which they described as if it were substantial. The island is now a low discus of marine deposits on top of a reef, and it must have been heavily eroded in the last half millennium, for today it is no more than 350 yards long. Smoke was rising from fires, and they took boats ashore and, records Bernal Díaz, 'found two stone buildings of good workmanship, each with a flight of steps leading up to a kind of altar, and on those altars were evil-looking idols, which were their gods. Here we found five Indians who had been sacrificed to them on that very night. Their chests had been struck open and their arms and thighs cut off, and the walls of these buildings were covered in blood. We called this island the Isla de los Sacrificios, as it is now named on the charts.'

They went ashore and traded trifles with nervous Indians. Grijalva managed to sail without either side provoking a fight. He reached another island, now attached by reclamation to the mainland, in the heart of the port of Veracruz. They had found the best natural harbour on the coast. They also saw a temple to the god Tezcatlipoca, and the corpses of two boys, whose chests had been cut open and their hearts torn out. Governor Velázquez had given orders to 'settle if they dared and if the land was suitable for settlement.' Grijalva was now convinced this was continental land and wanted to stay. Many were unnerved, and disagreed; Díaz's no-nonsense verdict was 'We found the mosquitoes unbearable and realised we were wasting our time.'

A compromise sent Pedro de Alvarado back to Cuba with all the loot they had traded, and the rest stayed. 'Pedro de Alvarado was a good storyteller,' notes Díaz, 'and they say that Diego Velázquez could do nothing but embrace him.' They grew over-excited about jewellery which contained little metal, and caroused for eight days.

Back in Mexico, the expedition petered out, but before they left, Díaz, intending to return, planted orange pips. The priests at the local temple watched this, and watered and weeded the unfamiliar plants which grew from them. This was the introduction of the fruit to the New World. In forty-five days, Grijalva reached Cuba and presented the additional gold they had obtained since Alvarado's departure. Velázquez's greedy soul was roused, and surrounded by ambitious men, he began to fear that when the portion of one fifth, payable to the king, reached Spain and created a stir, he would be replaced by some court favourite. A second seed had been planted, nurturing the bitter fruit of envy.

4

The Utterances of Fools

Governor Diego Velázquez gathered ten ships for a new expedition. There was no shortage of capable leaders, but whom could Velázquez trust? His secretary Andrés de Duero and the royal accountant Amador de Lares praised a certain Hernán Cortés. Cortés's secretary Gómara claims 'they promptly reached an agreement'. The deal was much more devious. Cortés agreed to share his spoils with the officials, if they could secure his appointment as leader ahead of more obvious candidates.

Velázquez gave Cortés the job, and they walked together to church, with the new leader at the governor's right hand, to spell out the approval. A local buffoon nicknamed 'mad Cervantes' ran alongside them, goading the governor: 'Take care, Diego, or he may run off with your fleet, for he knows how to look after himself.' A good slapping from secretary Duero did not discourage the heckler, who taunted, 'I'd rather go off with him to these rich new lands than stay behind and watch you weeping over the bad bargain you have made today!'

Díaz commented: 'Moreover all that he said came true, as they say the utterances of fools often do.'

Cortés was an interesting character. The month before I went to Mexico, I toured his homeland of Extremadura in September, when the furnace of the southern Spanish summer had scarcely abated. I wanted to see their Old World, the hearths the Conquistadors had come from. I visited Trujillo, home of the Pizarro brothers, who conquered Peru eleven years after the fall of Mexico, and of Orellana, the discoverer of the Amazon. Then I went to Medellín, the rustic original after which the Columbian drugs capital is named.

It was home to the Pizarros' second cousins, the slightly more respectable Cortés clan.

In Trujillo, the dominant impression, even today, is that it was made by the Moors. I drove across the featureless Trujillo and Cáceres plain in eye-melting heat, and parked a couple of miles outside the town. I climbed a jumble of granite boulders, crumbling back into their constituent minerals; the sand under my shoes glittered with mica. An old saying goes: 'Whichever way you go to Trujillo, you have to walk a league of rocks.' From here, on the north-west side, the suffering fields ran up the slope to a 600-yard line of ramparts running the width of the hill, spiked in the centre by the towers of the church of Santa María la Mayor. It was formerly a mosque, and before that, a Visigothic temple.

The air was sibilant with a barely perceptible breeze tickling through dry grasses. In a stone hut hounds whined quietly, hoping the door would open and their master would take them hunting.

When the Visigoths secured Spain around 600 AD, Trujillo was one of its oldest cities. In the eighth century the Arabs wrested control of the area, and in the ninth century it was inhabited by Berbers. It changed hands between Christians and Moors until the final Moorish defeat in 1232. Local nobility, vying for pre-eminence, kept the town bellicose for another two hundred years. But the past leaned down on them. The walls that enclosed them each night, as the seven city gates shut, were built by the Moors. The gateway into the towering keep guarding them was through a Moorish arch pinched in at its springing points to form a keyhole shape. The water they drank every day came from Arab cisterns, founded on Roman structures. I came across their cool waters with sudden pleasure as I wound through the narrow streets. All around were reminders of how far the town's sons travelled: gardens where brown maize leaves chattered when the breeze stirred, and on every patch of scrub land heavily fruited prickly pear cactuses, native to Mexico, wound their destructive roots into buried masonry.

It was a poor world, worked by humble families. Those Pizarros who made it home paraded their loot in the small town they had come from, building flashy mansions on the square. Francisco

Pizarro died in Peru, but his brother Hernán returned, acquired the plot where his father had owned a small house and garden on the square, and built a four-storey granite heap. This was his Essex manor, his Ponderosa from the Wickes catalogue, Florentine page. Granite is a brute to carve, and the bulk of the mansion is as plain and lumpen as their ambitions, but on the corner facing the plaza he set the new Pizarro coat of arms, which included seven Inca princes chained together at the neck. Up the hill is Casa Francisco Pizarro, which was home to the conquistador's synonymous great uncle. It is a small house made pretty with potted flowers and a creeper. There is a brightly painted mail box, on which I imagined a note: 'Señor Pizarro is out conquering new worlds and enslaving civilisations, but if you would like to leave a message there's no point, he is illiterate.'

From the ramparts of the castle at the top of the town, I could see the slope below, relieved by clumps of olive trees, but beyond that, as far as the eye could follow, was a plain of yellow grass. We can whimsically imagine past ages as simpler and easier, and be misled in the art gallery by idyllic landscapes of flocks of sheep, doing nothing all day but grow wool and mutton for happy peasants, asleep under a hedge with a bottle of Rioja. Life was brutal and brittle. Most of Europe lacked heavy grain-growing soils to feed its cities. Fernand Braudel, the supreme historian of the Mediterranean, put it simply: agriculture 'was an industry that was always in difficulty'. Spain was being devastated by three million Merino sheep wandering over Extremadura and Andalucía devouring the grass, exposing the soils. From 1450 there was over-grazing, over-farming and erosion. By the sixteenth century, few natural ecosystems survived. Even trees were scarce; Spain imported wood from around 1500. In the 1520s, one observer wryly remarked that the wood fuelling the cooking pot cost more than the food in it. Extremadura was a place where go-ahead people got out.

I drove into Medellín over a causeway crossing a valley floor green only at the river's edge. A yard from the bank the grass was parched, and the baking air shimmered up the hill towards the castle ranged along its ridge, terminating in a stubby round tower at one end, and squat square ones at the other. The ruins of a Roman theatre stood on the hill's flank. The town Cortés grew up in had a busy synagogue and mosque. This view would have changed little since the time of Cortés, as the town is hidden on the other side of the hill. Medellín's famous son may have conquered an empire and become a marquis, but his hometown's population is the same as it was in his day: two thousand five hundred. In the middle of the afternoon I photographed the main street without trouble, because I could stand in the middle of it. The shops and cafes were all closed: its inhabitants might have gone to the moon. One thing might not have surprised the arrogant and ambitious young man. His statue now stands in the square, above some demeaningly domestic topiary.

He was born in 1485 and, according to Gómara, Cortés's secretary-turned-biographer, '[a]s an infant Hernán Cortés was so frail that many times he was on the point of dying'. But he was an hidalgo, a corruption of *hijo de algo*, literally the son of a someone. The qualification was modest: being able to name all four grandparents. It whispers volumes about the society in which many could not. It may have become important because identifying your grandparents would prove or otherwise the absence of Jews or Moors in your blood. His grandparents 'had little wealth but much honour'.

Located in the wildest part of Extremadura, Medellín was a rebel town, which, during a four-year war of succession, had supported the failed claimant to the Spanish throne, and with Mérida was the last town to recognise Isabela of Castile. Legal records show the town did not calm down as a result; assaults and outrages continued to fill the court records. Despite this turmoil, Cortés had an education of sorts, although how much, is argued about. Aged fourteen, he was sent to the house of a kinsman of his father, in Salamanca, where he studied either grammar or Latin, depending on the source. Salamanca was home to Spain's oldest university, with scholars in many fields. When Christopher Columbus was required to explain his geographical theories, he was quizzed by the geographers of Salamanca. Cortés's family must have made

35

sacrifices for Hernán, hoping a lettered career would pay them all back. Instead he left early, after two years: 'either disgusted with school life or having changed his mind or, perhaps from lack of money. His return vexed his parents exceedingly, they being annoyed with him for having abandoned his studies. They had destined him for the law, the richest and most honourable career of all, because he was very intelligent and clever in everything he did.' He was also 'restless, haughty, mischievous, and given to quarrelling'.

He opted for a voyage to the Indies of the New World with Nicolás de Ovando, a favourite of Queen Isabela, who was sailing with a huge fleet of thirty ships and tens of thousands of colonists, to become the new Governor and Captain General of the Indies. Ovando knew Cortés personally, which would probably secure him a berth, and the young man's head been turned by the quantities of gold being brought back from the New World. The stock biography of a hero would see fate and sage judgement unite to take him where destiny beckoned. But while the fleet was being readied, Cortés, who in Díaz's words was 'overfond of women', was leaving a lady's bedroom by walking along the top of the garden wall in order not to wake her husband. The wall collapsed, the husband appeared, and was only prevented from killing Cortés by his mother-in-law's begging. Cortés's leg was injured, and perhaps through infection, he developed a fever, and, in short, missed the boat. Gómara takes up the story, and although Díaz thinks him a sycophant, the tale is no promotional puff: 'He decided to go to Italy, as he had first thought of doing, and set out for Valencia. He did not get to Italy, however, but wandered about idly for nearly a year, not without hardship and privation. He then returned to Medellín resolved to go to the Indies, and his parents gave him their blessing and money for the voyage.'

At some point he had begun the long training required to become a notary in Seville, handling day-to-day legal work, and he continued his apprenticeship in Hispaniola. This kept his Latin in use, and he would always enjoy displaying his credentials as an educated man, in a manner truly well-educated people do not need to do. What undoubtedly shows through in his writings and dealings is a knowledge of the law, and an understanding that in public life and the Court the law mattered, or at least making a show of proceeding according to law mattered. But when he quotes literature or the Bible, we sense a smooth talker with a stock of aphorisms, rather than someone drawing on a reservoir of deep reading. The hack lawyer, trapping a witness, may intone, 'Oh, what a tangled web we weave, When first we practise to deceive!' but it does not mean he is familiar with the other forty thousand words of Sir Walter Scott's interminable poem *Marmion*.

Oxford professor John Elliott has tracked down the sources of Cortés's quotes, and, even more interestingly, the places where the quotes reappeared. Quoting someone does not mean you have read the original. So he seems to quote Livy ('There is nothing like necessity for sharpening men's wits') and Aristotle ('There should be nothing superfluous on earth') as a cynical excuse for attacking Natives. But if he had read the novel *Celestina* published in 1499 he would have found both quotes already in his native Spanish. Professor Elliott concludes 'no world was so rich in imagination and so infinitely adaptable as the mental world of Hernán Cortés,' meaning he could make events seem whatever suited him. Subterfuge is a more valuable aid than any fine style or erudition.

Aged nineteen he made his way down to San Lúcar de Barrameda, on the estuary of the Guadalquivir river, which flows through Cordoba, then Seville, to reach the sea just north-west of Cádiz. The low sandy banks make modest scenery, but each August its beaches host the oldest horse races in Spain. San Lúcar is now a middling-sized town with the lowest personal incomes in all Spain. Around 1505 it was one of the base ports for the Indies trade, and would have given the country boy a sniff of the exoticism waiting for him over 4000 miles away.

He also quickly sampled how flexible ethics could be in his new profession of adventurer. His billet was on a ship belonging to Alonso Quintero from Palos, the home port, and training ground of Columbus's pilots, the Pinzón brothers. Palos now sits above a river so silted up the town has no feel of having been a port. I stayed in the dapper hotel on the main square, which is not named for the flagship *Santa María,* but for a Pinzón vessel, *La Pinta*. The town boasts one statue to the famous, and it is dedicated to the local boys, the Pinzóns. The Genoese Columbus does not get a look-in. Quintero was, like the others, carrying goods to trade in the Indies, where, because of their isolation, prices were high.

On 13 February the fleet sailed first to Gomera Island in the Canaries, where they took on supplies. One night, without telling any other captain, Quintero sailed off in order to arrive first and obtain premium prices for his goods. Within a day or so, a storm dismasted him, and he limped back to Gomera for repairs, and had the cheek to beg the fleet to wait for him. Surprisingly, they agreed. When they sailed, Quintero found his vessel swifter than the other ships, and let her pull away, but at some point their navigation broke down and they lost track of where they were. The pilot blamed the captain and the captain blamed the pilot. They were nearly out of food, and were dependent on rainwater for drink. Passengers and crew alike were fearful, confessing their sins, weeping, or just plain dying. To illustrate how remote, in travel time, they were from Europe, the return voyage of Apollo 11 to make the first moon landing took eight days, three hours and eighteen minutes. Cortés's passage from Spain, with a stop at the Canaries, had taken two months. On Easter Sunday they sighted Hispaniola. Last to arrive, their goods fetched the lowest prices. Welcome, Hernán, to your career.

Once in Cuba, Cortés made his intentions rudely clear. Allocated land to cultivate and on which to build a house, he replied that he preferred mining, and had come for gold. He was soon fighting Native chiefs in what was little more than a campaign of genocide. He then engaged in trade for five or six years. When Diego Velázquez was despatched to conquer Cuba, the only island of comparable size to Hispaniola, Cortés went with him as clerk to the treasurer. In the interim he had taken land, and the Indians to work it for livestock and mining. He proved himself able and diligent. He was, said Gómara, 'the first to own a herd and a house'.

In 1509, Juan Juárez from Granada arrived with four pretty sisters looking for rich husbands. One, called Catalina, had been told by an astrologer she would become a great lady. Cortés may have seduced her; he certainly created an expectation that marriage was on offer. When he tried to wriggle out of it he found Velázquez, as fond of women as he was of gold, was interested in another sister, and to help his own suit, Velázquez sided with the family. Cortés married. The tight-fisted Velázquez also knew Cortés was rich enough to defray a large share of the costs of the Mexico expedition, and spare his own pockets. According to Cortés, he paid two thirds of the costs and Velázquez one third. You could not trust Cortés, and Velázquez was so slippery he paid his own share with the funds of the absent Pánfilo de Narváez, for whom he held power of attorney. Cortés borrowed money extensively and put together a powerful force, three hundred men in six ships. Watching Cortés's thorough preparations soon gave Velázquez misgivings. Treacherous people seldom trust others, and he may have recognised a kindred spirit. But contracts had been signed and Cortés was enough of a lawyer not to be bullied out of them. Grijalva had still not returned, and searching for him became one purpose of the voyage, at least on paper. Grijalva would find his own way home shortly after Cortés had sailed.

5

The Shadow at my Throat

*All italic quotes in the medical interludes are
from* The Tempest *by William Shakespeare*

I begin 2012 worrying about my age; I will be sixty in October. In March, when I am in Rhosygilwen country house in Pembrokeshire, rehearsing for a speaking tour, I have to apologise for my voice weakening when the director repeatedly times me reading various extracts. A mild sore throat does not go away. In June I start coughing up blood. The locum at my GP's calmly says it could be TB or lung cancer, as though I wouldn't mind which. He orders blood tests; his clear hand writes URGENT in capitals then underlines it. He also gives me a throat spray 'which may help'. Phrases about plasters and fractures come to mind. The hospital X-rays me for tuberculosis. New Improved TB is now resistant to many antibiotics; it's making a comeback, isn't everybody?

I distract myself with the European Football Championships, but succumb to internet curiosity, and check up on throat cancer survival rates: 90 percent, not too bad. However, when they take hold they kill you very quickly. On Friday I go back to the same doctor and sit down. He asks, 'How can I help you?'

I remind him I may only have three months to live. He looks shocked. I am not too relaxed about it myself.

'There was nothing on the X-ray except that rib you broke.' 'First I've heard of it.'

'You don't appear to have TB.' 'And cancer?'

'Oh.' He looked hastily at his screen. 'No sign of it.'

Two weeks later I have an operation to repair a hernia, caused by dragging boats up icy beaches in Antarctica, as you do. It's work, and it beats an office.

It is a month before I go to ENT to see Dr Parikh at St Mary's Hospital, next to Paddington Station, for an endoscopy; a tiny camera will tour my throat. Two days before I had borrowed Celia's computer to use its big screen, and found she has been consulting too: the survival rate is actually 50:50 after five years, which was terrifying. I had found the statistics for a very benign and highly treatable form. I think of a ragbag of things I will never do, including reading all my books, lovingly collected. Books will not help me.

Dr Parikh shows me how healthy everything looks as the mini-cam goes into a pig's ear, that turns out, when I have adjusted my sense of scale, to be my nostril, and then down my throat. 'Everything looks fine,' he purrs. Abruptly, his tone changes. 'Right at the back, behind the tongue, is an area which is not normal: two little nodules.' Cancer is back on the menu. I leave, shaking slightly, and phone Celia from Winsland Street in the shabby backs of the hospital, surrounded by its oldest buildings and cheapest kit-built infills. My head is light and my heart hammering as I tell her, and hear her responding bravely. When I return home we collapse in each other's arms.

Professor Narula will perform a biopsy under general anaesthetic on 1 August. I also know him as Tony, my neighbour, and a Manchester United fan. I come back to consciousness after the operation to hear Tony saying, 'It's looking good. I couldn't see anything, so I didn't even take a sample for biopsy.'

So I am not going to die yet. I stayed awake until three in the morning, making plans for the life that had been returned to me. I might even have enough time to read all my books. But why am I coughing blood? On 14 August I have another long magnetic resonance imaging test and emerge feeling I have been in a fight. On 25 August, the Bank Holiday Saturday, Dr Parikh phones me at home. 'There is an alien feature deep in the base of the tongue, and the lymph glands on the left side are swollen. One option is cancer, a type that is rather good at despatching cells to start colonies in other places, especially the liver.' I know the rest: then you die.

41

There are two other options, neither very likely. My throat feels exactly like his detailed description of cancer, but I cling to consoling facts; no one in my blood family, not even one of the many smokers, has ever suffered cancer.

I know it is now serious because they have an ultrasound scan booked for me that afternoon. There is also a procedure with the gentlest of names, an aspiration. While I am conscious, fine needles are put through my neck to take minute samples; on these cells hangs my future. Something in me has changed – I am now in a serious fight – so the prospect of this procedure is nothing. I go home feeling stunned; emotions which have been on hold catch up with me. I feel apologetic to Celia. Not long before we first met she lost her husband of forty years after tests for brain tumours kept on, at every stage of diagnosis, revealing the worst of all the options was the one he had. His prognosis was brief and it ran to timetable. I am close to giving her a re-run.

For now, there is still love and life, and both are more precious for the threat of being curtailed. No self-pity. I sketch trees in Hyde Park, thinking of Edward Wilson, who learned to draw nature here, his lungs already suffering from tuberculosis before he was accepted to go south with Scott and share a canvas mausoleum with him.

As background for a long-planned trip to Mexico, I am reading Richard Eden's *Decades of the New World*, an Elizabethan translation of early Spanish reports. Eden was a fine stylist, and *Decades* was raided by Shakespeare for details in *The Tempest*. Prospero's isle has been a distorted paradise, a secret, a place to gender a new nation, and the shipwrecked sailors are thought to come from heaven, a detail stolen from Antonio Pigafetta's account of Magellan in Patagonia. But after the shipwreck spills uncouth sailors on their shore, Prospero's island is no longer a fortress against men and the disruptions they bring, no longer a barrier against real life. My life so far has been free of threats, but the uncouth invader is now at my throat.

Two days later, with Celia, I am back in the Charing Cross clinic of Peter Clarke, a top throat and head cancer specialist. He doesn't yet have the results of the aspiration, but Mr Clarke sees what Dr

42

Parikh saw. 'There seems to be an extensive area of altered tissue.' He also knows a few dermatological tricks. The next thing he says makes the skin all over my body tingle in shock. 'The discoloured tissue around the base of the tongue suggests cancer, and it is not at an early stage.'

'This isn't good news, is it?'

'No.'

When I travel to remote places people ask if I am afraid of wild animals. No, it's usually people who frighten me, though not much. Now, supposedly safe at home, I am attacked by my own body. The prognosis is poor, I'll die, and maybe quite soon. I notice they always talk of treatment, not cure.

We get off the busy train, and go down through the quiet side streets below Paddington. Their downbeat shops, locksmiths and cafes, refillers of printer cartridges, will become the backdrop to these memories. The landscape of this illness is being established: low-rent. In public, Celia is sympathetic and practical. Back home she stifles tears. I hold her and tell her to let them flow; she can be brave after she has cried.

We go to Tate Britain and find the flaring Turners, and the calming Constables. Walking back over the Serpentine Bridge I feel utterly empty, my sense of self gone. If I have no future, what is my 'now' worth? I stare bitterly at live green plants. They will return next year; I won't. This is my darkest moment.

What seest thou else in the dark backward and abysm of time?

3. Route of Cortés from Cuba

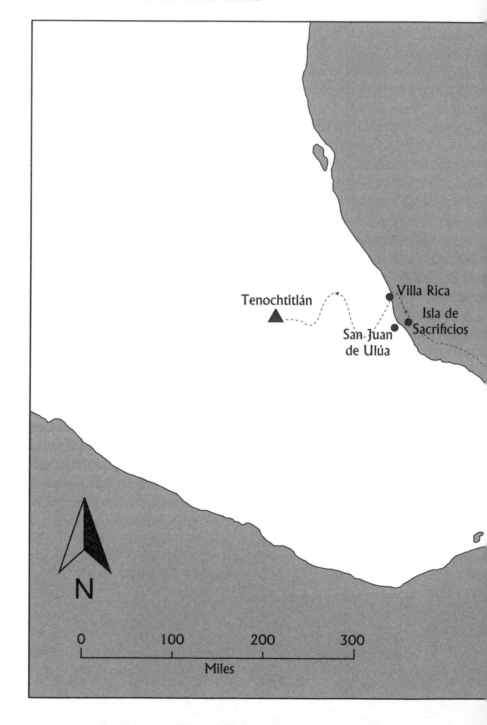

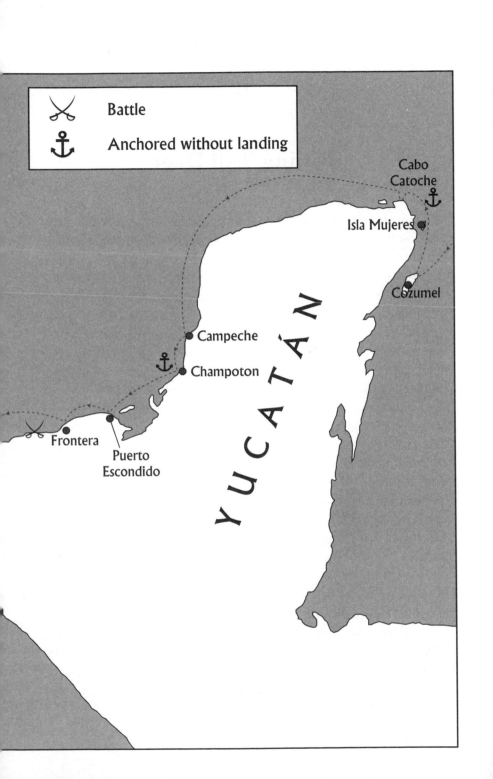

6

Riding Tall Deer

The morning after being thrown out of the bar, I left my hotel early trusting it was a coincidence that a policeman was standing outside my hotel in the empty street. I had bought my ticket the previous day, and my status as the only tourist in town was confirmed when, without checking my ticket, the woman in the booking office waved to me and pointed to my bus.

I spent a single night in Ciudad del Carmen, which until the 1970s was a sleepy town making a living by fishing and shrimping. The approach is dramatic, as the coast road rises up on a two-mile long bridge to cross a lagoon cutting inland in the shape of a low, wide U, leaving an island whose gulf side is in perfect alignment with the rest of the coast, concealing both entrances. This was Grijalva's Puerto Escondido: Hidden Port. In the 1970s oil was discovered offshore and the town boomed, but the fish market backing onto the sea is still here. Pelicans, egrets and cormorants gather to catch the trimmings thrown out by the fishmongers. I walked through it and into the dock area. Pausing until the security guard was preoccupied with his phone, which was not a long wait, I entered the port. To the left, rusting trawlers with the grace of toolboxes lay ranked in the mud. Out on the quay, a big Illinois-built truck crane was being used to load new machinery onto a small vessel. It was the type that stabilises itself on hydraulic legs with disc feet like manhole covers. The driver was Sarain Hernández Hernández, a stocky man in clean jeans and a plain white T-shirt; we chatted while he waited for the next delivery. 'Life is good here, plenty of work and the oil is all out to sea, so it doesn't spoil the town.' Looking over his shoulder at the lagoon, I saw a pod of dolphins leaping under the stern of the next ship.

He followed my eye. 'See! No pollution.'

When I stepped back to watch them he caught my arm. 'Be careful!'

Behind me was a hole in the concrete jetty just large enough to let a man fall through. 'I did that,' he said.

He nodded at one of the hydraulic feet. He looked as proud as a young father.

Next morning I turned up at 08:20 and was surprised to be sold a ticket for the 07:30 bus. The clocks had gone back overnight. My destination was Frontera, or more exactly somewhere in the fields around it, where Cortés fought his first battle in the Americas, and the sound of horses galloping was heard for the first time in twelve thousand years. There had been equines in the Americas since the emergence of the fox-sized *eohippus* fifty million years ago, but its descendants had been wiped out at the end of the Ice Age when rapid climate change inflicted a massive cull of large mammals.

The landscape so far had been lush but largely unfarmed. The fields around me now had more livestock, mostly doe-eyed cattle the colour of butter beans, wading chest deep in flooded fields, grazing like bovine swans. They ambled, footloose in time, with leaden-hoofed carelessness, their massive necks shouldering aside the years, weed streaming from the ogee curves of their horns. The fields of grass and water fed their bullish faith that the golden age had come to them in a sea of succulent grasses.

Frontera stands a few miles inland on the river now named after its discoverer, Grijalva. It is a square port town, bound in a rigid gridiron one nautical mile on each side. My hotel in the square was called Mar Mor, which I liked, as it is the word for 'sea' in Spanish then Welsh. I thought it would spoil things to ask why.

By day, there was not a lot to see. In the fish market one stallholder displayed a single fish, but it weighed 50 kilos and you could have used the skin for chainmail. Each scale was the size of half a hen's egg. The cheerful man cutting steaks off it said, 'This is a *sábalo*, a type of shad, and it isn't even a big one. We catch them on lines, sometimes a hundred kilos.'

In the evening I found one bar with two rooms. In front, facing the street, was a spacious quiet family area with no one in it. Through a scruffy curtain at the back, party sounds came from a smaller room overlooking the river which slid past the bar's back wall. It seemed a bad place to lose a fight, disposal of the evidence being so easy. It was the kind of bar where you thought of little but fights. Dives like this are safe for me now I am older. I wear the watch that looks even cheaper than the fifteen pounds I paid for it, I carry little money, and my compact camera is holstered out of sight on my belt. I am too grey to look threatening, and there would be far more fuss if a tourist were knifed, so they attack each other. A pair of big women in small skirts waved at me, and pointed to two empty seats at their table, which might as well have had *Get it Here* stencilled on them. When I shook my head and took out a notebook and pen, they howled with laughter and pointed out the weirdo to everyone else. It took time for my eyes to grow used to the fish-tank lighting, which a Farrow and Ball paint catalogue would have called something like Urine at Midnight. The floor seemed to be littered with tampons, but after a while I could see they were the screwed-up napkins staff tucked into the necks of the beer bottles to keep out flies. The noise from drinkers loose-tongued with beer yelling to *compadres* comatose on tequila would have frightened a hungry puma out of a butcher's. A woman as soberly dressed as a housewife leaned delicately to one side and spat on the floor. A young man winked at me, perhaps thinking if I didn't want women I might like boys, perhaps he was just friendly and a little drunk.

On the next table two men were water-boarding themselves with beer from a dozen bottles standing in an ice bucket, ten turned upside down, two to go. The one in a fake Lacoste polo shirt (available in street markets everywhere) made an expansive gesture to support some shouting he was engaged in, and elbowed his current bottle into the air, sending it to a neighbouring table where it skittled their empties to the floor. The management moved in firmly without confronting anyone. The man who had smashed the bottles understood it was time to go and paid the tab, but his friend continued arguing about it. Musicians filed in, setting up the corner stage. This was the beginning of the evening. Later on, everyone would be drunk.

Señor Miguel Paz Estañol is both Port Captain of Frontera and manager of two shipping agencies, and has offices just off the square, fronted by two well-educated young men in uniform, whom he likes to keep on their toes. Señor Estañol is sixty-five years old, with pale olive skin and Hispanic features that are rare in small Mexican towns; he is also a keen historian. We sat in his plain room, equipped with bland 1950s wooden furniture. Señor Paz wore a buff uniform shirt, and when he rubbed his hands together, which he did when gathering his thoughts, he revealed forearms whose tops were burned into melanomas with puce edges. Surveying his desk I saw his letterhead did not have a thrusting symbol of progress; his logo was a sixteenth-century sailing ship. Without notes, he recounted the early encounters in his quiet measured voice, giving all the dates, and pointing out locations on the hydrographic chart.

'Their largest caravel may have drawn as little as eight feet, but they could not bring them into the river or close to the shore, because of the sand bar across the mouth of the river, and shoals inside.'

'Would the river have changed much since that time?'

'It has moved position but not changed its nature. The midstream island has grown a little, but the river depths would have been much the same as now.'

'There are ships drawing much more than eight feet in the harbour here.'

'We have to dredge – it needs dredging again now.' He sighed. 'Will it be dredged? It costs money and this is not a busy port.'

I checked my notes. 'All I know about the location of the battle was that it was fought in the fields around the modern town: "It was near this same town of Cintla that we met them on the open plain."'

'Yes, the chronicler says "in the dry bean fields"; they were to the north.' He summoned one of the gatekeepers. 'Print a plan of the estuary north of town for Señor Harrison.'

'The battle is remembered every year. We hold a *Baile de Caballito*, the Dance of the Little Horse. A figure on a white horse slays Indians.' The map arrived. It showed the river running a little west of north, from the town to the sea. He stubbed a thick finger down on the east bank. 'Here!'

The first taxi driver would not take me, but I could not tell why, because although he had teeth, he spoke as if he did not. He pointed at another taxi, whose driver looked dubiously at the map, said 'Ah, the North Wood,' and named a high price. I talked him down and got in. Sempreano Jiménez soon warmed to the project. 'You've really come all this way to see this battle site?'

'And a few other ones.'

He whistled appreciatively.

The land around us was marshy meadows. The groundwater would probably have been better managed when Cortés arrived, but a swamp played a part in the battle.

Sempreano pointed. 'There's good fishing in the ponds, sweeter flesh than estuary fish.'

We drove around all morning, looked at the sea bar they could not cross, and the fields they fought in. I failed to picture the clamour of battle, the horses unsteady on their feet at first after weeks on board, because the tranquil domesticity of the landscape smothered imagination. I was looking hard, but standing in my own light. So I photographed symbols: lonely horses in flooded fields, and vultures staring at the flattened corpse of a skinny hound, its fur matted into the tarmac.

Sempreano took me down rutted cul-de-sacs, speaking to me, as some people not used to foreigners did, as though low fluency in Spanish was synonymous with learning difficulties. It had been a long morning and I realised I should not have bargained him down. I paid his opening price and added a tip. He now likes historians.

Cortés's fleet of eleven ships set sail from Cuba on 10 February 1519, with orders to sail in convoy to Cozumel. Díaz was in a ship piloted by Pedro Camacho, who came from Seville, and had sailed with Córdoba and Grijalva. The most senior soldier on board was the handsome and headstrong Pedro de Alvarado, the man Grijalva had rebuked for sailing ahead alone. When one of the other ships lost a rudder, every ship but Alvarado's hove to until it was repaired. He sailed on to Cozumel, where he further broke instructions by pilfering ornaments and food from a town. Cortés had to be seen to be enforcing discipline but judged it unwise to confront Alvarado so soon, and perhaps alienate him, so he clapped Alvarado's pilot Camacho in irons.

Cortés had to coax the Natives out of hiding, remarking they had fled 'for fear of the Spaniards, not knowing with what intentions they were coming'. No talk of being mistaken for gods, the common line in explaining the Natives' supposed lack of effective resistance. Speaking through the Native interpreter Melchior, Cortés compensated the Natives and charmed them with gifts. Melchior was never a fluent translator and Cortés could not know how much was lost or warped in translation, or how far he could trust the loyalty of a captive. Cortés had one hundred sailors and ship's officers, and five hundred and eight officers and soldiers. There were only sixteen horses, most from the plains of Córdoba, which were handy for the New World departure ports of Cádiz, Seville, and San Lúcar. Most of what we know of them comes from Bernal Díaz, who describes them as though they are independent volunteers. The much-vaunted superior weapons, firearms, were represented by just ten brass guns, four falconets (small cannon firing one-pound weight shot), and thirteen musketeers. There were thirty two crossbowmen. Their force would grow, but this simple list shows that two of the items usually cited as offering the Spanish technological superiority, guns and horses, were in short supply. The mass of any attack would be delivered by the third: steel.

These details are from the soldier and chronicler Bernal Díaz. We will hear from him many times, and any unattributed historical quotes are his. He has the ability that some soldiers and sailors have to file a report without frills or evasions. His life is almost a metaphor for the conquest. Born in the year of amazement, 1492, he died as poor as he had lived. He did not begin his history until he was seventy years old, and then only to vent his fury at accounts being published and given credence, written by men who had not been there. He is also splendidly grumpy with anyone who disagrees with him. The easiest way to abridge Díaz's book is simply to cut all the material vilifying other chroniclers. A special target was Cortés's secretary Gómara, who had written a fawning fabulation extolling his boss. Polishing one reputation may tarnish another; Díaz set out for revenge. I hate to think how many quills he got through in that first anger. But writing history needs a long slow burn, and he cast aside his manuscript in frustration at his unscholarly abilities, only to snatch it up again in later years and complete it aged eighty-four, deaf and blind, but having, unlike all the talismanic names, reached a remarkably old age.

In another time and place, one can think of Patrick Leigh Fermor writing in his early sixties of his teenage rambles across Europe, in ditches one night and a castle the next: the insouciance of youth revisited through the prism of age and wisdom. Looking back behind him from the 1970s, Fermor recalled the Europe of the mid-1930s and, like Díaz's Aztec memories, it was a world of wind-racked wraiths.

I like Díaz so much that I made a pilgrimage to the stately Colonial city of Antigua in Guatemala to see where he wrote it. The site of his former house was behind hoardings, where the shell of an old Jesuit church was being stripped down by builders prior to restoring it for use by an NGO. I slipped in through a tall Romanesque arch sealed with massive plain doors, and looked round as long as I could before being challenged and politely ejected. The foreman was not impressed by my press card proving I was a writer; they'd never heard of Díaz, never mind me. There was nothing left of his house.

His prologue runs, 'What I myself saw, and the fighting in which I took part, with God's help I will describe quite plainly, as an honest witness, without twisting the facts in any way.' The first great historian of the Spanish conquests, W H Prescott, said, 'he is among chroniclers what Defoe is among novelists'.

Cortés summoned Díaz and others to ask what they thought of the Natives at Cape Catoche on previous voyages shouting *Castilan!* He thought there might be other Spaniards in the area, a possibility no one else seems to have considered. He ordered Melchior to quiz the local chiefs. Only two days before, some Maya merchants in town had spoken to two captured Spanish men, slaves of different local chiefs. Native messengers were sent with a letter to the prisoners and trinkets to buy their freedom, and two small ships were despatched to Cape Catoche to pick them up. The letter first reached a man around thirty years old called Jerónimo de Aguilar, who went in delight to his master, Lord Xamanzana, Lord of Chectumal and struck a deal for his freedom. Then he went to the village of Gonzalo Guerrero, another sailor from Palos. His reaction was quite different. 'Brother Aguilar, I am married and have three children, and they look on me as a chief here, and a captain in time of war. My face is tattooed and my ears are pierced, what would the Spanish say if they saw me like this? Look how handsome these children of mine are! Go and God's blessing be with you.' Guerrero's wife was blunter, snarling, 'Why has this slave come here to call my husband away? Be off with you, and let us have no more of your talk.'

Aguilar pressed Guerrero, reminding him that this was not just a choice between two different lives here on earth. 'Do not destroy your soul for the sake of an Indian woman. Besides, if you do not want to desert your wife and children you can take them with you.'

Aguilar gave up, but he did not yet know how deeply Guerrero had committed to his adopted people. Guerrero was not nostalgic for Spain. He came from the village of Niebla, a short way upriver from Palos. Life there was so hard that he had witnessed famines during which people ate the dead. When his new Maya lord, Na Chan Can, ruler of Chactemal, had ambushed Córdoba at Cape Catoche, it was on the recommendation of his son-in-law and military adviser. That man was Gonzalo Guerrero. He had truly gone native.

Aguilar walked to Cape Catoche, where a canoe took him to the waiting ships. The six paddlers were so amazed by the sight of the Spanish fleet they began to turn around until Aguilar calmed them. On the flagship, Andrés de Tapia reported seven Indians approaching. One man stepped forward, wearing a ragged cloak with the remains of a prayer book tucked in it, and one ancient sandal on his foot, and the other tied to his belt. In broken Spanish he managed, 'God and the Blessed Virgin of Seville,' and they knew he was Spanish. Aguilar was escorted to Cortés's cabin where he squatted on his haunches. His ears and lips were pierced, his hair cut carelessly with a knife, and he was brown all over. Cortés asked the escort where this new Spaniard was. Close up, in the tiny cabin, Aguilar still looked like an Indian. In broken Spanish, he told his tale.

'I am Jerónimo de Aguilar, of Holy Orders, born in Écija, east of Seville. Eight years ago I was wrecked with fifteen other men and two women on a voyage from Darien (Panama) to the island of Santo Domingo, where I had differences at law with a man called Enciso y Valdivia. We were carrying 10,000 gold pesos and the documents for our case when our ship struck a reef called The Vipers near Jamaica, and could not be floated off. So we boarded the ship's boat, but currents carried us to this country, half of us already dead from want of any food or water, where the chiefs divided us up. Four were immediately sacrificed to their idols; the rest of us were put in cages. I had been intended for sacrifice, but one night I escaped and fled to chief Xamanzana, where I have been ever since.'

All the other escapees had died, except for Guerrero. Cortés avidly asked about the countryside around, thinking Aguilar would be the perfect insider guide.

'Having been only a slave, all I know about is hewing wood and drawing water and working in the maize fields.' Regardless, Cortés had a better translator of Maya, and a man he could trust more than Melchior. Aguilar's hometown of Écija is known as the Frying Pan of Andalucía, with a reputation as one of the hottest towns in Spain. It has fine baroque buildings and is thronged with churches. Aguilar's mother was well known around the town during the long years after his capture. When she had been told he was a prisoner of cannibals, she gave up meat, and became hysterical when she saw it cooking, screaming 'That's my son!' She haunted the principal church in Écija, dedicated to Christ the Captive. The Sunday morning that I visited, the porch shadows held beggars desperate in the face. One made noises in the throat, as if croaking though a ruined grating. A feeble arm gestured towards her plastic bowls. I gave to the elderly mother.

They sailed for the second time on 4 March 1519. Soon Cortés despatched his swiftest vessel ahead under Captain Escobar to find Grijalva's Puerto Escondido and see if it was suitable for a settlement. When Escobar's party went ashore, the greyhound that had been lost hunting during Grijalva's landing came bounding out of the forest, plump and well-fed. She now helped him stock up on fresh meat. At Champoton, Cortés proposed a punitive raid in retaliation for the attacks on Córdoba and Grijalva, or, as we might think, to kill people for defending their homes against armed invasion. He was dissuaded from doing so not by moral arguments, but by the pilots, who were worried about the wind changing and pinning them ashore.

They moved on to the fateful landing at Frontera, arriving on 22 March 1519. It was a regional centre with fine public buildings, including a pyramid temple. Forewarned of the ships' approach, the chief had ordered warriors from a wide area to come to his support. The motive was wounded pride. Neighbouring towns like Champoton had mocked them for not attacking the two previous expeditions.

Chiefs came out in a canoe and Aguilar translated for Cortés, who made what was to become a standard opening gambit. 'We have not come to do you any harm but to make gifts and greet you like brothers. But if you attack us you will be sorry.' The hand extended in friendship sported a knuckleduster. But the more Aguilar talked peace, the angrier the chiefs became. Cortés wrote to the Spanish emperor, Charles V, that he demanded co-operation 'for they were already Your Highness's vassals'. The Treaty of Tordesillas, 1493, had divided the New World between Spain and Portugal. In Spanish minds, they had the papal deeds to the land and people; now it was time for the tenants to hand over the keys and start paying rent.

Cortés went ashore with two hundred men, and saw a large town with stone buildings and a new fortified palisade around it. He said they wanted food and the chief told them to return to the square the next day. The Spanish slept ashore on the river bank, and used the cover of night to bring many more men ashore, but not the horses. Ominously Frontera's chief ordered all women and children to be evacuated. Next morning the Spanish were given eight turkeys and enough maize for ten people, a gold mask, and a few jewels. Cortés said he needed more food and wanted a basket of gold. The reply: 'We do not want war or trade. There is no more gold. If you want water, dig in the sand on the island and you will reach fresh water. Then, leave or be killed.'

Cortés returned to his moored ships and boats, sent out reconnaissance groups, and waited. At the end of the fifth day he parleyed but the conversation went the same way as before. Cortés ordered the Royal Notary, Diego de Godoy, to read out demands to submit to God and the King of Spain. The Maya attacked. Cortés brought ashore some cannon, and although the Maya were frightened by the first shots and lost ground, they soon rallied and replied with spears, bows and arrows, sling-thrown stones, and light clubs lined with obsidian blades. A skilled workman can flake obsidian to an edge finer than a modern steel scalpel. As light faded, Alvarado found a path through marshes to attack from the rear, and Spanish axes broke through the palisade and the battle turned into street-fighting. The Maya, lacking advice from cultural theorists, did not freeze. Díaz writes: 'Here they turned and met us face to face, fighting most valiantly and persistently.' Alonso de Ávila arrived with a third force and the fight began to move in their favour. When the townspeople retreated, the Spanish fortified themselves in the plaza of the temple for the night.

The only loss to the Spaniards seems to have been the desertion of their interpreter Melchior. The next day they found his Spanish clothes hanging in a palm grove. A prisoner, newly taken by the Spanish, said he had spent the night with Melchior, who had told them that the Spanish were only men, that there were few of them, and the Maya should attack them day and night. That evening Cortés cut three slashes in the beautiful ceiba tree in the square to claim possession in the name of the king, and offered combat to any man who disagreed. This was a formal act, witnessed by Notary Diego de Godoy, which caused grumblings among men close to

Governor Velázquez. The terms of Cortés's orders did not include conquest, and setting up a new kingdom. What is more, he had taken possession in the name of the king, without naming Velázquez. This is the first sign of him repositioning himself to act independently of both his boss, and the regional administration in Cuba.

The cutting of the tree had a different meaning for the Natives. The ceiba, with its massive trunk, was a sacred tree that held up heaven itself. Now it was scarred and weeping sap.

The day after this urban scrap, the Maya had by no means surrendered. More talks were held and Cortés spoke of representing 'the greatest monarchs on earth', but when he later wrote to those monarchs, his version of the incident plainly betrays how wilfully he is misreading events. Invited to be vassals, they 'replied that they were content to do so but required us to leave their land; and so we became friends': the kind of friends you deport.

A foraging party of a hundred soldiers under Francisco de Lugo came under sustained attack and were only able to retreat to the town when a second party under Alvarado heard the sound of arquebuses and came to their relief. Two had been killed and eleven wounded. Fifteen Maya died. The following day, Cortés brought every fit man ashore, and, for the first time, most of the horses. This was to be a battle waged with the full weight of the forces at his command. First they had to keep to the legal niceties. As a sop to Spanish conscience, the jurist Palacios Rubios had concocted a document known as the Requirement, which had to be read out before attacking. Here are the opening and closing sections, with some flourishes cut, but not changed in any other way.

'I, Hernán Cortés, servant of the high and mighty kings of Castile and Leon, civilisers of barbarous nations, their messenger and captain, notify and make known to you that God our Lord, one and eternal, created the heavens and earth, and one man and one woman, from whom you, and we, and all the people of the earth, were and are descendants, and all those who shall come after us. All these people were given in charge, by God our Lord, to one person, named Saint Peter, who was thus made lord and superior of all the people of the earth, and head of the whole human lineage; whom all should obey, wherever they might live, and what ever might be their law, sect, or belief; he gave him also the whole world for his service and jurisdiction.'

And so on. It closes with a threat.

'If you do not do this, or wickedly and intentionally delay to do so, by the aid of God I will forcibly invade and make war upon you, and will subdue you to the yoke and obedience of the church and of his majesty; and I will take your wives and children and make slaves of them, and sell them, and will do you all the harm and injury in my power, as vassals who will not obey or receive their sovereign and who resist and oppose him. And I protest that the deaths and disasters, which may in this manner be occasioned, will be the fault of yourselves, and not of his majesty, nor of me, nor of the cavaliers who accompany me.'

On this day, it was read to the Natives and translated into Maya. Often, it was, as the champion of Native rights Bartolomé Las Casas wrote, 'read to the trees' or, in another case, to a deserted village. Las Casas said he did not know whether to weep or laugh at it. But it squared the soldiers on the ground with the lawyers at home.

I summarise the Natives' reply: 'Sod off!'

The chosen ground was maize fields. Cortés faced five masses of Maya warriors, who had their own repertoire of intimidatory tricks. Their faces were painted black and white and their bodies protected with quilted armour. They wore feather crests to make them tall, they played trumpets and banged drums. Their tactic was to use their massively greater numbers, perhaps a ten to one advantage, to surround the Spanish, and rain arrows, darts and stones on them.

The Spanish found that fear of the cannon soon abated, and assaults with arquebuses and crossbows had little impact. Only when the Spanish could fight at close quarters did they make progress with their swords, but then the Maya, quick to learn and tactically astute, fell back and hurled missiles at them. Díaz and his fellow foot-soldiers began to wonder where the cavalry were. Only Francisco de Morla was there, riding swiftly to hotspots where his comrades were under pressure, observed with wonder by the Maya, who reported the aliens as riding on tall deer. At last, after two hours' fighting, the cavalry force of ten horses was unleashed. Having struggled to pass through the marshes, they now broke out behind the encircling Maya and speared them at their leisure. Rider and horse were taken to be a single centaur-like creature.

This is a fascinating notion, for Greek centaurs are believed to be a mythologised memory of peoples of the Aegean and Minoan worlds to first seeing mounted nomads from Asia come to the frontiers of Europe. In myth they are liminal beings, with unresolved natures, half-animal, half-man. In stories where they quarrel with men, such as when attempting to carry off the bride Hippodamia on her wedding day, they typically represent the animal side of human nature. Increasingly the Spanish would fulfil that role in their dealings with the peoples of the New World. In Dante's *Inferno*, centaurs guard the murderers and tyrants, next to the River of Blood. Some Conquistadors may reside in their untender care.

Fear scattered the Maya, and in another hour the battle was won. The enduring image of the day for both sides was Francisco de Morla beautifully handling his dapple-grey horse, ranging everywhere across the battlefield. Soon they were being mythologised in two realms: as a centaur by the Maya, and as their patron Santiago by the Spanish.

This was the first of many battles in which the Spanish would defeat much larger forces. Cortés was good at psychological warfare, and would use the horses, and the cannons' noise, to shock the enemy. The speed of movement of the horses allowed the Spanish to move instantly to support infantrymen under pressure. As they moved through Mexico, the shock was new each time, but if the first impact was not decisive; the Natives overcame their surprise. It proved difficult to kill an armoured horseman, but they studied hard how to do it.

The invading force were less battle-hardened than the locals, for whom warfare was part of the cycle of the year. But the nature of that warfare is key to understanding their vulnerability to a European force. Warfare was to intimidate, and to obtain tribute, hostages to sacrifice, prisoners, and slaves. Fighting was intended to injure and stun. Their obsidian blades were set deep in the club's shaft, to cripple, not kill. When a warrior took a prisoner, he tied and secured his victim. This kept him away from the fighting. Killing a man is much quicker.

Even though many Maya had been terrified, they still managed to injure five of the horses. One inhuman detail is glossed over in Gómara but spelled out in Díaz. It chills all the more because he reports it in such a matter of fact way. We 'sealed the wounds of our horses with fat from the corpse of an Indian we had cut up for this purpose.' For us, the stench of the concentration camp hangs over such use of a human body.

The following day, Maya nobles came to discuss the peace. Cortés determined to exploit the strangeness of the horses and cannon in a devious way. A brown mare was in heat; she belonged to Juan Sedeño, said to be the richest soldier in the fleet. There was also a stallion called the Drover, with a reputation for randiness. It was owned by Ortiz, a fine guitar player but a poor rider. At the place where Cortés would be, the mare was kept standing long enough for her scent to linger. Then both horses were partially hidden, with the stallion behind Cortés, and the mare upwind, behind where the Maya would stand. The nobles came at midday and suffered an introductory talk on the majesty of Emperor Charles V, and were warned that if the nobles were not truly contrite he would know because something evil would come out of the cannon, which was now fired. The nobles were startled and unsettled. The stallion was then led into view to stand alongside Cortés like a comrade. He scented the mare on the ground and began pawing. When he caught her scent from directly behind the nobles, he began to whinny and roar. Cortés addressed the horse. 'Do not be angry, they are friendly and have come to make peace.'

In Maya religion, animals represented forces in the spirit world, both good and bad. A large, swift beast, never before seen, had appeared before them, and spoken to its friends, the Spanish. They may not have thought it was a god, but it was thoroughly unnerving, and outside their experience. How could it be brought into their calculations about what was happening, and how they should proceed? For the immediate future, the object must have been not to provoke the Spanish and to move them on their way as soon as possible.

The next day men arrived with gifts of gold: four diadems, lizard ornaments, two dogs, five ducks, and two masks of Indian faces. They were not of great worth, but something else was delivered. It was of inestimable value: the key to the conquest.

7

Malinche

The very name Yucatán illustrates how hit and miss communication by sign and gesture can be. When a Spaniard asked where they were, the local Maya replied either *Uh yu ka t'ann*, meaning 'Listen how they talk', or a similar phrase meaning 'I don't understand your language'. The Spanish recorded the name of the place as Yucatán. It is well to remember this basic error when the Spanish claim that major matters, including sovereignty, were discussed and agreed.

The conquests made by small European forces in the Americas arrest our attention. They have been subject for the last century and a half to explanations that favoured a view of history where not only cultures, but the people in them, were at different stages on a ladder of progress, and the primitive had to give way to the advanced. We now see such approaches as racial and often racist, for even when differences in technology were cited, it was often in the context of being the product of superior cultures, created by superior peoples.

Some theorists now argue that the Spanish conquest was as much a victory for the power of writing and language as it was for technology. Mesoamericans had developed writing, but their scripts were a mixture of pure pictograms, where one picture, or glyph, represents a single object or idea, and hybrid techniques, where some glyphs come also to represent a sound. Without a flexible, fully phonetic writing system, theorists argue, knowledge could not be effectively stored and passed on, so technology and mental growth were shackled. Myths stultified Native thinking, and they failed to react and develop new strategies when strangers appeared from a strange land. Analysts who think like this tend to come from cultural studies backgrounds, and apply their skills to a historical problem.

One occasionally wonders whether the academics, and they nearly always are career academics, emphasising the paramountcy of language and writing in the conquest, would choose to fight a duel with a low-technology obsidian-bladed sword that could slice a man in two, or a first folio edition of Shakespeare. They are seldom historians first, and although they take a magnifying glass to a text or problem, they may use generalised versions of the events surrounding it, and some do not seem to know just how much Native leaders adapted, or accept how prolonged and heroic their resistance was. Leaders who hesitated, as Moctezuma later would, were abandoned without sentiment.

Paradoxically, Western first-world analysts talk about some indigenous civilisations as having failed, when they lasted far longer than the empires of Spain, England, France, the Dutch and others, which are their models for success: the supposed Darwinian victors in the cultural struggle. Such views seek a subtler theory of difference, but they still retain cultural taints uncomfortably reminiscent of racial theories.

Victory in Mexico, which Cortés will achieve by the skin of his teeth, despite all the traditional accounts of the heroic small force, will only happen when he outnumbers the opposition. Achieving that superiority depended on diplomacy, and that depended on a gift that arrived in Cortés's camp after the battle at Frontera. Twenty young women were presented to them.

One was probably called Malinalli. In the Aztec language, Nahuatl, Malinalli, is both a grass and the name of the twelfth day of the Aztec calendar. When she was baptised, the Spanish christened her Marina, but Nahuatl does not have the letter 'r' and, like Chinese speakers, Mesoamericans would have found it difficult to pronounce, saying something like Malina. The Aztecs added the honorific -tzin, making Malintzin, which the Spanish heard as Malinche, the name which has stuck. Even her name was an unstable thing through life, as had been predicted. Each calendar day had its own astrological significance for any child born on it, and day twelve, Malinalli, was the sign for difficult, unlucky, rebellious children who would be torn from their parents. The grass she was named after had a special use: it was strong enough to be pulled through flesh to make the wound bleed for the gods. It was pulled through the tongue.

She was about as old as the century, eighteen or nineteen, when she was gifted to Cortés. Grijalva's chaplain, Juan Díaz, wrote of her homeland, 'The people of this province excelled in beauty and stature all the other Indians.' It is also assumed that Malinche was beautiful because she was seen as a worthy gift for powerful strangers, and because, out of twenty women, Cortés allocated her to the most genteel of his followers, a fellow son of Medellín called Puertocarrero. Then, when the latter sailed back to Spain, Cortés took her for himself, and fathered a child by her.

She told Díaz she was from the village of Paynala. No village of that name now exists, but we know it was near the modern city of Coatzacoalcos. In that area she would have been raised speaking a dialect from the Zoque branch of the Maya languages. When the Spanish arrived, the area covered by the modern state of Mexico was home to a patchwork quilt of one hundred and seventy languages, of which sixty two still survive. When the translator Aguilar reached Frontera he would have been in his fourth different Maya language zone. He was lucky that at that time they were all mutually intelligible to him; some now differ too much to allow communication. Her home area was being pressed by Nahuatl-speaking neighbours from the west who called this coastal Maya language *Popoluca*, which you might guess, after saying it aloud, means babble. Only a hundred speakers, all ageing, still speak it.

Her father and mother were nobles, but her father died when she was very young, and her mother remarried, to another chief, and bore him a son. They wanted this son to succeed to their title, and thought to secure this by disposing of the daughter. Slavery and people trafficking were normal, as they were in the Mediterranean world. At night in secret, they gave her to some traders based a short distance along the coast at Xicalango. The Maya were polygamous, and when children were trafficked, they were often the offspring of concubines, less favoured wives, or previous marriages or liaisons. Because of longstanding trade links, the Nahuatl language of the

64

Aztecs was also spoken in this coastal enclave. Giving out that Malinche had died of illness, her parents took the corpse of a servant's baby who by chance had died at the same time, and buried her as their daughter. The traders sold her on to men from Potonchan, close to modern Frontera, who spoke Maya, which she now learned. As a slave, her life may not have been worse than that of any other person without privilege. We know she was intelligent, with an aptitude for languages. This would have made her more valuable. She would also have seen how different mini-states did business, and commerce and diplomacy were closely linked. This skill would direct the course of her life. A company as small as Cortés's could not succeed by force alone. He needed to harness force to diplomacy, and that required communication skills. Malinche spoke Maya and the Aztec language, Nahuatl. The rescued Spaniard Aguilar spoke Maya. Now they could talk to the two most powerful groups in Mesoamerica. For the duration of the conquest and well beyond, one person constantly appears at Cortés's side in the manuscript drawings of events, sometimes drawn larger than other people, to indicate her importance; that person is Malinche.

8

San Juan de Ulúa

Cortés had other business to attend to before he moved on: evangelism. Columbus had worn his brand of millennial Catholicism not just on his sleeve, but on his skin. For two years he wore chains under his shirt to mortify the flesh, concealing his masochism under a loose Franciscan robe. Cortés's religious convictions seem far more ambivalent, not to mention sane. He sailed under a masthead banner which read *Friends let us follow the cross and if we have faith, truly we will conquer under this sign.* His confessor Motolinía wrote that 'he had faith and did the work of a good Christian', but his fellow captain Diego de Ordaz said he had 'no more conscience than a dog'.

Any adventurer needing support from the Catholic court of Spain, and with the political nous of Cortés, would have paid at least lip-service to the faith, as not to do so would be like running for President of the USA as an atheist. But the chronicles show Cortés repeatedly taking time in a complex and often dangerously uncertain campaign, to commend Catholicism to the Natives. He gives it a priority no cynic would. At times his own behaviour will seem appalling when looked at a from a modern Christian outlook, but his Catholicism was not that of today, nor were the norms of society, or notions about the conduct of war. Nor, in any age, does the existence of norms mean they were or are respected.

Before he left Frontera, Cortés convened the nobles and lectured them on the evil of their religion: their idols were not gods but demons, and sacrificing people was wrong. He explained that the Spanish worshipped one god, and he gave them a painting of the Virgin Mary with the infant Jesus in her arms, and said they must worship them, because she was the mother of that god. The ruler agreed to build an altar to house the image, and two ship's carpenters built a large cross.

Cortés demanded the return of Melchior, the interpreter who had gone back to the Maya. The chief tactfully agreed, but after a decent interval, said they had been unable to find him. The truth was that when Melchior's advice to attack the Spanish started going wrong, and the battle ebbed from them, the Maya had sacrificed him to solicit a little help from the old gods. Religion done, vengeance thwarted, Cortés got down to business. Where were the gold and silver mines, where did their jewels come from? They answered truly that they had little, but they also encouraged the Spanish westwards, crying *'Colua! Mexico!'*

Their next destination was the safe harbour of San Juan de Ulúa, where the mosquitoes had driven Grijalva away. Within sight of it they paused at Isla de los Sacrificios to revisit the scene of human sacrifice. Friendly canoes come to greet them, the envoys remembering the names of Grijalva, Pedro de Alvarado and others. This area was part of the Totonac culture, and the Totonac spoke an isolated language which neither Aguilar nor Malinche could understand.

At San Juan de Ulúa, friendly Natives arrived again, and as the conversation is recorded in some detail, they must have been Nahuatl-speakers. They were subject to the Aztecs, and envoys would have learned the language of their overlords. Malinche spoke to them in her provincial coastal Nahuatl, and relayed the answers to Aguilar in Maya, then Aguilar translated it into Spanish: a chain of Chinese whispers.

Grijalva had treated these people well, and Cortés reaped the benefit. They remembered the tambourine player Benito, who danced with them, making them laugh, as he had done the previous year. They may have been thinking that if these strangers had come back, they might be useful allies against their overlords, but they would have guarded their words, knowing that spies were everywhere. Reports were already racing to the palace of their ruler, Moctezuma, telling him there were 'towers or small mountains floating in the waves of the sea. The people in them have very light skin, much lighter than ours. They all have long beards, and their hair comes only to their ears. They are moving here and there without touching the shore. My Lord, we have never seen the like of this, although we guard the coast and are always on watch.' The messengers reached the city of Tenochtitlán at night. The priests recognised the gravity of their news, and anointed existing prisoners with chalk, held them sweating in flickering red torchlight on a temple crowning a pyramid, and slit them open.

If the Native gifts other than precious metals were strange to the Spanish, what would the Americans have thought of Cortés's presents to take to their emperor? He sent two shirts, gold belts, two doublets, one satin, one velvet, with a matching scarlet bonnet for each and a pair of breeches. The next day, Easter Saturday, a man in a different style of Native clothes appeared. Behind Cuitlalpitoc was a veritable retinue. He was a regional governor, and had greeted Grijalva the year before. His mission was to observe these new men for himself and report back. The following day another personage presented himself: Teudile, the steward to Emperor Moctezuma, and also a provincial governor.

Cortés began his usual approach about representing the greatest lord on earth, Charles V, who 'had for many years heard rumours of this country and of the great prince who ruled it'. Cortés asked to meet the great prince of Mexico, in order to become friends and trade with him. What he got was a lesson in manners. Teudile replied, 'You have only just arrived and already you ask to speak to our prince. Accept now this present that we give you in our master's name, and afterwards tell *me* whatever you wish.'

Teudile presented a chest of finely wrought gold objects and ten bales of cotton, a fabric permitted only to the elite, all worked with feathers. In return Cortés gave beads, including some of glass, new to the locals, finely worked moss agate jewellery, and a chair, richly inlaid and decorated. On the beach Pedro de Alvarado led a gallop-past of the horses. Díaz had an eye for horses, defining men by their mounts the way we might judge someone by their car. Alvarado rode a sorrel mare, 'a great runner and very quick on the rein'.

In the background, specialist Aztec scribes were painting everything they saw: the strange ships, the cannons, horses and greyhounds, and full-length portraits of Cortés, all his captains, and interestingly, Malinche, whose importance was already apparent from reports despatched from other locations along the coast. Her behaviour added to the shock of the Spanish arrival. Women in Aztec culture were meant to be silent. They had no right to speak at important occasions, so her role in fronting the Spanish negotiations was disturbing to Moctezuma in many ways. In codices she is shown standing forward of the Spanish, or if Cortés is seated, standing behind his chair, shamelessly looking Moctezuma and other nobles in the eye, her long hair hanging loose in the fashion of an unmarried woman.

There is a two-word Italian phrase every translator knows, whatever their working languages are: *traduttore, traditore*. The translator is a traitor to the original. Malinche's role in the conquest secured her a highly-charged but ambivalent position in Mexican culture: an unsettling presence in modern Mexico's psyche. She was not Aztec, and she owed them nothing. Although Moctezuma would describe her as *ce ciatl nican titlaca*, 'one of us', he merely meant she was not Hispanic. The Aztecs called her an enemy, but not a traitor. She did not betray her own, but if today you call someone a *Malinchista,* the insult means you do not have Mexico's interests at heart. Whose interests would she cherish? Bereaved of her father, abandoned by her mother, traded as a chattel between different peoples, she had, for the third time, been dumped among people whose language she had to learn from scratch. In the enclosed universe of pre-Columbian Mesoamerica, the role of women was not a cultural choice, it was the way the world was made. Now Malinche was unmaking it with her speech. She became the Spanish voice in the New World, and that role would grow. Her voice allowed Moctezuma and Cortés to communicate. Without her, it would all have been *Popoluca*.

Teudile's alert eyes saw a soldier wearing an iron helmet in the morion style, a little rusty, but with patches of gilt to show it had once been smart. He begged to see it, because there was one like it in Mexico and it had been left by a departing god, Huitzilopochtli, who, it was said, would one day return. He asked if he could take it to show Moctezuma. Cortés agreed, but, never one to miss an opportunity, said, 'I have a sickness of the heart which can only be cured by gold.' Would they fill the helmet with grains of that metal and return it?

Teudile was soon on the road to the interior to report back. Díaz wrote that the Aztecs were 'convinced that we were of that race which, according to the prophecies of his ancestors, would come to rule the land'. But no one said so at the time, or for decades to come. There is no evidence for this alleged belief until nearly half a century after the conquest, when old men were narrating stories they had to reconcile with circular time. No prophecy: no event.

Teudile returned a week later, bringing a gold disc as big as a cartwheel worked all over with figures and designs, or as Cortés listed them in his inventory, monsters, the whole perhaps representing the sun. There was a silver moon disc, even bigger. It is impossible to guess what these were worth in those times. The gold disc weighed tens of kilos, and as I write, the price of gold is £42,000 a kilo. With the discs were the Spanish helmet, filled with grains of gold, and a great many gold ornaments of animals and model weapons. Cloths and featherwork added to the bounty. Charles V would handle an image made from feathers, unable to believe it wasn't paint until he had touched it for himself. Minute feathers from hummingbirds' breasts would create a blue-green iridescent sheen, and the finest ornaments would be topped with the long plumes from the tail of the resplendent quetzal, a bird hunted for Moctezuma in the distant rainforest of the southern highlands near modern-day Guatemala.

There was also a message from Moctezuma. He praised their prowess in battle at Frontera, and was pleased such knights had come so far, and that his own fame had reached such distant lands. Moctezuma wished 'to serve us in any way he could during our stay in that port. But as for meeting, he told us not to think about it, for it was not necessary, and he put forward many objections.'

Cortés excelled at these kinds of exchanges in which little can be taken at face value. He pointed out 'since we had crossed so many seas and journeyed from such distant lands solely to see and speak to him in person, our great king and lord would not receive us well if we returned without meeting him.'

The governor promised to deliver this message 'but he considered the request for an interview superfluous.' Cortés sent what gifts they could muster, the prize item being a Florentine glass decorated with hunting scenes. While he waited for a reply, he ordered Francisco de Montejo, who had been here with Grijalva, to look for a harbour suitable to use as a base. They returned with reports of another town on a hill above the coast, called Quiahuitzlan. When Teudile returned, it was with more gold, cloth and feathers, but 'as for an interview with Moctezuma, that was out of the question, it would be useless to send any further messages to Mexico.' Confronted by the rare sight of Cortés admitting failure, Díaz observed he was depressed by this news. A camp bell rang, and they fell to their prayers.

Moctezuma has been caricatured as a weak and hesitant ruler. He was not. He had held the throne for seventeen years, and incompetents were not tolerated. He had been an effective domestic ruler and military leader, conquering the Zapotec and Yopi peoples, and making the empire larger than at any time in Aztec history. He was also conservative and religious. He had introduced a rule that no one could look at his face, and put in reverse changes which had democratised appointments to senior positions. He now called for the opinions of the wizards on this strange arrival. A Native source reported: 'They knelt before him, with one knee on the floor, and did him the greatest reverence.' He asked them, 'Have you not seen strange omens in the sky or on the earth, or in the lakes and streams? A weeping woman or strange men? Visions, or phantasms, or other such things?' It sounds like Prospero interrogating Ariel. They said no. Moctezuma thought they were hiding the truth from him, and threw them in prison. Next day he instructed his steward to question 'whether sickness will strike, or hunger, or locusts, or storms on the lake, or droughts, and whether it will rain or not. If war is threatening Mexico, or if there will be sudden deaths, or deaths caused by wild beasts.'

The magicians answered 'What can we say? The future has already been determined and decreed in heaven, and Moctezuma

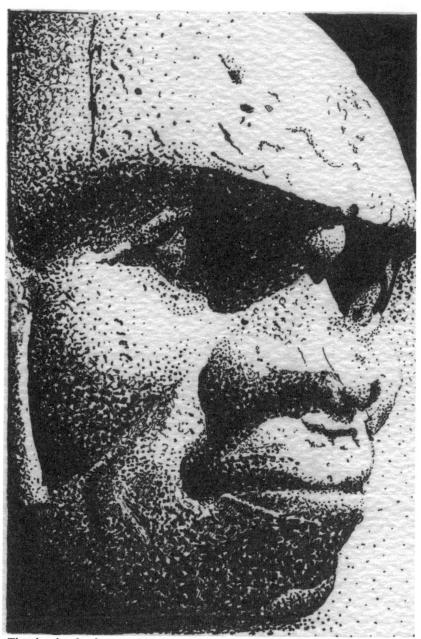

The depth of culture in Mexico: this colossal Olmec head testifies to a
sophisticated culture which flourished from 1500 BC around Venta near
Coatzacoalcos.

will behold and suffer a great mystery which must come to pass in his land. If our king wishes to know more about it, he will soon enough, for it comes swiftly. This is what we predict, he can only wait for it,' which is a long way of saying 'We don't know.'

Moctezuma persisted: 'Question them again about this mystery. Ask them if it will come from the sky or the earth, and from what direction it will come, and when this will happen.' The steward returned to the prison, but the wizards had vanished. The steward told Moctezuma that the guards were 'trustworthy men who have served me for years, but none of them heard the wizards escape. I myself believe that they flew away, for they know how to make themselves invisible, which they do every night, and can fly to the ends of the earth.'

The wizards' wives and children could not make themselves invisible. Their wives were hanged, and their children's brains dashed out against the walls of their own homes. The houses were demolished and the foundations dug up.

I had become a friend of ADO: *Autobuses de Oriente*, the Eastern Bus Company. Forget all the stereotypes about Latin American buses and livestock. These are comfortable modern buses, Volvos and Mercedes, which run to the busy timetable advertised on their user-friendly website. I think Britain is ready for something similar. The direct bus from Frontera to Coatzacoalcos was fully booked, so I had to change in Villahermosa which, despite its name (beautiful town), is a sprawling modern city where the armed guards at every door of the bus station either made you feel more secure or more nervous according to your state of mind. As we boarded, a uniformed woman scanned us for guns with a hand-held wand. She then walked the length of the aisle videoing our faces.

Coming into Coatzacoalcos we passed a road sign: Mexico 701 kms. Mexicans call their capital Mexico, seldom adding City. It was late afternoon, and three weeks' travelling, with barely adequate food, had worn me down. I discovered a cafe where two sisters cooked on a domestic stove. Their quesadillas were soft and easy to eat. I chomped away gratefully.

There was little to do on my day there except watch oil tankers enter the dredged harbour where the Spanish had been unable to cross the sandbar. It was easy to get lost in the gridiron streets with no landmark buildings, and every single museum was shut for no reason I could fathom. I was cheered when, struggling uphill wearing my blue shirt and Panama hat, a street vendor bowed and said 'Señor Anthropologist!'

The next night I returned to the cafe. Their quesadillas had sold out, and there was nothing I could eat. Back in my room with mini-market sandwiches, I saw how slackly my trousers fitted me. Never fat, I was thirty pounds lighter than before cancer. I was not supposed to be drinking spirits, but I thought today was a good day to be gentle with virtue. Tequila burned my throat like acid. I added mango juice. Slight improvement. When I drowned it in juice the pain was acceptable. I slept twelve hours.

I had given myself a target of three weeks to cover the coast and reach Veracruz, and was satisfied to be on the bus there on day twenty-two. I was a little apprehensive about Veracruz. Until now I had been in well-protected tourist areas or small towns and cities. Veracruz is the biggest port, and therefore the biggest drugs port, and it is poor. New statistics were announced in the local paper on the day I arrived; it was getting poorer. I would be there for the Day of the Dead, and I did not want to have any cheap headlines write themselves around me for the following day's paper. I found a hotel opposite one of the forts built into the old city walls. It was on the edge of the bay where the Spanish landed, but not a speck of natural landscape remains.

I needed to buy local maps to plan my route overland from here. At first, I mixed leisurely sightseeing of the town, the museums and forts, with enquiries about maps. On day two, leisurely was a memory, and I was quizzing anyone who would stand still about where I might find maps. By the end of the day I had no maps, but I had spent an hour with the municipal archivist, and Jamie Cortés Hernández, the regional archaeologist of the state heritage agency Conaculta.

Jamie was a portly fifty-year-old with a bristly, two-postage-stamp moustache, commemorative format. His office was off a courtyard, at the back of a Colonial building, which ambled back from a narrow frontage on a square. I asked about the exact locations of the first Spanish settlements here, and how they had changed sites.

'Initially they attempted settlement to the north of modern Veracruz at the place recommended by Francisco de Montejo on his reconnaissance. They arrived on Good Friday so it was called Villa Rica de la Vera Cruz, Rich Town of the True Cross; it is now called Villa Rica. Over twenty years ago I helped excavate a fort there. We found the walls, reduced to this height,' he indicated the seat of his chair, 'it was a standard design, oblong with a tower at each corner.'

I asked about my chances of finding the old roads used by the Natives and Cortés.

'Those roads followed the rivers, which move through time, so the modern highways haven't been built over them, but they have been swallowed up by the haciendas and buried.'

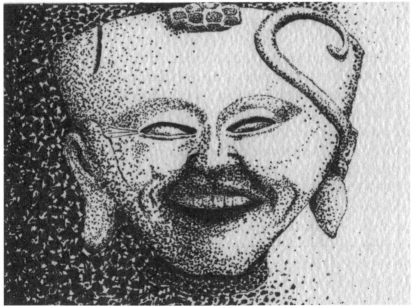

Mexico abounds in little-known mysterious cultures. Some of the laughing masks from the Veracruz Culture c.750 AD were found next to buried skulls.

The autumn weather was still fiercely hot and humid; it would break in another week. I had been hearing that for three weeks. In the afternoons I scanned the sky hoping to see the cumulus build into anvil-headed thunderstorm clouds to crack the air apart and let us breathe. They resolutely stayed small and fluffy.

Veracruz is a hustler's city in some parts, but a friendly place which I quickly came to like. My grandfather and great-grandfather were Liverpool seamen who had come here many times, and sentiment makes me well-disposed to the ports they sailed to. Some of the old dock buildings and offices would have looked the same in their day, only newer. Their designs were Colonial exports, and I have seen the same models since childhood: Liverpool, Valparaiso, and Montevideo.

When I travel alone, evenings are the tough time of the day to fill. Usually diary, dinner and a beer do the job. Neither was eating nor drinking easy, but needing forty minutes to eat half a main course did help pass the time. In the bars around the port, shaven-headed Russian sailors smoked in the non-smoking restaurants, and searched the menus for something familiar, before ordering a litre of tequila.

I wanted camping gas, which I never found, but I visited some interesting and distant parts of the city looking for it. I finally found the offices of INEGI, the national mapping agency, on the first floor of a bland back street, and a chubby, morose young man called Alejandro Negroe who told me they no longer sold maps.

'Where can I buy them? In a bookshop?'

'No.'

'Where, then?'

He seemed never to have considered where anyone bought the maps his office made. I explained my project, and without directly implying he would be responsible if I died emaciated on a circular desert trail with five sets of my bootprints on it, tried to make him feel a little ownership.

He sighed, blew out his cheeks, raised his eyebrows and held up a finger. 'We can give you the maps as electronic files. Is that any good?'

'Fine. Where can I print them?'

His arms impersonated helicopter blades. 'Anywhere.'

It took six hours running round town before I found somewhere with a machine to print A3 maps that was working and had ink left. I gave the assistant the memory stick and she opened the first map. I asked how much, she said, 'Nothing. We do not have a licence to print INEGI documents.'

'I have their permission. They said anyone can print them.'

'We can't.'

I repeated the medical consequences of me not having these maps. She looked at her watch. 'I'm supposed to have finished my shift seven minutes ago.' Over the last two days, almost entirely given over to asking the national map agency to sell me a map, I had developed a way of settling down in someone's space so I looked as if I wouldn't leave until they included me in their will. She pouted, 'The only person who can authorise it is the regional manager and he is in the other shop.' I showed the address to a taxi driver. The manager agreed, but made me swear to tell no one. By reading this you are agreeing to the same promise.

That afternoon I received an email from my younger brother, Neil, who seldom writes unless something has happened. It was titled Dad. Our father, at ninety-one, was still living independently at home. Alzheimer's disease, which my mother had been released from at the age he now was, was making this harder for everyone. My feelings about the time he had left were changing. There was little for him to enjoy, much more to suffer. The disease filled him with anger. Often it was directed at his bank, or the paper-driven care he was receiving from health and social services, and I could only agree with him. But no one suffered from the anger more than he did, since it drove out the little capacity he had left for pleasure. I dreaded opening the email, knowing there was not going to be any change for the better. It was simply a question of what kind of bad news it bore.

He had been taken into a care home. Neil wrote that Dad had become more confused, aggressive, and repetitive in his behaviour. It was hard to hear this news alone, so far away, and in weakened health myself. But it meant he now had supervision, and would not die because he had put the electric kettle on the gas hob and started a fire. He would not be arrested for abusing people who parked in his never-used parking space outside his block of flats. These were my fears for a man who, when the Second World War broke out, was seventeen years old, and the youngest person in MI5. He wanted to join the RAF, the most glamorous and dangerous service. They said if he joined he could never be re-admitted to the secret service. He joined.

The cancer had made me feel about ten years older, and in recovery, I was hauling back those years at a very slow pace. Now, when I looked at old people, I sometimes saw so clearly how much pain and weakness, even fear, shaped their lives. The pain had made me short-tempered, like him. Would that fall away, or would I be left with it? My father's decline seemed too close to bear. Wanting to find something to feel good about, I wished that being freed of his responsibilities would release him from his frustrations, leave him room for small joys. It would be a pleasure to meet again, for a little while, the clever and cheerful man, not the caricature for whom I was just an ear to rave into.

It was 31 October, All Saints' Day, the first of the Day of the Dead festival, a coincidence too blunt for ironies. Skulls were everywhere, including icing cakes, small sweets, and anything else that could made to look cranial. This is not a communal funeral, but a celebration of life before and after death. In Mesoamerican cultures, the bones were what endured after death, so they were symbols of life after death and rebirth. For me, they are a reminder of an X-ray of my skull with a shadow over the pituitary that must not grow or become denser, and of scans where I do not want to see any more lights come on.

In the country, cemeteries are decorated and families picnic around relatives' graves. In Veracruz, the public expressions of the Day of the Dead were mostly modern fun: the trams had been illuminated in Day-Glo lime green and skeleton drivers were placed alongside the living ones. I took a ride around the city centre on the top deck and enjoyed the crowds partying, lasers lancing the sky, the streets closed off for live music, and the squares turned over to bands, orchestras and dancing. I alighted in the main square, where a large silver band was playing dance music, and observed a woman slowly dancing on the spot, holding the hands of her father, facing her in a wheelchair. Her smile never wavered, his face never moved. My chest ached at her tenderness. I left quietly, making for my hotel, thinking of my mother's decline into trance-like consciousness in a ward at Cardiff Royal Infirmary where I held her hand for the last time, spoke to her, and listened to her incoherent responses; the sense of her world meant nothing in mine.

She still saw beauty; her eye followed the sunlight on the wall, filtered through a net curtain turning in the breeze from the open window. Other women lay catatonic or howling, thin, starved birds plucked of their dignity. The woman on the next bed, who had deteriorated sharply in the ten days I had been visiting, shrieked for a nurse in a voice that would have been torture to listen to had it come from a person in command of their mind. My mother looked me in the eye for the first time and said, 'You wonder why they let some of these mad people in here, don't you?' I smiled and asked her something, but her mind had gone away again. The reply came from her encrypted world, 'Da ree dooly sum.'

Toddlers in skeleton outfits begged for sweets. A schoolboy and girl in uniform sat with their legs over the side of the dock, sharing biscuits and sweets spread in the lap of her green tartan skirt, then kissing with earnest formality. Beyond them in the centre of the harbour a vast grey shape came out of the dusk, tended at the angular corners of its hull by a pair of tugs nipping skilfully around her like terriers penning an ox. The new vessel was an almost featureless slab of metal, high and with no visible superstructure. In minutes she slid out of sight behind the tankers and container carriers.

An evening breeze had sprung up cool and fresh, and luminous kites rose on it, their trailing ribbons curling up, then snapping straight. The streets seemed full of couples with newborn babies, the last of the Librans, conceived at Christmas or New Year like me, Celia and half my family; a clan born of carefree celebration of the season of gifts. A young woman in a Caribbean explosion of clothing lay along a bench with her head on her girlfriend's lap, resting her phone on her own drawn-up thigh to select music. Her sitting friend leaned forward across her face, obscuring the evening star.

Now I had my maps, the next day was left free for me to cross the harbour, to where the Spanish built their first serious defences. From the old town I could see the Fort of San Juan de Ulúa, which once stood on an offshore island in open water, but has been swallowed by the modern docks, so that just a moat separates it from the shore. The boatman for the launch which ferried tourists out to the fort was shooing away a stout lady stripped down to just her skirt, who was sitting on the stone steps washing herself. The fort's design became clearer as we motored behind to dock in what was now just a moat between the former island and the fort. The stern of a container vessel, the *Montevideo Express* of Monrovia, and the special container cranes that attended her, towered above us. In plan the fort was rectangular with a central parade ground. At each corner a lozenge-shaped fortification was superimposed so a V-shaped salient extended into the water. Once I had crossed the low pedestrian bridge over the moat, I could no longer hear the industrial docks, just fish leaping in the moat, watched intently by herons.

Pepperpot turrets fortified every corner. It was once rendered, but only patches remained, with lemon-coloured paint peeling away in a stylish moult. The exposed masonry was textured with delicate fan shapes, for there is no natural building stone around here, and the Spanish quarried coral reefs. I ran a finger along the convoluted surface of a brain coral.

When Cortés was here trading trinkets with the locals one day, a group of strange figures arrived from Tenochtitlán without introductions, and began to observe the Spanish and perform rites. These were magicians sent by Moctezuma to attack the Spanish. 'They concluded that the Spanish flesh was so tough it was impossible to know where their hearts were,' and slunk home to court.

Food arrived from the Aztec governor Teudile, but, probably to test what the Spanish beliefs and customs were, these Aztecs blessed it with a sprinkling of human blood from freshly sacrificed victims. The Spanish were disgusted, and spat and swore before refusing it. It seemed to fix the Spanish in an inflexible attitude: whatever skills and technologies they had mastered, these were truly savages. No quarter should be given, no trust extended.

I wanted to visit Isla de los Sacrificios, three nautical miles south-east of where I stood, but the boatmen told me the islet is now a bird sanctuary and landing is forbidden. From farther south on the sea front, I could see it a mile out, so flat a storm would wash right over it: a copse of palm trees, a lighthouse, and enough room for a helipad. The grey sea to either side flowed with white horses. The wind built up through the evening, and in the last light, the fronds of the palms in the park around the fort were trailing out on one side like wigs about to fly. When the rain came, it was nearly horizontal; pigeons on a ledge on the building opposite turned their faces to the wall. Above them the girders of the radio tower began to whistle through metal teeth. An American-style locomotive horn blew a single note of mourning while on a plastic roof beneath my window, something without music strummed its fingers.

I was done with the new Veracruz, but her abandoned sisters were waiting to the north.

9

My Christmas Tree

What seest thou else in the dark backward and abysm of time?

Within days I settle down to just being depressed, with passages of emptiness and fear, but no despair.

We begin to tell people I have cancer, and for some reason this makes me feel less optimistic. Within a day I am convinced I will not respond to treatment and will soon be dead. I began the year worrying about being sixty. I end it worrying if that neat number will be on my tombstone. Burial? Cremation? I've made no plans, maybe ashes to be scattered in the Southern Ocean, food for fish which might one day nourish the penguins.

John Donne wrote a much-quoted admonition to recognise we are a community of souls sharing a common fate: 'No man is an Island, entire of it self; every man is a piece of the Continent, a piece of the main[.]' From this moment the tide sweeps in for me, and I look across the deadly waters standing up in steep, short waves, separating me from the main. I am now an island. No one, not even Celia, is with me; she is on the continental cliffs, waving, holding her arms out, but a world away. You can go through this with someone at your side, but they are not in the same place, and cannot be.

One of my best friends is increasingly ill. Tan Pearson has been a broad shoulder and a beer-buddy through the years of break-up, when my home wasn't a fit place to sleep, as my then partner started dating another woman but still lived in our house. It becomes harder to get news as he becomes reclusive, and only replies to emails in the small hours, posting me web addresses hosting random trivia. A mutual friend, Richard, who visits me, does not see him around Pontcanna any more.

The classic cycle of adaptation to bad news was framed by Elisabeth Kübler-Ross: denial, anger, bargaining, depression and acceptance. I skip denial: the diagnosis has gone on so long that it is a relief to have a diagnosis, for it is easier to cope with bad news than extended doubt. I feel no anger, not against myself, since it isn't caused by bad habits, and not against my fortune; luck is luck, so there's no point in bargaining. I suffer from fear rather than depression. Acceptance takes a little while.

I have seizures about details: they may cut my tongue out and leave me dumb. What am I without words? Some people die when the tongue swells until it chokes them. Someone told me that cheery fact when Danny, who drank in the same Pontcanna pubs as me, was dying of throat cancer. I last saw him standing, skeletal, in Patel's store, quiet and resigned to his fate. Paperwork arrives for my pension, payable soon. There are two options for the balance between the lump sum and the income. In short, I have to gamble on how long I will live. I choose the live a long time option. If I die soon I won't need the money.

September comes, though in my diary, when the new month begins, I have written August again, each day, for weeks, without ever noticing. On 5th September, the day before the aspiration results that will define my fate, Celia and I go to Westminster Abbey and see the tombs of Elizabeth I and Henry V. It's a reminder that they actually lived, like me, that they were not just characters in the play of the past. In the floor, near the tomb of the unknown warrior, is a small stone dedicated to John Harrison. This one died in 1776; he was the man who solved the longitude problem. We walk along the embankment; by Hungerford Bridge my mood is plunging. We hug like parting lovers, holding on to what they have. I picture her, alone in the house for a second time: and it is intolerable, but highly likely. For the first time I am close to tears, catch myself, and straighten up, for her.

Tony, the consultant and neighbour, invites me for a pint on Saturday lunchtime. He tells me that four things make it likely that one would contract the common form of throat cancer, the 50 percent dead in five years variety. They are all lifestyle: be a spirit drinker and a smoker, with a history of syphilis and septicaemia. I score none from four. 'You are very young to have throat cancer at all. When you get the results, what you want to hear is that you are P16 positive, then the lymph glands are just reacting to a cancer caused by a virus. It's related to the one which causes cervical cancer.'

On 6 September, Celia and I sit sullenly as the train pulls out from Edgware Road, through Paddington, then runs overground out to Hammersmith. Crowds teem as we pass under the brutal flyover, which has an internal rot caused by gritting salt corroding its steel cables, a condition casually dubbed concrete cancer. Past the Apollo Theatre and, next to it *El Paso*, a Mexican restaurant so ruined it could be marketed as an authentic place to be fed, watered and shot. Past a tiny drab garden below the Guinness Trust flats in which a solitary shrub will bloom aromatically all the bitter winter to come, then the pub called *The Old Suffolk Punch*, a breed of farm horse Celia's grandfather raised and worked, the Maltese cafe specialising in cakes, and finally the main entrance to the hospital, with a Henry Moore statue in a pond, surrounded by benches and low walls where down-and-outs pursue the four qualifications for lifestyle throat cancer.

I see Peter Clarke. He has a kindly caring manner, but is serious. 'The samples from the throat tumour and the glands both hold cancerous cells. You are P16 positive: that means the cancer is HPV in origin ...' He continues to talk, but I am alone with my own thoughts. A part of me had still been fostering a little bit of denial, *perhaps it will not be cancerous*, but the muscles around my heart have relaxed. It is HPV; nine out of ten live, not fifty-fifty. My attention comes back to the room, where Peter Clarke is adding, '... relatively new in that it is being presented in numbers for the first time. Two years ago we might not have continued looking after your initial all-clear. It's in a good position to treat.'

I buy expensive hi-fi headphones; there will a lot of time spent doing nothing in bed. I wonder what other purchases are sensible: shall I buy a 2013 year planner? Spring bulbs? Renew my annual subscriptions to magazines? Should I bother to look carefully before crossing the road? Shortly after this date my diary entries stop for ten days. I am taking stock.

On 13 September I go for a PET scan, a misleadingly comforting acrostic. I wait in the area marked Nuclear Medicine, reading a John Sutherland essay on *Frankenstein*. The Positron Emission Tomography scan is preceded by injecting a radioactive sugar into my blood. It sounds like a new club-drug fashion, and will be administered by a slightly camp Romanian called Igor Petro. Perhaps that should be PETRO: Positron Emission Tomography Research Operative. After the injection, he says, 'You will not be able to read for one hour while you wait.' I pick up the paper. I can still read. He repeats, 'You will not be *able* to read for one hour.' He means *allowed*. 'Wrong areas light up when your brain is working on reading.' That's a matter of opinion, I thought. The bed faces a wall on which there is one thing to look at: a clock with a long red hand beating the seconds, 3600 of them.

I have bought Celia a semi-eternity ring of emeralds set off by small diamonds for her birthday in two weeks' time. When I return home I give it to her. We aren't married, so this is for solidarity, for unconditional love.

On 20 September the results of the PET scan come through. This should show a single bright spot in my throat caused by greater metabolic activity in the cancer. There is always the one-in-ten shot, that we would see more white spots away from the throat. Celia and I wait for hours in the chaotic day clinic in the central tower block at Charing Cross Hospital, which, confusingly, is now in Hammersmith. Peter Clarke has passed me on to the consultant in charge of chemotherapy and radiotherapy planning. When we enter the room of experts we enter the atmosphere of a funeral parlour. An image comes up on the computer screen. My neck and chest are lit up like a Christmas tree. I squeeze Celia's hand and stare out of the window at the drab terraces and the pocket gardens of Baron's Court in autumn decline. So this is the place where I find the terms of my mortality. Mephistopheles rising, arms wide in welcome. There is palpable shock in the air; no one had expected this.

The oncology consultant in charge of treatment passes on bad news as if it adds to the gravitas of his post. 'These are the lymph glands which have been affected. It could be sarcoid reaction, which is not nice, but not dangerous in Caucasians. Afro-Caribbean races can suffer badly with complications.'

'But if they are cancers it's bad news.' It is becoming my catchphrase.

'Very bad news.'

'I thought this type of cancer seldom metastasised.' I've boned up on the medical word for spread.

He gained momentum. 'Very bad news indeed. There are two kinds of throat cancer. You may have both.'

Tony had told me that the answers to just two questions were what really mattered. 'Is it advanced?'

'Yes.'

'Is it operable?'

'No.'

Inhale. Make yourself.

'Treatable?'

'We'll test these secondary sites, and decide on treatment when we have the results of the new aspiration.'

Celia asks other questions with a quaver in her voice. I scarcely register the questions or answers. We walk in Kensington Gardens and sit under a bench away from other people. I tell her I could not be brave without the certainty that I love her. Everything has shifted in that short audience from knowing all the signs were pointing to long-term survival, to now, this wretched *now*, with just a slim chance of survival remaining. I have no children. Over two relationships there were many pregnancies but none lasted more than a few months. The line stops with me. Mortality will be absolute: the halt of the generations. I feel physically and emotionally filleted. Pigeons and squirrels gather, expecting food. Will I live longer than that bird, this rodent? How long do the little fuckers live anyway?

Over another beer, Tony consoled. 'I've looked at your scans, and the hotspots look too symmetrical for ordinary throat cancer. As I said, you are young to have one type of cancer. I don't believe this idea you might have two.'

Aspiration: inspiration, the act of breathing, a breath, a sigh. Steadfast desire for something above one. More needles in the neck.

Part 2

Mexico! Mexico!

4. Cortes's Route from Coast to Tenochtitlán

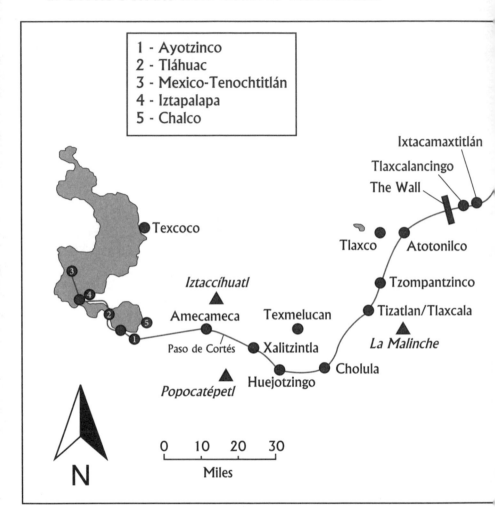

1 - Ayotzinco
2 - Tláhuac
3 - Mexico-Tenochtitlán
4 - Iztapalapa
5 - Chalco

Ixtacamaxtitlán
Tlaxcalancingo
The Wall

Texcoco

Tlaxco
Atotonilco

Iztaccíhuatl

Tzompantzinco

Amecameca
Texmelucan
Tizatlan/Tlaxcala

La Malinche

Paso de Cortés
Xalitzintla

Cholula

Popocatépetl
Huejotzingo

N

0   10   20   30
Miles

GULF
OF
MEXICO

Tlatlauquitépec

Teziutlán

Xalacingo

Altotonga

Villa Rica de
la Vera Cruz

Quiahuiztlán

Perote

Cofre de
Perote

Xalapa

Coatépec

Cempoala

Cardel

San Juan
de Ulúa

Xico

Antigua

Monte Grande

Isla de
Sacrificios

Ayahualulco

Ixhuacán

Pico de Orizaba

10

The First Foothold

Two early attempts at founding Veracruz were abandoned: Antigua and Villa Rica. The simplest way to visit them was to lodge in the small inland town of Cardel and make day trips, but I was not too excited about staying somewhere my guidebook enticingly described as a 'lively transport hub'. The Hotel Cardel stood on the corner of a large square and I had a room with a view where I could put a chair and watch life go by. I dropped off my pack and returned to the bus station.

After 20 miles, the coast bus north passed beneath an imposing hill rising steeply from the coastal plain. I was staring up at the fluted basalt cliffs which made up the hill's north-east ramparts when the driver slowed down, nodded at me and said 'Villa Rica.' The bus drew away, leaving me alone at the roadside near the entrance to a narrow road with luxuriant hedgerows. If you ignored the tree species it could have been a Devon lane in June. I strolled past the sign that read: *Villa Rica 168 inhabitants, located in the outer plan for radiation emergencies*. Its neighbour at the end of the long shallow bay to the north is Laguna Verde, home of both Mexico's nuclear power stations. Swish holiday homes with two-car garages sat behind high fences. Guard dogs barked, gardeners and cleaners clipped, cut, swept and dusted, but the owners were in town. The road dissolved into a sand track; I bought milk and chocolate at a small shop with little on the shelves except sweets and fizzy drinks. A radio played; a band of palm trees marked the head of the beach where, beneath frond-thatched roofs without walls, families picnicked, hammocks were slung, and outboard engines benched.

I was the only non-Mexican and as I walked along a sandy beach, on which purple trumpet flowers sprang from endless webs of vines, each family group took a turn to stare. At intervals lay tree trunks from which the bark had been ground off to reveal satiny white wood; I could not keep my fingertips off them.

Observing where the waves began to form, I could see the bay was shallow for a mile. The next headland to the south was five miles off, and the air between was laden with fine spray whipped off the wave tops. The shore was washed to a dull zinc. The shadows of clouds forming inland turned the brilliant fields and tree canopies to the dead green of dusty conifer woods. To my left, an outlying boss of land 100 yards across and as many feet high, was linked to the shore by a high bank of sand dunes, which I climbed, panting, while swallows zinged round my shins. They flew how I wanted to run when I was a boy: lightning and ballet fused.

The outlier was covered in dense scrub that looked ideal for snakes, and a loose mat of twigs and dry fronds, perfect for spiders to hide in. I had given up researching dangerous wildlife after beginning with scorpions, and finding out Mexico has 200 species. I did recall a coral snake whose nickname is the 20-minute snake, (your life expectancy after the bite), and it was not easy to forget the fluffy orange caterpillar of the southern flannel moth, whose hairs are venomous and can kill sensitised victims. The adult moth looks like a tarantula-rottweiler crossbreed. I sweated up the hill, less from the now oppressive heat, more from fear of a sudden needle bite and then the sear of some exquisitely-refined toxin exploring my nerve endings. All I suffered was scratches; every plant had thorns. From the hill I could see, over the slight promontory opposite, a scatter of stylish modern villas gleaming above green lawns. The old Villa Rica was under them, and, Jamie the archaeologist from Conaculta had told me, under the dune causeway, but above ground there was nothing to see of this first European settlement in the Americas since Erik the Red wintered in north Newfoundland soon after 980 AD.

The bay of Villa Rica soothed the eye. Perhaps it was the steady roll of the breakers coming into the broad bay, beneath the hypnotic drift of the spume drawn in on the wind. Although the bay was shallow, behind the outlier and spit there was protection from the northerly winds that caused the Spanish the most problems.

Looking back inland through binoculars, the hill with basalt ramparts had a ledge running north from it, on which I could see a low stone mass. This historic site was very much above ground: the Totonac settlement of Quiahuitzlán: The Place Where it Rains.

I crossed the causeway over marshes where two purple gallinules splashed into flight: coot-like birds with indigo and viridian feathers set off by eye-shocking crimson and chrome yellow on the beak. This bird is believed to be the miraculous 'heron' seen in Tenochtitlán presaging, in the mirror on its head, the arrival of the Spanish. Cortés climbed this road about 1 June 1519. To spare the horses, they did not always ride, but that day he wanted to impress the chief, and he ordered everyone to mount, and told his men never to appear surprised by anything. They must always seem in control. I was visiting Villa Rica and Cempoala in reverse order to Cortés. When Cortés arrived, the Quiahuitzlán chief had been forewarned by the chief of Cempoala, and had prepared a hospitable welcome, though some accounts say that when the moment came most of the inhabitants ran away in fear. I was greeted by sulphur-orange butterflies chasing through the air, and a velvet-black species whose wing tops were sprayed with flecks of white set off by four vermillion blood drops on each wing.

At 500 feet, I emerged onto the ridge I had seen from below. The best description of this curious site is that it was a fortified city cemetery, begun around 850 AD by a small local culture with architectural influences from the Toltecs, based far away, north-east of modern Mexico City. It was then taken over by the Totonacs, a regional power. From 900 there are signs of Aztec influence, and it was later brought under their control. A series of small plazas, now lawns, divided by knee-high walls, led to one plaza which at a first glance was scattered with stone beehives. A closer look revealed they were miniature temples the size of a large doll's house, made from a shelly concrete, which gave them a seaside municipal look. These were burial vaults in which selected bones were placed: the arms, legs and skull. I sat down among them, my feet dangling over the scarp facing the sea. The richness of the forest was a marvel. After 5 minutes studying the tree canopy, I could not see two trees of the same species. I found my favourite, *Bursera simaruba,* locally called *chaco*, widespread because it is virile: a green branch stuck in the ground will root, and it out-toughs hurricanes. The sinuous boles are smooth in a sensual way, but the papery surface of the bark is red and peels, giving it a new nickname: the tourist tree.

The Spanish were greeted without signs of fear or surprise, although they were much stared at, particularly their beards. Native American peoples have little facial hair, and usually remove what does grow. On a tree trunk above my head I saw a five-pointed star of mauve petals with its centre formed of a purple cowl above a tongue whose base first turned yellow then cream tiger-striped with coffee-colours. It was *Laelia gouldiana*, named after a vestal virgin, and one of the most beautiful of Mexico's 1200 species of orchid. When Cortés stood where I was, other visitors arrived, in embroidered cotton, which was reserved for the elite, and their hair slick and drawn back. As they swaggered into this plaza, they sniffed a type of fragrant blossom which only people of the highest status were allowed to smell. The Lord of Quiahuitzlán began to tremble. He had encountered aliens from Europe without batting an eyelid, but these men with scented flowers frightened him. Servants walked before them whisking insects from the air, and with superb aplomb, they passed Cortés, his captains and their terrifying horses, and did not deign to notice them. Village servants scurried to bring them luxury foods and chocolate to drink. They were Moctezuma's stewards, his tribute collectors.

In Quiahuitzlán, and other places ahead, we have the victim's perspective of what it was like to live as a subject nation under the Aztec Empire. They were always resentful, often frightened. Cortés put his tongue in his cheek and observed to the local chief that Moctezuma would be very pleased to hear Cortés and his friends had been so well received. The chief blanched. He knew Moctezuma would look on any amity with extreme suspicion, suspecting an alliance to challenge his rule. So when Cortés suggested he arrest the stewards, the local dignitaries were appalled, but the chief thought for a moment and seized the collectors. A collar with a pole was attached to their necks in the fashion of criminals, and a steward who resisted was given a beating to encourage the others to acquiesce.

This move might have occurred to anyone, but Cortés's guile is illustrated by what he did next. He released two of the prisoners and summoned Aguilar and Malinche to talk to them. The stewards were both affronted and rattled, and babbled that these coastal people were barbarians, and, they stupidly continued, given half a chance, would rise in rebellion.

Cortés freed them, asking them to return to Tenochtitlán and assure Moctezuma of his good intentions. He despatched a vessel to carry them north out of Totonac territory. Moctezuma might have distrusted Cortés, but in the end the chief's men had seized them and Cortés's men had freed them. In the morning, the chief bought the story that the stewards had escaped, but he wanted to kill those who remained. Cortés magnanimously pleaded that they were only acting on orders, and his offer to shackle them and imprison them on his ship was accepted, as it distanced the chief from the remains of the problem. Cortés's strategy had left both Totonacs and Aztecs feeling he was on their side.

The chief was certainly decisive. He held a brief conference with his nobles and said he was ready to rebel provided Cortés led the army, which must have made the Spanish swallow hard. They had planned to keep Moctezuma onside for as long as possible. This would show their hand prematurely. So Cortés asked 'How many men can you put in the field?'

'A hundred thousand.'

We can take it this was not a head count; it meant 'a lot'.

Cortés was not an experienced field commander but he had grown up in a frontier town and the Spain of his lifetime had been constantly in conflict with its neighbours, its competitors and itself. He began to apply those lessons in earnest, and his strategy would soon emerge.

Before he left to go back to Villa Rica and consolidate his new base, he went through the formalities of swearing in the Lord of Quiahuitzlán as a loyal servant of a man whose existence he had been unaware of at breakfast the day before. He formally founded Villa Rica de la Vera Cruz on 28 June 1519 and took a hand in planning the layout of the plaza, church, barracks, and, to show this was a place where law ruled: the stocks, prison and gallows. Soon a general arrived from Tenochtitlán with two nephews of Moctezuma, bearing a message that Cortés's service in freeing the stewards would cause Moctezuma to overlook the discourtesy of staying without permission at a Totonac town. He was accepting Cortés's line, but with his eyes wide open. The ambassadors had words ready for the question they knew would come again. Moctezuma was both unwell and busy. It was hard to say when a meeting could happen, but it could be considered. Cortés had made a little headway.

I followed Cortés's route down the hill and and stood with my thumb out for the next bus, which was so full my seat was on the steps inside the front door. The fortress passed by, high above to my right. The day had been deeply satisfying, real sites looking much as they had 500 years before. I had climbed the same road as Cortés and followed his footsteps, to a very Mexican kind of place, a fortified cemetery, and looked down on the bay which nurtured such grand dreams. I felt I also had a foot in the door.

Back in Cardel I strolled at dusk around the square, which had a small-town plainness about it: almost prim. There was a second, low-budget, commercial area behind it where the unfenced railway ran through a strip of cheap shops and ramshackle stalls. It had a pulse to it that the square lacked. Hen chicks were for sale in plastic bags like goldfish at a fair.

As dusk fell, great-tailed grackles congregated in their thousands on the wires and in the tree canopies around the square. These birds are built like slender magpies, but with a lighter, down-curved beak which comes to a sharp point. The males are glossy blue-black, and the females a dun colour, and they have an astounding vocal range. In this first month I had often heard a strange bird-call, and scanned around me to see what new bird it was, only to see another grackle.

I had been tricked by melodic tunes, wild shrieks and whistles, and hoarse cackles. They filled the parallel wires in long arpeggios, and fruited the trees. Slowly the birds would quieten to roost, then a tree would erupt and a cloud of shrieking birds would fly in a mob round the square, over the water tower that looked like a Martian in H G Wells's *War of the Worlds*, and return to start claiming roosts all over again. I could never guess when they were done.

The square was also filling with people, and a band dressed in matching white trousers, blue shirts and Panama hats was lining up under the colonnade of the town hall to play for the evening tea dance. Another group of people in different matching outfits arrived, and drove round the centre in open top pick-ups with machine guns fixed to a frame above the tailgate: the military police. I looked at the pensioners starting their slow waltz with fresh admiration, and waited for them to start a riot that would justify the police presence.

Another bus took me down the coast road back towards modern Veracruz, but stopped short and left me in a lane leading down to a sleepy estuary, and, as it said on the arch spanning the road: Antigua Vera Cruz. Nearby: Pop. 963. I walked through farmland and scrub, stopping to watch a pair of altamira orioles patrol the stubby trees of their empire in orange and black, showing off as if lesser birds were subject to sumptuary plumage laws. A white goat peered at me with the haughty look of being both the emperor and his sardonic jester.

The village was still half-asleep, despite the curse of Mexico: cheap, powerful hi-fi systems. From a concrete house of two rooms, with all windows, doors and shutters closed, came an ear-shredding disco-mariachi beat. Was someone inside sitting in a chair staring at the wall not knowing if they were waiting for madness to begin or end, flies on their lips?

In the pleasantly shabby square, two vultures tumbled, fighting, from the tower, only to square up to each other again onto the ground, shaking their feathers into line like bar-room scrappers straightening their collars. A newspaper-seller on a tricycle with a megaphone taped to the handlebars was playing a recording of the headlines, making the opening of a school extension sound like the outbreak of war.

The ancient church was nicely proportioned but suffered from black and green moulds on the white and sky-blue plaster interior. The polished floor was of red brick parquet like the 1950s hallways and kitchens of my childhood. To me, the plaster images of Mary, Christ and the saints were crude mannequins from a country fairground. But that was the point: this was not fine art but a text written in headlines for a people with limited literacy. The statues were not complicated by obscure symbolism; each face was engraved with emotions written in bold and underlined, whether beatific trance or the agonised pain of their heart, body or mind writhing across a bloody face, emotions a field worker could understand, especially patient suffering.

As I left the church, I could see ruins along the left-hand side of the square, set in a well-trimmed garden. A spare, dapper man with wire-framed glasses and a courier's bag slung crossways from his shoulder headed purposefully towards me. 'My name is Wenceslao, I am an archaeology and anthropology guide.' I could not imagine how many days he must sit in the square and wait while tourists did not come – he must live like a spider, seizing on the rare flies, cocooning his source of nourishment and eking it out. I was happy to hire him as a guide to the ruins, for what was buried by the dunes of Villa Rica is here still standing around the square.

'The first building in this range,' he said, 'was the *Casa de Contratación*, the counting house. All valuables gifted, found or stolen, had to go through here before being redistributed after one fifth had been deducted to send to the King, in payment for his approval of expeditions to the New World. At the time it was built, all the gold and silver in the New World came through these doors. The guard house was next door.'

In 1523 Cortés laid out these buildings and lived here for a while. There was little local stone available, just the rounded local river stones. At Cempoala the Totonacs had learned to build great pyramids of this difficult material, but the Spanish avoided using it as much as they could. They hauled coral from San Juan de Ulúa, and imported slim, Roman-style bricks made in Cuba. The floor was grey tiling made locally and in good condition. Wenceslao kneeled against the foot of a wall and I joined him, waiting for my eyes to become accustomed to the gloom. 'See!' He pointed to two tiles, each of which had a paw-print in it. 'Coyote.' He pointed to the second, quite different one: 'Jaguarundi!'

500 years ago a coyote had trotted across a yard where the tiles were drying and left its signature in history. The jaguarundi is a dark cat a little bigger than a domestic cat, active night and day, which put its silent paw in the clay, and perhaps uttered the high-pitched chirrup that is its only sound, and continued on its gipsy foraging. Most of us expect nothing grander to stand for us in time than a moment's footfall saved forever, in the corner of a dark room.

It was moving to duck through the doorways, knowing that the famous names of the conquest had stepped over those same thresholds. The character of the buildings is dominated by something that both attacks the walls and holds them up, the *amate* tree, one of the strangler figs. Wenceslao showed me a sapling making an innocent-looking start on the side of a wall. A twiggy seedling sporting five leaves had no niche to lodge in, but a web of roots, far larger than the plant seemed to need, was spreading over the masonry. These roots will take over the entire wall. They can envelop a tree in a mesh, stealing its light and nutrients, until it dies and rots away, leaving a hollow trellis as a cenotaph. The roots do not delve into walls, as those of the prickly pear do, but sheath them. The core block of these Colonial buildings was now a mould on which a copse of vast *amate* trees had clamped itself. The utilitarian rooms had been transformed into a creeping, organic wall and roof. It is surmised that the inspiration for gothic naves in medieval cathedrals was a forest glade, with columns and arches standing for the trees and branches. The rough ruins were becoming chapels of living trees, and the trees could not be removed without the walls beneath falling in a heap. This hybrid is how it will be preserved: a tableau of nature trying to strangle the past, but only succeeding in strengthening it.

In the square, the town hall's plain single-storey facade has a low red roof in Roman tiles. Renovations disguise its age; it is the oldest town hall in the Americas. At the rear I glimpsed the crude masonry of the original. Nearby is a church, the Ermito Rosario, even older than the one in the square. Work began in 1523, just 2 years after the fall of Tenochtitlán. Although it is tiny, the first nave was only half this size. The join is easy to see, as these amateur builders changed from a semicircular concrete roof like a cement Nissen hut, to a low ridged tiled roof. Massive buttresses betray a lack of confidence in their walls. Wisely, they did not attempt to build a tower. Instead, the west facade rises a little higher than the roof and is pierced by a triangle of three arches, each hung with a bell. There is the simplest of piscinas set into the wall and the first church baptisms were held here, in the first church in the Americas.

Beneath a blossoming tree, a donkey tied to a garden fence looked no more ambulant than the tree. I remembered being alone in the Peruvian Andes with Dapple the donkey, who suffered from motion sickness, or to be more exact, was allergic to motion. I thought this donkey was staring at me oddly, and suffered a pang of fear that donkeys were telepathic and now they all knew about me.

Round the corner, Wenceslao pointed to a flat concrete slab that had been the overhanging corner of a flat roof, but now hung straight down, held only by internal reinforcing rods. 'Knocked down by a tree. If it had fallen a metre to the left it would have demolished the house.'

I looked around. 'That was unlucky. There are hardly any big trees.'

'Not since 11:30 in the morning on 17 September 2010. That's when Hurricane Karl hit us. Its centre passed directly over the town. If we had been in this street that day we would have been waist-deep in water. No matter how massive the tree was, it came down. Only one tall tree was left, a Norfolk Island Pine.' He pointed to the tree; it belongs to the same genus as the monkey puzzle, but grows its branches in neat layers. All the way up its trunk, fresh green branches were sprouting. Only at the top had branches survived the hurricane, where the whippiness of the trunk had taken some of the strain. The poor thing looked like a toilet brush. 'And the *amates*,' he added, nodding back at the ruins. 'When they are that size, nothing moves them.'

We walked past even vaster trees, which the Spanish are supposed to have moored their ships to, and out onto a suspension footbridge over a muddy green river. The river is still called by the Native name for the town: Huizilapan. The ships could not come into the river, and the gold and silver were lightered out. I looked down as the sliding waters bore memory away. With the modern village hidden in forest, and just a few wooden boats in sight, it was easy to imagine Spanish barges, loaded with heavy chests, nosing clumsily downriver and over the surf of the bar, to the anchored ships, whose pilots anxiously scanned the horizon for signs of the weather turning. Once full, the ships would turn out to sea and head northeast, either putting in at Havana, on the west end of Cuba's north coast, or heading past, looking for the westerlies to drive them home to Spain. Here, from this muddy bank-side, out beyond this bend, the wealth of the new continents began to pour out. A larger ship might take fifty tons of silver which would be worth, at modern prices, over £20,000,000. Thousands of such vessels sailed. Had it been invested it would have made Spain a superpower, but it was spent, and how stupidly we will see later, in Acapulco.

Wenceslao was knowledgeable about history, plants and everything to do with his home town, but he was chippy about people who got things wrong: other guides, maybe travel writers. As we passed the school he pointed out murals commissioned by a former president of Mexico. 'Look, he has Cortés in three ships instead of eleven, and they are the *Niña, Pinta* and *Santa María*, Columbus's ships. People like that are running Mexico!' The grumpy spirit of Bernal Díaz lives on.

11

In the Land of the Fat Chief

Cempoala is a small town, a twenty-minute bus ride north and a little west of Cardel. The bus took some finding. It had once been white but may have been parked in the small side street out of shame. Its destinations were painted in whitewash on the windscreen by someone keen to know more about writing but new to the game. The dashboard looked like the bench of an untidy workman and I could see the road through the hole around the gear stick. In other words, it was a proper bus. The driver was a cheerful, chatty man who already knew every passenger but me, so he asked about my trip. As I was leaving, it seemed a safe time to ask why the tea dances were guarded by armed soldiers. 'There are two roads running inland from Veracruz, and Cardel lies on the less used one. It is the one the drug carriers prefer, and we are at the crossroads of five routes so it is good for distribution.'

'Drug distribution depot' might have made a more colourful strapline in the guidebook than 'lively transport hub.'

Before Cortés came to Cempoala from San Juan de Ulúa, he staged a coup over his own expedition. His purpose was to be independent of the established Caribbean power base in Cuba under Governor Velázquez. Before he left Cuba, Cortés had discussed with friends the possibility of settlement, but he had no mandate for it; officially he was looking for Grijalva, and trading. Velázquez would do all in his power to prevent him setting up a second power base in the region, and he had many supporters in the expedition, but by no coincidence most of them were now sailing north on Montejo's reconnaissance cruise.

Cortés's allies and enemies agree on what happened next: 'all the people with one accord required the said captain to settle the land.' Many of them had become disillusioned over the slim pickings remaining in Cuba and Hispaniola, and saw Mexico as their chance to get a lucrative first grab at new land. Loyal Velázquez supporters became furious, and Cortés seemed to capitulate to them, giving orders to return to Cuba. The majority pro-settlement faction then protested so vehemently that he threw up his hands and allowed himself to be talked out of Cuba. The senior captains publicly acted a charade of requiring Cortés to show them his commission from Velázquez, which they declared accomplished. He could now write his own orders.

Cortés's first letter to the king recounts events up to the start of his march inland. Unlike the ones that follow, which are straightforward first-person narratives, it is written in the third person. It makes everything sound oddly formal, like a civil service account of events, while Díaz's account reads like a report from a front-line correspondent. When Cortés describes his coup, the use of the third person allows him to distance himself from events, and place the initiative in the hands of the men: 'all this was accompanied by certain intimations that that we would protest against him if he did not do as we required.' Using 'we', he appears to be merely one of the men backing Cortés. He becomes the servant of popular will, not the leader of a revolt.

Contract fulfilled, Cortés resigned, and was elected civil and military commander. Friends and allies, nearly all from Extremadura, were appointed to key posts. It was stage-managed to smother dissent, in the manner of a modern party conference. From this day, Cortés would declare that all policy decisions, including the action to invade the Aztec empire, were made by a lawful council. He defended this with a good knowledge of the reforming code of law published by King Alonso X of Spain, *The Seven Chapters*. It provided that in Spain men of good standing in any community could form a council to govern locally and not just make laws, but set aside existing laws. The community in Mexico comprised Cortés's force: no votes for the Natives.

Out of these changes came another one without parallel: Cortés would be entitled to a fifth of the booty, putting himself on an equal footing with the king. The rest would be distributed to all men, according to rank.

In the first week of June 1519, Cortés set off overland to see the harbour at Villa Rica. On the second day they were met by a welcoming delegation of Cempoalans. The view enjoyed by the mounted horsemen would have been similar to mine from the bus, looking over the extensive flat valley floor to orchards and rich, well-irrigated fields. In Nahuatl, Cempoala means Place of Twenty Waters. Even Cortés found time to sell the beauty of the land to the king, though his account has a little of an estate agent's sales pitch about it: 'The country inland is likewise very flat with most beautiful meadows and streams; and among these are so beautiful that in all Spain there can be none better.' Offers in excess of 10,000 castellanos.

I was dropped off outside the gates of the Totonac archaeological site, and lay against the least populous patch of an ant-filled wall, waiting for nine-o'clock. The exceptionally well preserved site shows what the Spanish saw of the local civilisations. A delegation invited them to come to their city, and apologised that their chief, who was impatient to meet them, was unable to come in person. The reason given told them that at least one person in town was prosperous: he was too fat to move. The advanced scout who was the first to see Cempoala galloped back to say there was a city whose buildings were plated in silver. A closer look revealed white-washed stucco. Díaz records that for the rest of his life the man could not mention silver without someone saying, 'Well anything white looks like silver to you.' Funny for the first 30 years, you imagine.

The chief came out to embrace them. Because his name, Tlacochcalcatl, is not easy to say or spell, the chroniclers simply called him the Fat Chief. Room was made for them in a palace with suites of rooms and courtyards. Cortés was welcomed so cordially he suspected a trap, and set up his quarters with the cannon deployed. The city's central area was sealed by rampart-like walls, a point not missed by the Spanish.

I walked through the gates and onto a huge level expanse of lawns with monuments on every side, and in front of me a large step pyramid dominating the plaza. Trees with long, delicately fronded leaves grew to monumental size. One canopy was 50 yards across. I would be the only visitor there for the next 2 hours. A shrine had been set up for the Day of the Dead and a stepped series of trestle tables, laden with food, drink and candles, rose like an altar to a back curtain painted with skeletons in elegant nineteenth-century dress. It was in the style known as a *calavera,* literally *skull,* popularised by the greatest printmaker of the Mexican Revolution: José Guadalupe Posada. Birds had found the cake and it was pitted where they had delved.

To the left I was excited to see for the first time that one of the temples had a round rear elevation, a design used only on shrines dedicated to the god Quetzalcoatl in his aspect as Ehécatl, the wind god. No corners may obstruct his flight. Every building was constructed of the only material to hand, round basalt stones from the nearby River Alcopan. There can be few less tractable materials to work with, perhaps only the flint nodules which medieval church builders used in East Anglia, which are like stone tubers. Cempoalan masons graded the stones carefully by size, and laid them on rows bedded in cement. So many shells were used in the render which covered these stones that they gave a glitter through the whitewash, producing the blinding reflections which had deceived the Spanish scout, his eyes misled by his heart's greed. The render is almost wholly gone, so the stones lie bare again, rows of giant black mint imperials. In front of the pyramid was a miniature temple which formed a seat where the Fat Chief and his ancestors and heirs could overlook the stone dais on which human and animal sacrifices were performed.

Across future decades, settlers, friars, philosophers, lawyers, and royalty would argue about the status and rights of the people who built such cities. To our minds their arguments seem more medieval than modern. They did not have mental worlds distorted by prejudices and errors; prejudices and errors *were* their mental world. It was in great part through these debates that the medieval reliance on the Greek philosophers of antiquity, especially Aristotle, was broken. Scholars in the Americas were in a strange place intellectually and culturally, as well as geographically. Many asked, 'If Aristotle did not know of the existence of these continents, in what else was he ignorant?' José de Acosta (1540-1600), author of the first encyclopaedia of the New World, found himself laughing away Aristotle's theory of the uninhabitably hot torrid zone, not because he had thought of a new and brilliant argument, but because he was climbing an Andean mountain near the equator, and shivering under the midday sun. The medieval system for describing things was all they had, and it had been creaking back in Europe, but they had to stick with it because without a system they could not describe what they found. José de Acosta was a Jesuit who spent the years from 1572 to 1586 in the Caribbean, Ecuador, Peru, Bolivia, Guatemala, Nicaragua and Mexico. He has one of the most interesting minds of all the chroniclers, and encapsulated the paradox of the New World, that you can only describe an alien world to someone who already knows it: 'The things of the Indies seemed, after I had had personal experience of them, to be both the same as I had heard them and not the same. Indeed I found them to be the same in that those who told me about them had not actually lied to me about them; but nevertheless I judged [the whole] to be different and very unlike what I had first thought.'

Nothing made less sense than the problem of the existence of these new races and their status. Scholars all approached the problem through the writings of Aristotle (384-22 BC) filtered through the commentaries of Thomas Aquinas (1225-74 AD), his great Christian interpreter. The work of one of the bright new generation in Salamanca University, Francisco de Vitoria (1492-1546) showed that when Aristotle argued that men of barbarian races were natural slaves he contradicted himself. If whole races are not true men, but only barbarians fit for enslaving, those races could not become fully civilised. This meant they were incapable of fulfilling their potential, their *telos*. But Aristotle himself had said that god creates nothing intrinsically incapable of fulfilling its purpose. Therefore, there is no such thing as a barbarian race. To Vitoria, this meant God would not make imperfect races incapable of salvation. If they are men they can be saved, and cannot be natural slaves. It began to look awkward for Spain's previous king, Ferdinand II, and anyone else arguing for slavery, for it gave Indians far more rights than were convenient. Pro-slavery apologists ended up arguing that Natives were technically free men, but slavery was the way to exercise that freedom, for their old world had failed, and they were not equipped to live in the new Europeanised world. In the liberal Dominican friar Las Casas's copy of one such paper by Palacios Rubios, the man who wrote the preposterous document to be read before battle, you can still read his sarcastic note in the margin: 'a contrived argument for tyranny'.

However contrived the argument became, making a legal case remained important because foreign princes were challenging Castile's right to conquer lands and enslave peoples over whom it had exercised no historic claims. When Columbus brought home slaves to sell in 1495, Ferdinand's wife Queen Isabela forbade it '[b]ecause we wish to be informed by civil lawyers, canonists and theologians whether we may, with good conscience, sell these Indians or not'. As any responsible buyer might ask, are they ethically sourced slaves? She decided that they weren't, and made Columbus return them to America. The religious fervour that followed her death in 1504 demanded that her delicacy be respected. Her widower Ferdinand II, on the other hand, thought his Papal Bull to rule in the New World was also a mandate to enslave: had not Pope Nicholas V in 1455 given rights to Afonso V of Portugal to reduce the infidels of west Africa to 'perpetual and hereditary slavery?' So the question was passed on to the lawyers and theologians of Salamanca.

The Vatican's expert on the Pope's rights to sovereignty over pagans, Cardinal Cajetan, had a three-point test, including the argument that peoples were liable to conquest and slavery if they had heard the word, but chosen not to believe. To decide where New World Natives stood, it became important to know whether Christ's word had reached the Americas before Columbus, and if America's Natives had migrated from lands where the word was known. Either would make them fair game.

When the Spanish saw cross-like symbols among the temple carvings, and observed the use of white cotton robes like priests or monks, they wondered if a debased form of Christianity had arrived, then fallen into paganism. To explain how, it was convenient to conjure a visit from St Thomas. Tradition credited the apostle Doubting Thomas with spreading Christ's word outside the Roman Empire, especially India, where he remains the patron saint. But it soon became obvious they were a long way from India and St Thomas. That left migration.

José de Acosta postulated that the unknown west coast of the Americas was connected to Asia by a land bridge, and that man and animals had migrated across it. This meant they could be sons of Adam and have souls and share original sin. It did not show they had had any prior contact with Christianity. This made them human and blameless, suggesting they had rights.

That slavery in general was fair trade was never in doubt; it was one of the staples of the Mediterranean and the North, and always had been. Spain even imported white slaves from the Balkans and the Black Sea. By 1500, the slave markets of Seville and Valencia were among the biggest in Europe. Interestingly, no one grew very exercised about the use of black slaves, and this was not a racially based decision but a political one. Black slaves came from countries where Europeans had few ambitions to settle, and were brought to African ports by local traders. The New World was different. Spain was fully engaged in colonisation and government under Papal authority, and was under an obligation to convert these lands to Christian belief.

In Salamanca the arguments did not so much simmer quietly, which implies modest energy, as marinade in cold storage, until one Sunday morning in 1511. In Hispaniola, just before Christmas, the Dominican Antonio Montesinos preached to senior dignitaries, including Columbus's son Diego: all landed slave owners. Montesinos had been there fifteen months, time enough to see how things worked, and he tore into his smug congregation. 'Tell me by what right of justice do you hold these Indians in such a cruel and horrible servitude? On what authority have you waged such detestable wars against these people who dealt quietly and peacefully on their own lands? Wars in which you have destroyed such an infinite number of them by homicides and slaughters never heard of before. Why do you keep them so oppressed and exhausted, without giving them enough to eat or curing them of the sicknesses they incur from the excessive labor you give them, and they die, or rather you kill them, in order to extract and acquire gold every day.' To make sure they appreciated the personal consequences he went on to say the Spanish were 'all in mortal sin and live and die in it, because of the cruelty and tyranny they practise among these innocent peoples.'

We have this account from the only man in the congregation who agreed with him: the Dominican Friar Bartolomé de Las Casas. For Las Casas, as for Cicero, the universe was a single joint community of gods and men. Las Casas wrote: 'All the lineages of men are one. All the races of the world are men, and the definition of all men, and of each of them, is only one, and that is reason.' For both Montesinos and Las Casas, religion was at the heart of their lives, not a coat of spiritual varnish on a secular life. After all the debates, practical needs had overcome all arguments. The labourers forced to work the mines and fields could not legally be owned or traded. They were subject to a system of feudal duty, like serfdom, where labour was traded for pastoral care, an education in Christianity, and the provision of life's barest essentials. The award of land, and Indians to work it, was called an *encomienda*. In the New World slavery had not been abolished, just rebranded.

The *encomienda* as actually practised was a cruel sham in which the estate holders did not even bother with a minimum of religious instruction; the Bolivian silver mines became death camps. For this failing, preached Montesinos, both Spanish and Indian would go to Hell. Las Casas, never knowingly undersold in his rhetoric, describes the *encomienda* as 'a mortal pestilence which consumed these peoples, invented by Satan and all his ministers and officials to drag the Spaniards down into Hell and all Spain to destruction.' Everyone knew it, but it was in no one's interests to say so. It was not even in the Dominicans' interest, so Montesinos's regional overseer mollified the estate holders by suggesting the sermon had been prompted by Satan.

From the moment the Spanish saw Cempoala's busy prosperous streets they knew they were not dealing with barbarians but with a prosperous culture. The smallest estimate of its population was 14,000. Cempoala was a well-run city with government, laws, religion, and commerce. All its principal buildings were made of stone, not adobe – further evidence of sophistication – and it was not even the Totonacs' grandest city. El Tajín, their metropolis, would soon entrance me. Cities were seen in medieval and early modern thought as essential to man fulfilling his potential. Bartolomé de Las Casas, who went from being a slave owner to a defender of Native rights, wrote a history with ten chapters devoted to the cities of the Aztecs and the Incas, precisely to show that their sophistication was incompatible with any notion that these peoples were barbarous.

The Spanish themselves were obsessed with founding cities in America, however puny. Heaven itself was the celestial city, and civilisation could not be delivered without cities. They were islands of rationality in a sea of ignorance. 'Beyond the city', said Aristotle, 'only beasts and gods.' The countryside represented the opposite. It represented not just ignorance but fear; it was untamed; wild men lived there. For the Greeks it was home to centaurs, fauns and satyrs, beings made in rough facsimile of man but cruder, primal versions of ourselves: the things we nearly were. The polymath Paracelsus (1493-1541) regarded New World Indians as belonging to the same category. Christianity itself needed cities: the Latin root of the word pagan meant a countryman, because it was there that conversion was hardest, the old religions most obdurate.

Bernal Díaz is always generous about the peoples he meets. He said of Cempoala: '[A]s we came among the houses we saw how large a town it was, larger than any we had yet seen, and were full of admiration. It was so green with vegetation that it looked like a garden; and its streets were so full of men and women who had come out to see us that we gave thanks to God for the discovery of such a country.'

Each time I read those lines they become sadder to me. The Spanish destroyed all those cities. Only Díaz reflects on the loss, and he does so with poignant regret. Writing those words in old age, he had lived long enough to know the Spanish dreamers had died still living the nightmare in which those cities were destroyed, or woken up years later, still screaming.

Of course, Cortés's men were not holding seminars discussing philosophical tracts from Salamanca. Two practices made it easy for the men on the ground to stay with the idea that these were barbarians: human sacrifice and cannibalism. The Greeks specified barbarians were ferocious and cruel and loved eating human flesh, and men who ate other men were never considered fully human.

Cortés soon got down to business with the Fat Chief: exchanging modest gifts, and spinning the pretence of being ambassadors for Charles V, rather than licensed freebooters who had just torn up their licence. The Spanish had just learned that Charles was now even more powerful. He had been elected Holy Roman Emperor, a just reward for the millions he had spent buying votes. The Fat Chief spoke of Moctezuma, and 'heaved a deep sigh and broke into bitter complaints against the great Moctezuma and his governors, saying the Mexican prince had recently brought him into subjection, taken away all his gold jewellery, and grievously oppressed him.'

He warned of the difficulty of taking Tenochtitlán, built on water, and reachable only on exposed causeways. But his next words must have pleased every Spaniard's ears: 'The people of Huejotzingo hate the Aztecs, the people of powerful Tlaxcala hate the Aztecs, Itlilxochitl, candidate for the throne of Texcoco, across the lake from Tenochtitlán was the enemy of Moctezuma.' My enemy's enemy is my friend. Adding the Fat Chief's Totonac empire, four nations might be allied to the Spanish cause.

Cortés said he could help. For the first time he conceives of forging alliances against the overlord city of Tenochtitlán; he would repay the chief's hospitality with service in arms. He spent two weeks there, during which he found five slaves held for sacrifice and released them. The chief was horrified. 'Our infuriated gods will send locusts to devour our harvests, hail to beat them down, drought to burn them, and torrential rains to swamp them if we fail to sacrifice.' Surprisingly, the advice to return the slaves came from two priests, Fathers Olmedo and Díaz, who counselled 'it was not yet time to suppress the ancient rites'.

Firstly, Cortés had to go to meet his ships at Villa Rica. The chief lent him 400 porters to carry their gear, almost one per man, and from now on the soldiers would never again carry their kit: a vital advantage in a campaign which would take them from tropical jungles on the coast to freezing high plateaus and over high passes with thin, chill air. Malinche and Aguilar told Cortés that these subject chiefs were required to provide professional porters for Moctezuma, and as Cortés was on good diplomatic terms with Tenochtitlán, receiving its gifts, all the provinces would feel bound to extend the service to him.

News came in that one of Cempoala's tribute towns, the now vanished Tizapancingo, had refused to pay tribute to the Aztecs. It seemed that rather than punish the satellite, Moctezuma's troops were merely organising before coming to the centre to punish Cempoala. Cortés led his force the 20 miles to Tizapancingo. He lined up outside, the Aztecs lined up opposite, and after taking a good look at the horses, the alien men, and their alien beards, began to scatter. He surrounded them using the horses' speed, disarmed them, but killed no one.

At this time an additional ship, left in Cuba for repairs, arrived at Villa Rica with men and horses. Also on board was threatening news. The Crown had awarded Velázquez new rights to colonise. He would come gunning for them. Cortés decided it would be a good time for the king to see solid evidence of the good work he was doing, and sent some loot to Spain. Cortés grandly turned down his right to claim a fifth, and persuaded the others they should forego their shares to buy the king's attention with the biggest gift they could summon. The men chosen to take this booty home were his friend from Medellín, Portocarrero, and the able Francisco de Montejo. Both would speak well at court, Portocarrero was reliable but had not contributed much to the fighting. Montejo was a leader of the pro-Velázquez faction and would be a danger removed. The ship was to sail directly to Spain, going nowhere near Cuba. The treasure in the holds was not as much as many had expected. Despite the misleadingly detailed inventories: 'Two pieces of grey cord, with some wheels of feathers,' there were elephantine gaps. Large acquisitions such as the gifts from the chiefs of San Juan de Ulúa did not appear at all. At least half the loot ended up compensating Cortés for his investment to date. No one else kept anything.

Thanks to the porters, the Spanish walked with lightened step. I was going to do the opposite.

12

Across the Plain

In Cempoala's supermarket I bought whatever light foods I could find. My pack was at the limit of what I could carry, because I was physically still weak. A local man my own age helped me put it on, and pointed the way, emphasising 'Keep on past the cemetery,' which made me feel I did not look any healthier than its horizontal arrivals.

There were few places where I could walk part of Cortés's route, but I thought I could hike as far as the next town, Actopan, in three days. The River Alcopan wound along my route, and I planned to go no more than a mile, then rest up for a picnic lunch along its banks and begin walking again when the heat abated. However, the surrounding land was planted with sugar cane right to the edge of the road, so there was nowhere to sit and rest. I could feel the heat of the asphalt road through the soles of my boots, and my socks were already drenched with sweat: a fast track to blisters. I put gel pads on the balls of my feet where my blisters always start. I hoped my hours walking barefoot on the sandy horse-trails of Hyde Park had toughened my skin. The first small village, Mata Verde came quickly, and I gratefully let my pack drop, lowered my bony frame onto the iron bench in the miniature square, and drank milk, and munched peanut brittle. The council office had a porch with a little shade, in which two men sat without conversation under the Mexican flag. When I stood up to go they had disappeared silently into the light and heat. The road changed to a rough surface of river cobbles, tough to walk on. In the next village I passed a group of construction workers eating lunch outside a cafe. My wave produced cries of greeting, and when, shortly after, they passed me in their vans and on their mopeds, returning to site, each one offered me a lift. When I explained I was walking to Actopan they plainly thought I had already spent too much time in the sun.

In half an hour I reached their camp where they pressed me into the shade and gave me chilled water to drink, and refilled my flask. 'We are building a major station on a gas line. First we have to build a secure compound.' A huge walled yard was almost complete. Ahead, I saw trees and the hope of shade, and soon I could hear the river. 'There's no bridge' they had said, 'but it's all right, you can wade it.' Soon I was looking at a bright river dividing in two around a midstream islet. From the first channel I learned that it was flowing faster than it looked, was deeper than it looked, mid-thigh, and I was no stronger than I looked. I had a heavy bamboo walking pole, cut in the woods on Quiahuitzlán hill, and used it to brace myself against the current, but when I crossed the deepest section, the current began to carry my leg from under me before I could plant my boot. If I fell, I didn't know how I would stand up with a wet pack, or, if it fell off, when I would see it again. When I reached the islet, I threw my pack in the sand and lay down to get my breath back. Then I ate a snack. Unable to find a reason to postpone matters longer, I loaded up. The second half was worse, but I made it. There was no one to applaud, no headline: Middle-Aged Man Crosses Pretty Stream.

Including time at the ruins, I had been on my feet six hours and the muscles of my left leg were complaining about it. I made it to the village of Santa Rosa, my goal for the day, content that I had walked with a full pack for four hours. In the village shop, a somnolent lady admired my dashing, scarlet face before pulling a rocking chair onto the porch and putting a bottle of cola in my hand. I asked about camping and she sucked her lip and said she would call her husband. Abie arrived, a big man running to corpulence, who phoned his uncle, who managed the football team. 'Sports pitch is out, football training tonight.'

He led me round the back and through a barbed wire fence where he insisted on taking the pack from me, winced at its weight, and dragged it over the lowest strand of wire, ripping the fabric through.

We were in a copse of large trees out of sight of the road, but with views through the trees to sugar cane fields where horses were tethered to feed on the cut stalks. In the other direction I could see teenage boys warming up before football practice. I nodded happily to Abie.

'Anything you want just ask at the house.' The air filled with flies and mosquitoes, so I gathered dry sugar cane leaves, which light easily. When I had a small smokey fire, I pitched my tent and sat outside it, propped against my pack. I drank a half-litre of water before opening a beer to celebrate cocktail hour. Milk mixed with powdered dietary supplement was my starter, followed by tuna, cold refried beans and sweet soft rolls to mop up the tuna oil. I shifted my tired legs and decided I must jettison a few things to reduce my pack's weight. Then I looked around and wondered what.

The football pitch, backlit by the sun filtered through trees, was almost gold; the sides faded to deep green. The boys' shouts grew tired and then, in straggling groups, they left the pitch, the last one with his head down, holding the ends of his sleeves and stretching them taut. Weaving fireflies bid for mates. From the ashes of the sunset came a delicate sliver of new moon caught in the old moon's arms. I built up the fire as my head torch became a magnet for insects, and set my wet boots to steam while I taped up the tears in my pack. A chestnut mare moved towards the river and tore at moist grasses bent over by their own lush weight.

I was an eavesdropper on the village edge, noting the sudden burst of loud music, mopeds and motor scooters riding up and down hoping and wishing that next time there would be a pretty girl, a beautiful boy, leaning by a tree smiling only for them.

I was very happy. It was the 5 November. A year ago, I had stood at a sixth-floor window in the main tower block of Charing Cross Hospital overlooking the Thames at Hammersmith, gripping my drip stand to steady myself, and watching fireworks rise from parks and gardens, sparkling the sky and the river. I was finishing Dante's *Divine Comedy,* and finding books two and three, Purgatory and Heaven, less interesting. For entertainment, it was all downhill after Hell. Now I was self-sufficient, an autonomous human being again, not a patient attached through tubes to a hospital. I relished my soul's content.

When I lay down to sleep in my polyester walls, it was like being in a scanner. Human noises fell away, and the insects' calls span a cocoon of noise around me, sending alarms over the dark fields. For now, the morning and its miracle of light was a distant promise, and the night cries must be answered.

The alarm sounded at 05:30. At breakfast, my dry throat could not swallow anything more substantial than a bread roll and half a litre of orange juice. I was looking for the right road out of the village when a mother shepherding her children out of the house to school deputed one, ten-year-old Jimi, bright and smart, to guide me. He soon acquired a bubble of friends curious to meet the stranger he had captured.

My road led down to the river which here was slow and shallow, but very wide. A rotund man was pushing his bicycle across it. To avoid walking all day in wet boots, I waited for a lift. Immediately a vehicle came into view, a JCB; I put out my thumb. He laughed, stopped, and pulled my pack into his cab. I rode on the step, swaying as the massive wheels churned through the boulders. I arrived as the same time as the cycle pusher, who stood regaining his breath. Ahead, the asphalt road climbed gently between hedgerows and I put my head down and began. The cyclist mounted with feet fanned out like a ballerina's, his face shaded by a broad-brimmed straw hat. I said hello and detected the faintest acknowledgement from the shadow. We kept pace up the hill since he walked any slope that would have required the least bit of effort to be applied to the pedals.

The only traffic consisted of small open-topped cattle trucks taking workers to the sugar cane fields which stretched away over the whole valley floor. The informal uniform was loose-fitting trousers, replica football shirt, straw hat or baseball cap, and a machete wrapped in cloth at the hip. The average wage of field workers is $150 Pesos a day: £7.50. Field workers are casual labour, paid by the day, and work is seasonal. The GPS in my palm cost five weeks' wages. By United Nations standards, half of all Mexicans are poor, but 60 years ago the figure was nine out of ten.

They stared down at me, and I waved, but the waves they returned were listless, half-hearted. Some lorries were lined with a wall of faces as impassive as livestock. Fieldwork keeps body and soul together, but the only fat men on the lorries were the drivers.

By 10:30 the heat was up. The road continued through fields of sugar cane twelve feet high which stifled any movement in the air. I had drunk a litre of water and my shirt was wet. I sat on the only rock at the roadside. It had an inconvenient point on top, like a chair at an inquisition into buggery. I took off my boots, still damp. My gel pads had come off my feet in the river yesterday, and my soles were tingling. I put on new gel pads and dry socks, and felt better. I ate a second breakfast of bread and tuna, and headed on. The road levelled and changed to dirt. I passed through a hamlet called Buenos Aires, good airs, and sure enough, some trick of the land funnelled the morning's slow air-drift into a light breeze, drying my sweat. Round the corner by a lone house under old trees at the edge of the cane, a middle-aged man in a vest sat in the shade of his shed hitting a piece of metal with a hammer. It makes us feel we are men. He was Leuche Andrade, metal-worker.

'I keep busy repairing anything thing that breaks.' He held up a right-angled bracket with two holes in it for bolts, one of which had torn into the surrounding metal, ploughing up a collar. 'It's from a tractor. I'll weld metal over the edge of the tear and re-drill it.'

'Do you come from round here?'

'Not originally, this is my wife's house. But we've been here eighteen years.'

I looked up and down the road where nothing came and nothing went. A cat appeared on a heavy bough overhead and stopped mid-stride. Her back dropped and her head turned to stare down on me.

'Do you like it here?'

'*Muy tranquillo.*' Very peaceful. The answer I knew he would give. I saw he had a gas-powered torch. I gave him my camping stove. 'I cannot get fuel for it. It's yours.' He would fix up something to make it work.

I went on, and the tap of his hammer resumed. The cat came to him rubbing its sides sensually along the rough serge of his trousers.

Hernán Cortés, from an anonymous 16th century portrait.

The author at Bahía Iglesia, abandoned by 1650, the year Columbus thought the world would end.

Tulum, where the Spanish first sighted Maya ruins.

Villa Rica from the island. The first Spanish settlement lies beneath the smart houses to the right.

The marshy site of the battle at Frontera.

Valladolid: the procession of the Most Holy Sacrament.

Antigua's ruins smothered by the roots of strangler-fig trees.

Portrait of Moctezuma by Antonio Rodriguez c.1690.

Cortés and Malinche meet Moctezuma,
depicted in the Lienzo de Tlaxcala.

The dead takeover the trams, Veracruz.

Riding Cortés's route from Xico to Monte Grande.

Cholula's church stands on the world's largest pyramid.

Icing cake Baroque; Sanctuario Ocotlan, Tlaxcala.

Iguanas Greens, one of Malcolm Lowry's
mezcal drinking dens in Cuernavaca.

Popocatépetl from the pilgrimage bus going over the Paso de Cortés.

Coati mundi, one second before it steals my lunch.

Cornish mine engine at Real del Monte.

Ceramic portrait of Eagle Warrior, from the Templo Mayor, Mexico City.

Temple of the Sun, Teotihuacán. Its footprint equals that of the Great Pyramid of Giza.

My next water stop was interrupted by a rustling in the grass behind me. I had taken off my boots to rest my feet, so rather than stand, I twisted round to look. Five feet away the grass was alive. The writhing coils of a small snake rose out of it, and, attached by its fangs to the snake, was a spider the size of my hand. It was the kind with a large soft hairy body and thick legs that you know is up to no good. It had come out of its lair in the rocks and seized the passing snake. After half a minute the snake threw off the spider which stood where it landed facing the retreating snake, but not pursuing it, afraid of the biter being bit. Then the spider turned to face directly at me. I set a personal best for boot lacing. Suddenly alert to every noise, I heard the tinkling sound of a myriad trickles of water. The field over the ditch was the first of many growing bitter yams, in irrigated land as wet as rice paddies. Their huge leaves were green hearts, rich on the eye after the walls of rustling yellow cane.

In the early afternoon I reached a small village and sat in the shady porch of *Vicky's Groceries* drinking a Coke. Two men on motorbikes came in, nodded, and cooled off with a quart of *Sol* beer, which would kill the pain if they fell off. Soon the lane finished at a T-junction with the metalled road to Actopan. I had crossed the coastal plain. The narrow road carried fast traffic and had nowhere safe to walk. A taxi carried me the rest of the way, rising into cooler hills, to the Hotel Lagunas, a bare basic room with no view and little natural light, but there was hot water to wash both me and my clothes.

Cortés's departure from the coast was more fraught than mine. Villa Rica was no fortress. It was at risk of being raided by other Spanish expeditions, or of the fleet being taken by dissidents among his own men. One plot was leaked to him. Men of the Velázquez faction planned to seize a ship and sail it to Cuba in time for Velázquez to intercept Cortés's Spain-bound treasure ship. They had a pilot, another Palos mariner, Juan Cemeño, and sailors to man it. One ringleader was an old enemy, Juan Escudero, who 4 years before had imprisoned Cortés at Velázquez's behest. Escudero was under no illusions as to how he would be dealt with. After a court

119

martial presided over by Cortés, he and the pilot christened the new gallows. Others were whipped, and Gonzalo de Umbría, a good soldier, was whipped, and then suffered an ancient punishment for slaves, having part of his foot cut off. The rest were left in jail long enough to reflect on pain and eternity, then released.

Cortés ordered the pilots to inspect the ships and declare that they were rotten. They duly announced that the vessels were suffering from *broma,* or water beetle. The word also means joke. You imagine no one laughed. The ships were grounded and partly broken. Despite the legend, he did not burn his ships. This misunderstanding arose a quarter of a century later when a copyist struggling with bad handwriting mistook *quebrando*, breaking, for *quemando*, burning.

When Cortés's force crossed the plain the future was beginning to come into focus. As he put it in the beginning of his second letter to the king, 'I decided to go and see Moctezuma, wherever he might be. I assure your highness that I will take him alive in chains, or make him subject to Your Majesty's Royal Crown.'

In a straight line it was 250 miles distant; overground it would be around 400 miles. Guided by a combination of their Totonac allies and Aztec ambassadors, they went on a loop north, whereas the road usually travelled was much more direct. It is hard to say why. Cortés often received contradictory advice, and had to decide whom to believe. The Aztecs certainly had orders to paint a picture of a trail full of hardship and danger. The Totonacs proved honest and steadfast throughout the campaign, and insisted on routes which took them through the states most likely to come to their aid. One of their chiefs, Teuch said frankly, 'I went to Tenochtitlán once as a boy. It is large and strong, and if you go there you are certain to be killed. But if you do go, I shall come with you.'

I knew nothing about Actopan except that it was on Cortés's route, so I went out to play. It was a dapper, secluded place that not even Mexicans visited. The butcher's shop had half a cow hanging in the open air outside. One family brought their furniture onto the pavement each evening and settled down to chat to passers-by. But I could not photograph anything discreetly, because I was stared at the whole time. When I asked permission to take a photo, people turned away, froze into rigid poses, or just said no. They were very adept at spotting my attempts at clandestine photography.

There was bunting everywhere. In Mexico, bunting is quick to go up and slow to come down. The church tower was strung like a maypole and painted the colour of lime ice cream, with holly green detailing. My favourite building was the cerise and mauve kindergarten whose snappy official name was 3ODJNOO18Z, Zona 9O, Sector XV, Actopan. Its local name was Kindergarten Albert Einstein. In Year Two they move on from toilet training and knowing the colours of the rainbow to unified field theory and the special theory of relativity.

For supper, I found chicken and rice and made a fair fist of it, but looked in vain for an open bar. By seven-thirty the town was shutting down. I bought a bottle of beer from an old lady's vegetable stall, and went back to my room feeling weak in the lower end of my hamstrings. When I walk a lot they stretch, but reluctantly.

The morning was fresh after the humidity of the coastal plain. I looked for the post office, to send home redundant maps and paperwork, and was told which street it was in and that it was just outside the market. The owner of a children's clothing shop saw me walking past for a third time, so I decided to forestall a call to the police by asking her where the post office was. She walked with me to the industrial shed next door and pointed at a rusty box at knee height. The word *correo* does for both post box and post office.

'The market?'

She pointed at the shed. 'When does it open?'

A shrug, and she left. That was pretty well all there was to do in town, apart from admire the glossy spotted leaves of croton plants flourishing as bushes everywhere. When I first started work after university I tried to cheer up dull Cardiff flats with potted crotons. They sulked, and I would spend winter afternoons reading, to the intermittent sound of another leaf pattering to the windowsill.

The countryside around was pretty and a swift river confined one side of the town centre. A high suspension bridge took me to the other bank to walk through woods and scout for trails. None of them led far. The through-routes were all well-trafficked roads, and there were no walkable alternatives. I would be back on buses.

I consulted the chroniclers to prepare for the next stage of my journey, and I read Patrick Leigh Fermor's *Time of Gifts*. He had some powerful letters of introduction which secured him hospitality at the schlosses whose vineyards supplied the finest cellars of Europe, or he landed in a house of unchaperoned noble nubiles, who kept him secret and no doubt satisfied. I contrasted this with my trips, where meeting a friendly mule-skinner makes my day.

My next stop was Xalapa, and local advice was forget the buses and share a taxi, which I did. There was already a young man in the front passenger seat, every inch an office worker and too important to speak to other people. The road climbed up the valley side. Every scrap of level land was planted with sugar cane, yams, mangoes, grapevines and other fruits. The main street of the next village was lined with lorries waiting to fill up with farm produce. We stopped to pick up two field hands. One talked like a ventriloquist, barely moving his lips; I suspected his front teeth were missing. He asked endless questions about my trip, or rather he asked the same three questions many times. His friend remained silent except to whisper to the ventriloquist. *Where is he from? How rich is he? Does he like Mexico?* We kept climbing in tight curves that threw us to and fro in the seats, until at the top I could see that what had looked like hills around Actopan was actually the edge of flat plateau into which the river had cut a steep valley.

Xalapa is a city of 400,000 people. I loved the hotel from the moment I hammered the massive outer door with a knocker that would have sat well on a cathedral, and entered the owners' high-ceilinged office-cum-living room, overlooking a landscaped patio with salvaged architectural details deployed as garden ornaments. It was once the home of Ohio-born engineer and philanthropist William K Boone II, who came to oversee work at a hydroelectric plant and never went home. On my bedside table was a glossy brochure with a cover picture of a Welsh town I knew well: Hay-on-Wye. Xalapa has picked up Hay's arts festival franchise. I was the sole guest, and lodged in a modern extension at the rear of the long plot, with a first-floor balcony touching the branches of a chirimoya tree where birds and small mammals came to feed from the soft fruits, sold in Britain as custard apples. Beyond it I had views over the basin in which the city centre lay. As evening fell and rain threatened, the city fell dark grey but no lights came on. I laid out my kit, cleaned my sandals and boots, and reorganised the pack. The evening grew cold. The city lies at almost 5000 feet so temperatures are nearly twenty degrees Fahrenheit cooler than sea level. After five weeks of hot humidity, the chill felt even sharper than that. I ate the rest of my camping supplies: tuna in oil and refried beans. Without the distractions of a campfire, I realised they smelled like cat food. The room had air conditioning for the summer but no heating. I dressed warmly before settling down to read Díaz's chronicle and Cortés's letters.

I woke at five-thirty and wondered why they had arranged the clocks so it was dark at six in the evening, and light for 3 hours before breakfast. In the first light I was treated to a view 40 miles to the south-west of the city. When Cortés first saw the Sierra Madre Mountains he wrote: '[T]here is one which is much higher than all the others. When the day is very fine one can see the peak rising above the cloud, and it is so white we think it to be covered in snow, and even the Natives say it is snow, but as we have not seen it clearly, and because this region is so hot, we cannot be certain that it is.' The volcano was known at the time of the conquest as Citlaltépetl, or star mountain, and now its snows shone pink against the first blue of the sky. Today it is known by the more prosaic name of Pico (peak) de Orizaba, and at 18,491 feet high is the highest mountain in Mexico. This morning, clouds covered the base of the mountain so all that was visible was the peak, a floating ice pyramid. It brought a vow from Cortés: 'We shall endeavour to see and learn the secret of this and other things of which we have heard, so that we may render Your Royal Highnesses a true account.' He often uses the word secret. The truth of the place is hidden; he will find it and name it properly, christen the places and the people, claim them for the known world, and complete their half-formed existence, ready for salvation and the last days. The calendar days blow into the wind, their pile lessens. Time will return to its roots.

In half an hour Pico de Orizaba had vanished into the haze. Clouds and fogs keep the land's secrets, frustrate disclosures. Earn your knowledge.

I left the comfort of my Xalapa room for two nights to visit the greatest ancient city of the coast: El Tajin, just outside the vanilla capital of Papantla.

13

The Place of Invisible Beings

El Tajin was only 70 miles to the north, but the bus route took three sides of a rectangle and four hours. Papantla's only good hotel was full, the receptionist explained with a look of surprise, as she checked her records, and I looked longingly at the sun warming their swimming pool. I descended to the second choices, past a stand being erected for the mayor to open a new flood relief scheme, and chose the Hotel Las Arenas because it was no worse than the others, and was on a very quiet street. When I put my key under the bedsheet I could still read the room number through it.

Papantla is a town of nearly 50,000 people, set in fertile land growing cacao, maize and vanilla. Vanilla is a vine orchid, the world's second most expensive spice after saffron. For 300 years, Mexico had a monopoly protected by nature. The flower's male and female parts are separated by a membrane, so it relies for fertilisation on a single genus of stingless Mexican bee, the *Melipona*, or mountain bee. Vanilla was taken to French colonies such as Réunion, and Madagascar. It grew well, flowered, but would not fruit. *Melipona* bees were taken to these countries but always died. Even after the Belgian botanist Charles Morren discovered how the bee fertilised the delicate pale flower, while drinking coffee on his patio here in Papantla, no one could mimic it artificially. Where farmers, entomologists and botanists failed, on the Indian Ocean island of Réunion, a twelve-year-old slave boy called Edmond Albius solved it with a sliver of bamboo and his thumb. The flower opens only for one day, and pollination is best done after 12 hours, so the operation remains very labour intensive. The reward is one pod per flower. Vanilla was for sale everywhere, but I went to the market for something else. My tourist Panama looked naff compared with the local cream-coloured cowboy hats, woven from a cotton paper mix, and known as double stones, because the crown was impressed on either side as if with blows from rocks. I paid about a third of what I had handed over for the first one in the Gift Shop for Foreign Fools outside some Maya ruins.

Because my cancer had been caught at a late stage and was diffused through the base of my tongue, the radiation dosage had been high, and had burned and constricted my throat. My saliva glands barely worked, so swallowing was difficult. Mucous formed to protect the wound, and wrapped itself round food until I gagged. Nearly half my calories were still being taken through a powdered food supplement. I became an addict of guacamole and *malteadas*: milk flavoured with real vanilla, but I struggled with dry food, like the ubiquitous tortillas, and rice without sauce. Anything advertised as a little spicy was the strength of a madras curry. If the menu said spicy, it was a biohazard. I would have found it overwhelming when well, but with a raw throat, it was inedible. A reliable meal was spaghetti bolognese, and if I could persuade them to leave carrots out of it, I was a happy traveller.

Back at the hotel I watched the rain feed a six-inch deep flood teeming down the road beneath my room. The patio doors would not quite close to keep out the noise of the buses and trucks that laboured all night up the hill outside. The street had only been quiet when I arrived because it was closed for the mayor's speech. It was one of those days when you wonder what you have done with the wisdom of forty-five years of foreign travel. To console myself, I posed with my new hat in front of the mirror. At least I had proved it was waterproof.

The morning was dry and the bus stop was positioned outside the good hotel. If I stood sideways, I could not see the swimming pool. I was the first visitor at El Tajin and walked alone onto the plaza, which was bounded on either side by rectangular pyramids whose longer base fronted the square. I explored the grassy avenues and plazas of a city which flourished from 600 to 900 AD, and survived for maybe two centuries beyond that. The ruins were unknown outside the locale until Diego de Ruiz, a tax collector, came looking for illegal tobacco plantations. It is now set in woodland in the open countryside, but an artist's impression showed the site in its heyday, with walls plastered, and painted red. The picture was vaguely reminiscent of the Forbidden City in Beijing. The site rises at the rear and the later buildings were added here, skilfully linked by walls and ramps. The whole site, including satellite residential areas, covers four square miles. Who built it is debated, but it grew out of the coastal Huastec culture, and the area later fell within the Totonac influence. El Tajin was one of the civilisations which existed alongside that of Teotihuacán, the massive centre north of Mexico City whose ruins the Aztecs would visit, like Saxons gazing at Roman remains, wondering where such marvels had come from. The old Aztec name for El Tajin meant 'The Place of Invisible Beings', perhaps a name given when it was an abandoned ghost town. The meaning of the current name attracts varied translations, hurricane and lightning bolt among them.

When Teotihuacan declined, El Tajin rose. It is famous for the Pyramid of the Niches, built as a seven-tier step pyramid of which the top level, housing the actual shrines for sacrifice, is now missing. The oblong, deeply recessed niches create a rhythm along the facades, which was copied elsewhere, but this is the original. There were once 365 but the main purpose is not believed to relate to the calendar, but to the rain god, known as Aktzin to the Totonac, and Tlaloc to the Aztecs, a deity vital for the growth of the crops. As I started to take photographs the god awoke and the heavens opened. The only way to escape the cloudburst was by curling on my side inside a niche a size smaller than I needed. They were once painted black to emphasise the shadow, and may have represented caves. The underworld lay behind my back. Caves were important in Mesoamerican mythology, variously as the birthplace of man and animals, and through associations with springs, with the rain god.

I watched the visibility close in, and puddles form in the hollows of the lawns, and begin forming rivulets. In Native cultures, little children have been made to cry so their tears would bring rain. Little children have been killed to water the fields and fill the streets with streams like this.

I considered the melancholy, aqueous world sideways for 10 minutes, before enough body parts complained to send me running for a shelter 100 yards off, far enough for my trousers to be soaked by the rain streaming off my waterproof jacket. I soon decided it was not going to stop, and continued my tour: a good call as it didn't let up for 24 hours. I walked back to the site's most famous structures: the ball courts. The ball game existed by 1600 BC, and continued to be played widely until the conquest. In north-west Mexico, where there was little Spanish settlement, versions persist today. It was performed as an elaborate ritual from Mexico to Honduras, and was played in simpler forms as far away as Arizona and the Caribbean. More than 1500 courts have been discovered, and the second biggest group ever found is here at El Tajin, which has twenty and counting. There is no standard plan or size, though the pattern is usually similar for any given region and era. Their area is anything from the size of a tennis court to a small football pitch. They resemble real tennis courts, the ancient form of lawn tennis, where sloping gallery roofs form part of the playing area. The

A large, low banked ball court at Uxmal.

English king contemporary with the conquest of Mexico, Henry VIII, was a great enthusiast. A Mexican ball court's sides are always enclosed, usually by a low bench, from the top of which a stone bank slopes up to a flat area with shrines and places for spectators. The ends are sometimes closed off, often not. Sometimes it seems that a crowd could have watched; in others, just a select few.

The game used a rubber ball, and, when Columbus saw it played in Hispaniola on his second voyage, it was the first time Europeans had seen rubber. The balls were so lively compared with the wood, leather or cloth balls in use, they thought they might be bewitched. Throughout Mesoamerica this liveliness was associated with vitality, rebirth, fertility, movement, and various celestial bodies, especially the sun, moon, and Venus.

Rubber is easy enough to find in Mexico. Some 2000 plants produce a latex with rubber in it, but the best source is the tree *Castilla elastica*. When the bark is cut, latex runs for up to 5 hours. The white fluid that made balls that seemed alive was naturally associated with vital body fluids. In Maya, the word *k'ik* means blood and rubber, while *k'ik'ei* is semen. Once gathered, it can be rolled into a ball and dried, turning grey or black as it does so. This is not a stable form of rubber, and it was not until 1844 that the American Charles Goodyear added sulphur to vulcanise the mix and make it durable. The Maya achieved the same result, by adding to the mix the sap of the vine *Ipomoea alba*, which obligingly grows on the rubber tree. It fixes the long polymer chains of rubber molecules with sulphonic acids. Where rubber objects were placed in wet dark conditions as offerings they have survived: in the case of one cache, for 3600 years. The tree likes hot humid conditions and does not grow well at altitude, so the Aztecs were quick to exact it as tribute. Production was industrial in scale. One province was taxed at 16,000 balls a year.

The Aztec balls were solid, but it is possible the Maya used hollow ones modelled around a human skull. The game operated a little like real tennis, but with a line on the ground instead of a net. In the classic version, the ball was served by hand, then kept in play by arms, hips and thighs. When a team failed to return the ball before the second bounce, they lost the point. It weighed up to eight pounds, so protective hip guards and leg guards were developed to prevent broken pelvises. It is likely that two players from each side were engaged on the court area, while the rest of the team protected the end zones. Scoring was complex. Some courts had stone rings set high on the side of the court, one either side of the centre. If the ball was passed through one, which was extremely difficult to do, the game was won. Other events could take a score back to zero, so games went on for hours, sometimes days. The longest on record took a full week.

The courts were large and expensive items, and the game was not a simple sports event. The ancient Maya book the *Popol Vuh* blends myths and history going back half a millennium before the conquest. It does what most religious agendas in the ancient Americas needed to do: it explained how the earth and man originated, and why the rulers deserved to be in charge. But it does so with great poetry, as my opening quote in this book shows. When the world was made, its gods were great ball game players. Two mortal brothers called One Hunter and Seven Hunter played the game so loudly they disturbed the Lords of the Underworld, who tricked the brothers to come to the dark realm of Xibalba to play them. The gods won, killed the brothers, and buried their bodies in the ball court. To humiliate him, One Hunter's head was hung in a calabash tree. A young goddess, Xquic, came to see the sight. His head spat into her hand, which we can read as ejaculating. Xquic found herself pregnant with twins, and was thrown out of the Underworld, climbing to the surface of the earth to give birth to Hunter and Jaguar-Sun. When they grew up they excelled at the game and surpassed their murdered uncle and father in skill. They, in turn, were summoned to the Xibalba where they outwitted the Lords of the Underworld, and when they played the ball game, the twins won, and recovered the bodies of their uncle and father, and placed them in the sky as the sun and moon.

The game was a sport as well as a ritual, and the two roles were not contradictory; who but the gods would decide which man deserved to win? There were some professional players, and successful ones could become the intimates of kings, for their games attracted divine approval. Nobles also sponsored teams and gambled on matches: quite how much, we shall see.

Carved on the side of an El Tajín ball court.

The ball court at El Tajin has some of the most important carvings of any ball court along its sides; they include the maize god. Like the annual cycle of growth, death is necessary to bring life. The whole myth can be read as a the death and resurrection of the vegetation god, the maize god. A British folk song has the same mythic idea as its root.

> *And these three men made a solemn vow:*
> *John Barleycorn should die*
>
> *They ploughed, they sowed, they harrowed him in,*
> *throwed clods upon his head,*
>
> *And these three men made a solemn vow,*
> *John Barleycorn was dead.*

It is hard to decode meaning when the living tradition is extinguished. The myths point to the ball court, often at the lowest part of a city centre, symbolising the entrance to the underworld.

131

The palaces and administration buildings on the main level represent earthly life, and the pyramids, heaven and afterlife. This is reinforced by small details. At the Mayan site of Chichén Itzá the defeated players are shown surrounded by the *Datura* vine, which is both hallucinogenic, giving access to the spirit world, and poisonous, helping you to the land of the dead. The ambivalence is made more acute by the fact that the plant's poison varies in potency, some samples being five times as toxic as others. The line between heavenly visions and death was fine and fickle. The carvings show butterflies. Some species can eat *Datura,* and they also symbolise re-birth through their metamorphosis, entering a state without apparent life, to transform themselves from creatures crawling the earth to flighted beauties. Reptiles also feature strongly, and, as so often, represented the underworld, but they have another significance, because they are also capable of moving between the worlds of earth and water.

El Tajin's carved frieze also contains more deeply disturbing images. Rulers are often depicted playing the game. It seems that on certain occasions the game was played by nobles re-enacting a recently fought battle against captives, doubtless brought tired or beaten to the arena. In the South Ball Court, as the rain began to trickle through the grooves shaping their plumes and masks, I could see the conclusion of the game, the death of the maize god so he could be reborn and give life, enacted in the execution of a prisoner, as an obsidian knife descends to sever his head and reward the gods with precious blood. The defeated sprawled, their spurting arteries watering the dust.

The ball game could also be used as a kind of divination, in which the gods would favour the person who was right. Sixteenth century histories of the conquest, argued that the events of the conquest had been foreshadowed, and to a degree, foreseen. Unfortunately not every portent was recognised at the time. Time and history had to be returned to its smooth cycles, so events in the years leading up to 1519 were pored over until scholars could see how the gods had told them what was coming. Before signs appeared, a wager which belongs in a fairytale was decided on a ball court. Nezahualpilli was

Lord of Texcoco, which shared the lake shore with Tenochtitlán. He was a highly respected ruler and one of the finest Nahuatl poets. When his son was found sending love poems to his own stepmother, the punishment prescribed was death. Nezahualpilli was principled enough to execute him, and man enough to cry as a father. So when he came to tell Moctezuma that his fortune-tellers were predicting Mexico would soon be ruled by strangers, he was taken with the utmost seriousness. Moctezuma consulted his soothsayers, who denied it. Nezahualpilli suggested the gods settle it on the ball court, and they agreed on the best of five games. Moctezuma wagered his whole kingdom against three turkeys. Moctezuma won the first two, and it seemed all was well. Then he lost the next, and the one after that. The decider was also lost. The gods seemed to be mocking his pride. Nezahualpilli did not take the kingdom.

Wet and cold, I sipped coffee in the cafeteria and fed every other biscuit to a stray dog. There was a large and stylish modern museum of the site but I found the exhibits hard to study in the dim light. I asked one of the helpful staff if he would switch on some lights but he said, 'No.'

'I can't read the information.'

He shrugged. 'There's no electricity.'

'Have the power lines fallen down?'

'No, we haven't paid the electricity bill.'

Water began to come through the roof. It was a fine building but not being maintained. Mexico is not a poor country, but the money is not always where it needs to be. Public money is especially likely to be siphoned off. The assistant saw me looking up to the roof.

'It makes me ashamed, I am proud of my heritage, of this building, but ...' The unfinished sentences of Mexico. The conviction that change, above all things, is difficult.

14

Into the Mountains

Papantla bus station's dark hall was like an old-fashioned railway waiting room. A young family entered, the husband guiding a frail father by the arm. They sat him down, bought his ticket, then left. The father's calm demeanour vanished. Immediately he looked lost, then, agitated. Seeming to come to a decision, he took out his lunch pack and found a slice of bright pink iced cake. The familiar treat calmed him.

Bus stations were a part of daily life, and I now felt relaxed in them, unlike a reconnaissance trip I made to follow a later Cortés expedition to Honduras, where a guard with an automatic weapon boarded at dusk and took his reserved seat on the back row by an open window, so he could shoot down the length of the bus inside or out. Murders of bus drivers were still running at one a day.

The storms were lingering, and the sky deepened like a mood, making the room so dark that when I bought a newspaper the assistant greeted me with *'Buenas noches'*, before giggling at her mistake. I saw quick clips of the coast: a storm beach stoked by a brown fury of surf driving to the shore, breaking 200 yards out, the waves curling tightly over on themselves. A side-wind stripped off the spray in arcs; it would rip your face like hail. Gardens behind walls fronting the swollen river were filling silently with water; a garden table with four chairs still neatly disposed, was going under. We passed a crash where police stood, arms akimbo, round the frame of a small car smashed beneath a white articulated lorry. It was inconceivable anyone in it could have survived.

Back in the room in Xalapa, a small insect that had been on the wall above the television the first time I had arrived was still in exactly the same place. I admire such patience but would not want it for myself. I downloaded Malcolm Lowry's novel *Under the Volcano*. Autobiographical, it is a tough read, because he observes his own dissolution in all its self-deceit. We all lie to ourselves. Alcohol is the fuel to go farther, and make our lives a lie. He never again produced anything so fine, but most novelists never summon the courage to go there once. I planned to track down his old haunts.

In the last of the light I saw a mouse-sized body appear in mid-air in front of a yellow trumpet flower outside. It moved sideways to the next flower: a hummingbird's weightless delicacy, probing the strawberry stains in the funnels. I thought again of Lowry.

I visited the house General Santa Anna lived in from 1842-56. He bought the remains of an inn set up by Juan Lencero, one of Cortés's soldiers, at the top of the long climb from the coastal plain. A vast fig tree at the rear of the house is the only thing datable to Lencero's time. Santa Anna built a villa and a church in which, one month after his first wife died, he married the fifteen-year-old María Dolores de Tosta. A Xalapa-born boy, Santa Anna was the quintessential Mexican public figure, from his name (Antonio de Padua María Severino López de Santa Anna y Pérez de Lebrón) to his life. He became an army hero, a general, and was called the Napoleon of the West, not least by himself. He fought for the Spanish against independence, then with the nationalists for it, and became Mexico's president eleven times. Despite an initial victory at the Alamo, he lost Texas in 1836, when it declared itself a republic. After his defeat by a much smaller Texan army at the battle of San Jacinto, he was found hiding in a marsh dressed as a private.

Irrepressible, he led the army against a French invasion at Veracruz in 1838, an invasion officially instigated by France's overpowering national destiny to compensate a French pastry chef who had lost his shop in army looting 10 years before. Or maybe it was imperial greed. Santa Anna failed, France was bought off, but he lost a leg in the fighting, which allowed him to play the self-sacrificing saviour and return to power. Two incarnations of his cork artificial leg were captured during subsequent battles; the original was buried with full military honours and periodically dug up by

135

his enemies, in one instance, to use as a baseball bat. In 1848, serving as a general between presidential terms, Santa Anna lost all Mexico's other northern border states to the USA, permanently halving his country's size. He was then exiled to Jamaica and Colombia. He was so avaricious that he was nicknamed Fifteen Claws; in later life his corruption was discovered, and after a treason trial, all his estates were confiscated. His failed project in exile was to replace rubber carriage tyres with *chicle*, natural chewing gum. Aged eighty, after further exile in Staten Island, Cuba and St Thomas in the Virgin Islands, he took advantage of an amnesty and returned to Mexico, where he died two years later. Otherwise his life was uneventful.

For a time, his house became a girl's school, apposite given the age of his wife, and is now a museum with landscaped grounds. From the villa, I went to Xalapa botanical gardens. After a sunny morning the sky remained for hours as if a cloudburst would fall any minute. The enclosed valley containing the gardens sang with the sibilance of restless canopies and rustling bamboo; their springy green lances, candy-striped with yellow, fanned outwards, but the dense hearts of their stands were impenetrable citadels of calm. One genus of plant personified the strangeness of the world the Spanish had entered: *Aristolochia*. One dreary winter, I had tried to grow *Aristolochia grandiflora* from mail-order seeds, and failed. Seeing one in Xalapa smothering a large pergola made me see my failure as a blessing. A foetid smell hung in the air. The flower is coloured the purple of old bruises mottled with cream, and is one of the largest in the plant kingdom. A long trumpet opens up like a wind-up gramophone to the size of a dinner plate, and at the narrow end curves over on itself into the shape of a poultry corpse, accounting for one of its many common names: the duck flower. The 300 species in this disturbing genus all have the same strategy for fertilisation; they emit the odour of dead meat to attract flies. *Aristolochia grandiflora* first opens as a female flower and when a fly enters the funnel, traps it in sticky hairs like those on sundew. The flower now changes sex, lets the fly fertilise the male organs with its female pollen, then releases the fly and shuts off the smell.

Extracts from the plant have shown potential for treating Parkinson's disease and arthritis, while the Greeks, by association with the flower's uterus shape, used it to help women after childbirth to expel the placenta. But US drug regulators have banned all human consumption, because it is more carcinogenic than tobacco. It is a sombre plant, but it nurses beauty. Swallowtail butterflies feed on it to make themselves unpalatable to predators. I went out of the gardens into the louring dusk, and waited a long time for a bus back to town, night birds calling.

Back at my room, a ladder-backed woodpecker with red, black and white plumage was the last bird to leave the *chirimoya* tree. A wet cloud filtered through its branches, licking the down-hanging leaves until droplets coalesced into globules which slipped to the drip point on the leaf's tip, and fell with the lightest of taps to the leaf below. Ferns glistened, and when backlit by the nacreous glow of the street's lamps, they bristled with rough strings of industrial diamonds. Pale grey plates of foliose lichens seized on the smallest glow to maculate the tree's trunk and limbs and break up the mass of their lumber. Every morsel had been coated by the mist and the billions of minute movements made a noise, faint but defining, like the background waves in space, ghost pulses of the first creation.

A wall of beige-grey light hangs two streets away. My world has shrunk to an amphitheatre on the hill. The traffic is muffled, and the dogs stopped barking long ago, their tails tucked tight in half-dry corners. It is beautiful when the world becomes simple, as if under snow, and our choices narrow with our sight, and thoughts focus, stripped of extraneous detail. We are left with the essential grey bulks of our existence, and the drip of leaf on leaf, and thought on feeling.

From Xalapa the Spanish swang south-west to Coatepec, a small town with just 3 miles of urbanised countryside between it and the expanding edge of Xalapa. I found a hotel owned by local coffee farmers and decorated with sacks of produce in the foyer. Coatepec's street corners and doorways were posted with vendors selling captured birds and wild orchids. The latter are the reason for the town's Orchid Museum. It was set up in the back garden of Dr Isaias

Contreros, effectively as a conservation and study centre for endangered orchids, and he curated it for 40 years until his death. It took over their large rear garden, so they bought adjacent land. I was shown round by his widow, Zita Fernández: a full partner in this enthusiasm.

The first thing she did was give me a magnifying glass, 'They come in all shapes and sizes.' Some of them were minute even under the glass. Orchids hybridise easily and the varieties are astonishing. We stopped in front of one popularly known as the white nun. It possessed the simplest, and often most moving beauty: plain white with a touch of colour, in this case a patch of yellow shining at its very heart. It was *Lycaste skinneri alba;* whose fused stamen and pistils really did look like a nun at prayer. Fernanda said, 'When we received funding and became a public museum the President of Guatemala agreed to cut the ribbon. We put the white nun in front of all the others in his honour. He loved it and asked its name, I said "Mr President, it is your national flower!"'

Back in the street, a demonstration by striking teachers passed by. The well-heeled citizen next to me said it was all about pay, and slapped his newspaper disapprovingly. But the demonstrators told me it was more about political interference in teaching methods and the curriculum. One poster read *We want to teach children to think, not to recite.* An articulate woman with fierce green eyes carried a banner for parents supporting the teachers. 'The government are telling lies, saying the teachers won't accept being appraised; it's not true, teachers are happy to accept that. The politicians want to force the schools to look after the maintenance of the buildings. We want them to be teaching!'

My over-designed hotel room was luxurious in everything except light. I needed the reading lamp on in the middle of the day. In the minds of Mexican hotel architects, it seems to be forever midday in June, with sun-stricken guests passing out from heat exhaustion. Winter must come as an annual surprise. When I went out for supper, the courtyard seemed even less well-lit than usual, and the street dark. There was a deadness in any spot where lights did not shine directly. The air caught at my throat and my lungs tightened.

Then I saw, on both sides of the road, a slow beauty, sliding from the terracotta eaves at streetlamp height. Fog pinned the traffic's fumes in the narrow gully of the street. It moved with delicacy and grace as if an armada of ponderous galleys in the darkness above had turned at anchor, on the day's ebb, and pushed the vapours aside to drain into the channels of the town. I was looking at Venice from the bottom of a canal.

A crystalline haze haloed each street lamp. Walkers hunched their shoulders, outlines were softened while bodies darkened. Any figure standing beneath a light assumed an aura of quiet intent. Silhouetted in the doorway of a brilliantly-lit pharmacy, four folk musicians in rustic riding clothes stood watching a programme on a giant television screen. A rich and shiny blonde family were being domestic by a sunny lake. One musician took off his hat to watch, holding it by the brim, as if in church. His thick, black hair was roughly cut. His guitar was held ready to play, but he just stared at the young mother on screen and blew her a kiss, his breath clouding the damp air.

At dawn I climbed the hill above the town. Mist lingered in the hollows of the plain. Smoke plumes rose from slow fires in fields. An olive bird like a female chaffinch landed by me, delved in the grass and cocked its head skywards, grasping an insect by the thorax. It squeezed, and the insect's four wings fluted up into a slender glass to catch the light one last time before its farewell toast.

Pico de Orizaba was closer, dominating the old road ahead. Warm, humid vegetation gave way to temperate fields and then thin scrub, before yielding to moorland then bare rock up to where the snow wiped the slate clean.

The next town a few miles farther to the south-west was Xico, a smaller and more picturesque version of Coatepec. I stayed on the edge of town in a second-floor room with no windows; but it had wooden doors onto a large balcony which overlooked the old stone bridge crossing the river in the steep-sided wooded valley which bounds the south side of the town. I took a chair and an hour to enjoy where I was. Among the finer feelings, it is common to underrate smugness. Much of the traffic was equine, riders going out to the farms on fit strong, compact horses to work, or to fetch firewood, which they piled on patient donkeys. The bridge was a gateway into an older life. The countryside out there was far more remote and unchanged than anywhere I had seen so far. At night, the river's chatter was a constant backdrop to hoofs slithering on the cobbles.

Xico is old Mexico. I could see into old-fashioned rooms, plain, with photos of smooth passive faces from a generation or two before, the men's hair oiled sleekly back, the women's tied tightly to the skull. The prints were cheap, with little detail, the skin as smooth as if it had been airbrushed. They stood among the household devotions to the Virgin of Guadalupe and Christ. Some living rooms looked like chapels of rest, as airless and unlived-in as the unused front rooms in my grandparents' terraced houses: shrines to guests who never came. I quickly warmed to Xico; it still possessed a heritage that Coatepec was self-consciously re-inventing. Its side-streets were what old Extremaduran streets once looked like, seen by me only in black and white Spanish films. The buildings were unrestored, their lines and edges softened by age, their surfaces a little crumpled. One side of the street was slaughtered by the midday sun into a blinding slash of heat and light, the other was a dark sash; you could walk into it and disappear.

At the top of the town, near the border where the town centre's heritage gave way to simply old, the *Bar Renacimiento*, the Rebirth Bar, sported a pair of swinging saloon doors. I stepped in braced for a torrent of noise and found one sober customer talking to the proprietors. The walls were plastered from floor to high ceiling with bullfighting posters. A few were souvenirs from Madrid, the rest were for corridas at Xico. The first bullfight to take place in Mexico was organised here for Cortés's birthday, after the conquest. A man in his thirties served me beer, and nodded at the seated older gentleman behind the bar. 'My father-in-law is the aficionado, you can ask him anything.'

I did.

The son-in-law relayed my question to his father, although we were all speaking Spanish, and he responded 'I am Feliz Morales, and it's true, bullfighting's my love,' which was not what I had asked. So it went on. Like my own father, the old man was losing contact.

The son said, 'The big arena, that's where they have the bullfights.' 'The one like a circus big-top?'

'Yes, but it's permanent, the Alberto Balderas Stadium.'

I was impressed. The steel cables supporting it were like ship's hawsers. On one side, the cables were anchored to the ground on the other side of the road, and lorry drivers who did not know of the hazard risked being cropped if they did not weave across the street.

'How often do they hold bull fights?'

'Most years, not every year. It's an expensive business.'

Especially for the bulls.

Next morning I was up before dawn and walking through the streets at first light. The sky was clear and the moon just one night past full. Only half a dozen other people were about, all men, walking to work, sometimes knocking quietly on friends' doors, trying to rouse them for work without waking the street. My road led out of town through banana estates with coffee bushes planted between to enjoy the shade. Mexico is well suited to grow the high quality Arabica strain which prospers between 3000 and 4500 feet. Climate change is warming this zone, and plants at the lower end of the range do not thrive. Many estates do not own the land above to plant higher. Prices have also been variable, and the costs of extracting and processing the meagre two and a half pound of beans from a mature bush are always high, so some estates have simply been allowed to grow over.

I heard my destination before I could see it. It was like distant traffic, but softer. There was a viewpoint on the lip of a gorge. A tissue of cloudlets stayed in the same place; they were the vapour pall above Texolo waterfall. A path led me to a narrow pedestrian suspension bridge 30 yards long crossing a slot-like gorge falling 250 feet to a small tributary stream. I felt fine until a butterfly crossed in front of me and my eye followed it out into the void above the drop. I felt as if I had walked off the bridge after it. Some of the maple trees were enormous, and beneath them were tall cycads corseted in lianas that sent down curtains of aerial roots. I thought of the botanists who went deep into equatorial rainforests, staring at the trees rolling on forever, in endless variety, the vegetation gods making them mad by excess.

A second bridge crossed the river above the falls, where the water was squeezed into a rock sluice before flying out into a tunnel formed by the overhanging trees. Below me was a steep chute, where it gathered into a river again before launching out from the top of the cliff. There was a path dug out of the hillside that scrambled its way to the foot of the falls though dripping forest. I sat on a rough bench, and listened to the roar drowning out all other sounds. When water falls so far it makes its own time, breaking into smaller drops and finer spray, and slowing up. I could choose whether to see it as moving or something endlessly renewing itself in the same place. I let myself go with the idea that I could hold it still, and I slid into a near trance. Two people were on the far shore looking at me. They stood like the women in the foreground of Vermeer's painting *View of Delft*, with a still calm in which time becomes irrelevant; reality has slowed to a halt. They have arrived at where they are meant to be; their stillness is not captured for a moment, but complete, and here they will stay. With the strange certainty without evidence that dreams lend us, I knew the figures were Celia and I, back on the same shore. Time shook. I was on the bench; water was falling, clocks moved again. There were no people, just the plunge pool and, high above, the spider's web footbridge I had crossed. It seemed to hang on a prayer.

Walking back I found a dead specimen of a butterfly that I had been glimpsing in flight. It had deep black velvet upper wings with a single band across that iridesced blue-green-turquoise. The undersides seemed not to belong to the same creature, but to have been cut from a Japanese print. On a white background, black and scarlet were interspersed by black lines. In the centre of each wing was a black circle with the number 88 in it. It is so clear the local name for the butterfly is simply *ochenta y ocho*.

Something about the falls had been familiar. Back in the hotel, the internet rescued my half-memory: the waterfall had been used in the film *Romancing the Stone*. My delicious lunch was a dish described in the menu as real vegetarian-style trout. I recalled the speciality of the day in a Xalapa restaurant: *Real Arab Empanadas with Ham*.

A procession came down the main street: young people in brilliantly-coloured costumes, which were hybrids of Native cotton clothes, Spanish dress, and for the girls, a third influence, the style known as *China poblana*, an oriental fashion confected in the nineteenth century. Rockets were held in the hand and lit with a taper. There were no sprays of colourful sparks, just a deafening explosion. If I did not see the rocket rise, the explosion made me jump out of my skin. It echoed round the surrounding hills like gunfire. Small children did not so much as blink, babies did not cry, dogs did not bark or hide. I was close to doing all four. A life-sized effigy of Christ the King was carried through the streets shoulder-high on a small platform, venerated with incense, just as the old gods and their priests and kings were censed with copal resin in smouldering pots. The road kept rising into the town's poorer areas, past children joyously rioting their way through the afternoon break on the school playing fields.

A man leading two skinny horses laden with a milk churn roped to each side, was delivering fresh milk door to door. The road headed straight at the steep hill on the edge of the modern town, though I believe the top of this shanty suburb was the centre of the original town, because it was a defensive position commanding the slopes down to the river. In 1519 Cortés was welcomed here after his allies, the Totonacs, presented his credentials as an ally against Moctezuma and his tax collectors. Cortés's secretary-biographer Francisco Gómara called it 'a strong place on the side of a very steep mountain, to enter which two paths like staircases had been cut; and if the inhabitants had defended the entrance, our foot-soldiers would have had great difficulty in reaching it, to say nothing of the cavalry.'

With each block I passed, the houses became a little shabbier, and were in worse repair. Paint peeled, tin roofs were rusting, the children played with sticks and stones and mud; there were few toys. The homes were home-made cabins pieced together from roughly cut wood, cast-off plywood and old doors. Woodsmoke leaked through walls and roofs which were unpainted, unless the wood had paint left from its previous use. I stopped taking pictures; it was too much like poverty tourism. But the children and the mostly young adults I saw here were not failures, they had not given up. Their clothes were clean, they tended their gardens, and kept pets, chickens and pigs.

The road petered out and fields of maize began. The countryside was green and lush as far as the eye could see. Cortés was leaving this, and climbing higher, into the interior.

That night I went to an Italian restaurant where the waiter regretted that the spaghetti bolognese was finished. I was wondering what else I could manage to swallow when the owner, Pedro Córdoba, came to talk to me, alone among the tables of his large restaurant. "I recommend the pizza.'

I explained about my throat. He visited the kitchen and returned. 'They'll cook some more spaghetti. Where are you headed next?'

'Ixhuacán.'

'It's my hometown! Tourists never go there; they turn around in Xico and go back to Xalapa. The season here is short, they come for a month in July when we run the bulls, like Pamplona. That's it.' He gave me the names of his relatives. 'Ixhuacán is a small town, just ask, everyone knows everyone.'

'Is this country I can ride across? I would like to see it as the Spanish did.'

'No one rides horses on the roads, it's too dangerous for the animals. They use them in the lanes to go to and from the country, to go to market. You can get to Monte Grande that way, on the back lanes. Where are you staying?'

'Hotel Coyopolan, by the river.' 'I'll see what I can do.'

The fog had come in again and I walked down the stony streets to the muffled sound of my own footsteps. It was so quiet that the dogs were lying in the road. A single vehicle came into earshot behind, sidling slowly closer through the murk. It was hard to tell how far away it was, as the engine was muffled. It seemed to be at my shoulder. It suddenly braked and pulled close to me.

'Señor!'

I jumped. A solidly built man I had never seen before was staring at me from the passenger seat. He turned to his companion, hidden from my sight. I looked up and down the street. It was just me, the big American pick-up truck, two men, and the sleeping dogs.

'Yes, that's him.' They got out. One carried a long knife wrapped in cloth.

15

The Ride to Monte Grande

I usually keep out of trouble on my trips. That was why the farce in the bar at Champoton had been such a strange experience. The horror of getting into trouble in an obscure part of the globe is that your world changes in a moment. The vehicle's other door opened and Pedro the restaurant owner got out. 'Did I frighten you?'

I was laughing an artificial laugh, so he knew he had. 'This is my chef, Ray Fernández, he has a friend who keeps good horses, he'll bring them round in the morning, and go with you.' The morning, for Ray, was eleven o'clock, and for his friend Rodrigo an hour later. In the meantime I looked at the amateur mural in the mini-park opposite the hotel. It showed Cortés's route, from Xalapa to Tenochtitlán, with Xico at the centre, and the passage that awaited me, moving west then north onto the high plains. Alongside were cartoon portraits of Cortés and Malinche. He looked like a seventies country-rock guitarist dressed to play Shakespeare, and she looked like a Disney princess from the Arabian Nights.

Rodrigo was round-faced, round-bellied, round-eyed and wore an old-fashioned heavy cotton tracksuit. He had come with two horses; both were strong and nice on the eye. A chestnut was the compact size of local riding horses, the other was larger, a stone-grey mare with dark brown socks and matching tail and mane. My confidence in Ray as a guide was dented when Rodrigo indicated the larger horse and asked him, 'Do you want this one?' Ray looked aghast, and shook his head. I mounted her and settled in the saddle. There was a high pommel with a flat top the size of both my spread hands. It was a working saddle for cattlemen.

My mare handled beautifully, and we crossed the bridge and

began to walk them up the steep wooded hill and out to the south-east. There were more horses than vehicles, and the landscape was lush parkland, with long deep grass studded with copses. The hedges were full of an acacia with giant thorns and tiny, mimosa-like leaves. There was little livestock, although you would have thought cattle would only have to look at the fields to fatten up.

Crossing small stone bridges and fording streams, I thought of Cortés, although only a dozen had mounts and they often walked to keep the horses fresh for any skirmishes. I realised that when I pictured him riding through the countryside, he had a smug smile on his face. In Spain he had never seen such fertile land as I now rode through. He must have been mentally carving it into estates. The participants often remark how like Spain it is. Galicia, in the maritime north-west, might have been, but they had never been there. The Spain they knew was parched and starved. A hawk broke from the hedge without fear, flapping lazily to a tall dead tree in the bordering field, and settling to watch us go by. Occasionally there were bee-eaters, which might have reminded them of Spain. Ray pointed to a group of what looked like fruit trees.

'Oranges?' I asked.

He shook his head. 'The orange ball is not the fruit, it's a kind of case. It will open up to reveal a flower, then the flower makes the real fruit, which is a different shape and colour.' Like Spain, and very different.

Occasionally we passed field workers, or men working in kitchen gardens round their cabins. When they saw us they stood transfixed, as if Adam had planted them there with the first hoe. They awaited the seasons, their faces incurious moons.

We climbed relentlessly. In Britain, it would have taken us from arable land through sheep pasture to moors, bare rock and snow. In Mexico there was just more green land. A black and white cow stood in the field above us right next to the hedge. An orange sack at the end of a string of tissue hung from her vagina. She had just given birth. The horses seemed agitated. I sidled mine closer. The calf lay in the grass. The cow sniffed it from time to time, but did not lick it clean. The calf's flanks were still. It had been still-born. The mother needed time to realise that this was not a living thing, and her longing to nurture would have no outlet. The trees were now shaped as much by the growths on them as their own form, because their trunks, limbs, and branches were carpeted with brilliant green moss, and a hundred bromeliads sprang sheaves of leaves. After 3 hours we came to the top of a broad-topped ridge and followed it, still climbing, gradually crossing over the ridge and opening up views into the valley in which Ixhuacán lay. It took time to accustom myself to the sheer size of the landscape. The top of the main ridge looked close, but it was another 50 minutes before we finally reached it. The cloud had sunk low and it was starting to rain as we rode into Monte Grande. For the last few miles the road seemed to circle the village rather than approach it. Cloud was banking up on the west side of the village, a dark wave building, rolling slowly across the slope towards us. The gloom stole the colours, and smells became more distinct; woodsmoke stood still and fragrant. The village was a humble place without even the pretence of a square. There was a green and turquoise church that could have seated every soul in the parish, where an old lady with skin the colour and texture of cured tobacco lowered her bony knees to the cement floor, and prayed with her palms over her face, one hand trembling like a forest leaf which feels a breeze that does not touch its neighbours. Monte Grande possessed a small school and a shop, with little in it, where we tied our horses. Ray, who had not brought so much as a water bottle, bought food elsewhere and cheekily ate it here, but he was so charming to the ladies who ran it, they were soon looking for kindnesses to do us. I was brought a chair in which to watch the rain build determinedly to a downpour. Thunder moved through the hills around.

On the back of each saddle was a tight pack which unrolled into a poncho big enough to cover my body, legs and much of the horse. I only lacked a Colt 45 to have a complete Clint outfit. The first lightning bolt was close but my horse only broke into a trot, and soon settled. The few lights which came on before we left the village glowed brightly. The storm crossed our path and moved along the ridge we had come up. The road was threaded with streams, and puddles where foam built up, then shot out in white snakes, writhing down the hill. The black and white cow was standing in the darkness by the body of her calf, two hours after we had first seen her.

The rain drummed on my hat, but it and my poncho kept me dry from head to foot. For the whole ride down the mountain the storm circled us, never more than a few miles away, sometimes almost above us. After the first thunder and lightning, the horses did not seem to notice it. Sometimes they slipped on wet rocks; Ray was almost thrown. Having settled to riding he became nervous again, and from there I took the lead for the remainder of the journey. There were a few other riders. We waved but spoke no more than *Buenos noches*. A few large birds could not settle to roost, and their cries were the only noises beyond the rain, the tousling of the trees, the streams, and the clip of hoofs. I felt part of the night.

Ray caught up. He too was grinning.

'Tomorrow I am going to Ixhuacán. Do you know anyone there?'

'A few family, and I know the boss's people.'

'Are you doing anything?'

He caught on. 'You want to hire horses there and ride back to Monte Grande, complete Cortés's route?'

'Interested?'

'No! One day like this is enough!'

Within an hour darkness was complete, and the road ahead was barely visible. I was tired; all the muscles that only riding uses were aching. I concentrated on keeping my back straight and letting my pelvis rotate beneath me. Even holding my arms forward with the reins was difficult. But riding through this night storm was something special which would soon end. When orange street lights became visible on the farthest ridge I knew it was civilisation waiting, towns: comfort and the everyday. In half an hour we were sliding down the paved hill to the bridge by my hotel. Rodrigo was standing under a lamp in the porch, his hand to his eyes. I surrendered my poncho and my alter ego.

The country buses to Ixhuacán went a long way round, winding through all the other small towns in the area. First, I had to bus back towards Coatepec, and wait at the side of the road for the half-hourly bus. A well-dressed woman was waiting with country people she studiously avoided. She drew my eye, although she was frowning and not beautiful. Taxis pulled over, and she turned them down with a faint shake of her head. Cars slowed, and men drooled at her. Buses for everywhere I had ever heard of came and went. When, after half an hour, another jalopy rumbled up without Ixhuacán on the windscreen, we exchanged a faint roll of the eyes. More buses. I nearly boarded one to Teocelo because it was a nice name and there was a bus going there. After an hour a bus came for Ixhuacán. The smart lady did not get on. Where was she bound? She was carrying only a handbag. Had she arranged to meet someone, been jilted or stood up?

My road out led into a towering gorge where trees clung on to any slope less than vertical. After a slow morning, the drive lifted my spirits. In places half a mountain had been cut away to force the road through on a narrow ledge with precipices above and below. We burst out into an open valley. A straggle of houses consolidated into a row of properties, some with picturesque wooden balconies where maize cobs were hanging to dry. I was deposited on the bottom of the main square outside the Three Kings Church, where a two-story high decoration in maize kernels and leaves was being erected. The driver said, 'Ask for your friend's family in the town hall.' The square was a fine space with Colonial colonnades on three sides. The buildings were peeling, but it felt more real than the heritage facades of Coatepec and Xico. The town hall filled the top of the square. After the staff recovered from their surprise that I had intentionally left the bus to spend time here, I was sent to other offices, occupied by people who were all very pleasant, but none of them had heard of the relatives whom, Pedro had assured me, everyone knew. I was directed along a bunting-striped street to the town's only hotel, but when I reached the corner opposite the next church, there was a handsome two-story Colonial house with no sign of being other than a private home. I knocked the door, waited, then knocked louder until I had crossed the pain threshold for knuckles on 200-year-old oak. The men at the vehicle valeting service over the road encouraged me, but whether to be helpful, or just have a longer laugh at my expense I was not sure. Eventually a face appeared; it belonged to a smartly

150

dressed woman, who unlocked the door and pointed to the doorbell just above head height, where children and idiots could not find it. 'We don't advertise rooms any more, just friends and people who know.' I climbed up the metal spiral stair jamming myself several times with the backpack. The door at the end of a dark corridor opened out into an enormous room in which a three-piece suite was almost lost, despite there being two double beds in there. There were no windows, just twin wooden doors onto a narrow balcony which, due to a dog leg in the road, looked straight down the street leading to the square.

The Holy Kings Church was a parish church as large as a cathedral, and there were at least three other churches in town. I marvelled at the statistic that the percentage of churchgoers in Mexico is no higher than in Britain. People of all ages came in to sit briefly, or pray, or make the sign of the cross in front of a favourite saint. The life-sized statues of saints were dressed in real garments of a quality few parishioners could afford. Two ladies with richly thick hair moved between statues, where they performed their round of worship. One wore her grey hair in plaits which fell to her waist. The white hair of the other was swirled around her head and held with a wooden pin. The latter settled just behind the main west doors, standing as far into the shadow as she could while still catching enough light to read her prayer book. When she opened it a quiet certainty strengthened her repose; she became a column of stillness.

What was left of the day, I footled away pleasantly walking the length and breadth of the town. Rockets went off at regular intervals, and the explosive noise bounced back off the mountains as if the town were being shelled. I returned to my room when the clouds that had been standing on the peaks to the west decided to fall on the town. At night you can measure prosperity by light. Ixhuacán was dark. The shop over the road was open but in darkness.

I woke at four when a lorry turned the corner below my room and revved up the hill. I could feel its weight through the vibrations, and imagined Saturn V rockets were being delivered to the outlying villages in an arms race to make a noise for Jesus. Cockerels took the rumble as a hint that the day was beginning and began to crow. When no light appeared, a dog took offence and barked without pausing for breath for 15 minutes. No one calmed it. An extraordinary noise joined it, a roaring scream. Was it a toddler in an uncontrollable tantrum, or a pig in pain? Now thoroughly awake I read until dawn, when I piled on clothing, and pulled a chair into the corner of the balcony which the sun reached first. Because, to the east, there were no mountains delaying the sunrise, a low light came straight up the side street and threw long shadows over the pale concrete crossroads.

Horses were ridden to the stores, loaded with a sack of grain or maize, and led home. In one photograph I caught a hoof with the point barely touching the ground as it lifted. Its shadow worked like a reflection, doubling the image. The eye looked for ripples, before remembering the road was set concrete, and its step would not be recorded, like the curious coyote which dabbed its paws in the wet tile at Antigua. The morning commute brought a man with a pig on a lead, which seemed to know the route and trotted cheerily along like a dog. Another man led a goat on a lead. Turkeys, native to Mexico, abounded, confined in sacks with their head left outside. Before the conquest it was one of only two domesticated animals kept for food, the other being a small dog.

The lady who owned the hotel returned from business.

'You are travelling alone?' she asked, as though it were inconceivable.

'Yes, it is work, I am writing a book.' I never felt this came over as convincing in a country where most people bend their backs to work.

'You must have supper with us tonight, what would you like?'

I tried to think of something which would not be too much trouble, and I was sure I would be able to eat without choking and putting everyone else off their food. 'Vegetable soup would be fine.'

'I'll put some chicken in too, is that okay? Wholemeal bread or tortilla?'

I could have kissed her. I had not had good bread since I arrived. When I went down for dinner, her daughter and her family were there, including a charming toddler called Cecilia, who was delighted to meet someone new. To my grateful embarrassment, a separate meal had been cooked just for me. I showed them pictures of my home, on my iPad, something I do not do unless the person is affluent, as they were. They probably thought my terraced mews house rather underwhelming compared with their Colonial pile. They were more interested in our car. A Mini Cooper is a luxury import in Mexico.

After a night's sleep without screaming and barking I felt ready for a walk to the next town, Ayahualulco. Ixhuacán was set at 6000 feet in a large valley from which the route to the west climbed steeply through a gorge to a notch in the hills. One hedgerow plant was new to me. It was a small shrub with a fruit like a crab apple. But what caught my eye was the leaf, which was shaped like a maple, but with fierce long spines standing vertically from it. Part of me wanted to test the sharpness of this extraordinary feature. A more sensible part whispered that if it looked vicious it probably was vicious. That night at supper I showed a picture to the women of the family and they exclaimed together *mala mujer*, bad woman. *Cridoscolus angustidens* has the most irritant sting in the plant kingdom. The forest thinned as I reached the base of the notch and the road bridged a stream. I sat on the concrete parapet and thought how British the scene was. No doubt Cortés would have thought how Spanish it was. On the floor of the side valley green, meadows flanked stony streams tumbling against a backdrop of towering hills, cloaked in a mix of pines and junipers, like Gwynedd in north-west Wales with the vertical perspective out of control.

I kept thinking how I could describe these landscapes. There are really only two ways of describing something strange: comparison and catalogue. Comparison can seem a lazy and crude short-cut to describing an object. This was a new world, it was not filled with the things of the old world, it was especially not populated by degraded versions of familiar species, where pumas were lions which had not developed manes. President Thomas Jefferson was so infuriated by Count Buffon's championing of the theory that species degenerated in the Americas, that he sent him a stuffed moose so big it took twenty soldiers to carry it. But what use is the catalogue

153

technique? *The puma is a sandy-coloured feline quadruped eight feet long weighing 220 pounds* is businesslike, but how would you describe an armadillo? It would read like a tool catalogue: Gradgrind teaching metalwork.

At the top of the gorge, the road ran Roman-straight for a mile until I found Ayahualulco's first building, a small new Jehovah's Witnesses church, spick and span with a chain-link fence around it on tubular steel posts, giving it the air of a pumping station. Small workshops followed. One man was spray-painting the metal headboard of a bedstead. I lunched on hot pork in a bun at an open cafe in the square, run by a man whose hair was thinning strangely, leaving tiny clumps, so they looked transplanted.

At the top of the town a gang of hard-bitten men lay in the grass swigging cane liquor from Coke and Sprite bottles, while their starved horses with shabby coats and muddied legs looked on. A new road went straight up the hill serving new houses and cabins. It had a frontier feel to it, enhanced by the smell of wood fires. A piglet had made friends with a horse, and rooted wherever it dipped its head to graze. There were occasional sheep, the first I had seen. I left the town behind and walked a beautiful grass road, through fields tinged with a golden light that brought out autumn colours dormant in the maize. Whole families were gathering the cobs or stacking the stems into stooks. Papery yellow leaves sheathing the red stems were rustled by the wind brushing through: rumours and lies. My lungs felt the thinness of the air, and the trees were now all juniper or pine. The highest maize fields are the last to be harvested, and work was beginning on these. When the path began to wind over the hill at 7000 feet, I stopped to check my GPS and was aware of being watched. In the centre of a field a line of hats and headscarves topped the faces of scarecrow field workers staring through unblinking eyes. A turkey vulture made low passes.

At 7500 feet I came out onto the road leading north to Perote, where the Spanish shivered, and the Cuban Natives with them died of cold.

16

God Knows How
My People Suffered

As I left my hotel next morning, the owner's husband appeared for the first time. Lively and intelligent, he had lived in Ixhuacán all his life. When I tried to coax more biography from him he gave it sparingly, as though he were paying a stonemason by the letter. The bus stopped outside the hotel, and as I got on the chatty driver asked, 'Are you warm enough?'

I nodded.

'Good, there isn't a heater.'

We followed the route of yesterday's walk, then detoured into every village. Through the window I saw snatches of daily life, like cinema news shorts. In one village, a new church was being built, in the same neo-baroque style in which they had been built for 300 years. The driver lost concentration coming down a steep hill and we hit the gully at the side of the road before swerving out and alarming a small flock of sheep driven by a boy no taller than them, wearing a lime-green sweater with more holes than wool in it.

The earth changed to yellow, matching the maize leaves. Field-hands were standing motionless as often as they were moving; birds gleaning the debris alighted on them. At a hamlet called San José de Aguazuelos the road levelled out, the hedgerows disappeared and we ran across near-moorland with short cropped turf and drunken lines of maram grass wherever water gathered. Cabins and unfinished breeze-block bungalows were scattered about. Work on the bungalows had stopped, money gone, but a boy on a poster was grateful to a politician for his new supply of clean water.

To my right the Cofre de Perote was in view, a massive, gently sloping shield volcano. When it first came into sight, its peak nursed the only cloud in the sky. Soon they were gathering all around and a wind whipped their tips into thin shreds, imitating the silk on the maize heads which lay in the khaki-coloured fields like dirty birds. I had expected there would be no arable farming on this high plain, but still the maize grew. Mexico seems to grow enough to feed the world, but it still needs to import.

Maize is the wheat of Mesoamerica. The growth of cities began with the discovery of a process known by the cumbersome word nixtamalisation, a compound of two Náhuatl words, *nextli* which means ashes, and *tamalli*: dough. Maize is soaked or cooked with mineral lime or ashes, and the alkalis not only soften the kernels and loosen the husks, but make more proteins and vitamins available to digest. It turns a useful food into a superfood. Portuguese trade spread this Mesoamerican plant around the world, but in parts of Africa and India where the technique of nixtamalisation did not travel with it, the poorer people who are over-reliant on it suffer from vitamin deficiency diseases like pellagra, whose symptoms are dermatitis, diarrhoea, dementia and death: another deadly foursome.

Even treated maize falls short of being a complete diet. It lacks the essential amino acid lysine, but beans, another staple, are rich in lysine and niacin. Maize and beans make a complete diet, but a dull recipe. Add chilli, and you have taste.

Squalls hit us. The driver grinned. 'How do you like the climate up here?'

'Just like home,' I said.

The small town of El Triunfo arrived, The Triumph. It was not finished. Reinforcing rods topped every building, barely a wall had been rendered. Dust coated everything, including the animals in a big compound in the middle of a town that seemed, against all reason, to be a working farm. Agave cactuses were sending up the towering flower spikes that signal their orgasmic eruption of fertility before death. The plant does not, despite the nickname century plant, do this after a hundred years, but when the roots have exhausted the water or nutrients, or perhaps, in this place, when they had exhausted hope.

We reached the town of Perote, where the road became an American-style strip with the usual logos fifty feet high, shouting the names of supermarkets, petrol stations, tyre-fitters, taco takeaways, burger bars, warehouses, and cheap motels in walled courts like depot yards. The driver stopped specially for me, and pointed down a side street towards the main square. For some time I would be in towns not in the guidebooks, so I would find a hotel for the night by starting in the main square and working outwards. In this case there was somewhere on the square which had just been revamped. Now empty conference rooms overlooked the pleasant square, while the bedrooms had various views of the same concrete wall.

It was a hustler's town, and despite the bleak landscape, was the base of Mexico's first President, General Guadalupe Victoria. The war for independence from Spain was drawn out over many years and, at the lowest ebb for the separatists, Guadalupe Victoria refused a pardon, or surrender, and for several years, until the end of 1820, lived off the land in the jungles of the north-east, becoming a mythical figure, appearing in towns for provisions, looking like a wild man, then disappearing again for months. Once independence was secured, the San Carlos Fortress, a stone shipwreck beached in the scrub on the edge of town, became his barracks and home. His second-floor room was like all the others except for a strange marble fireplace: a massive surround with only a small, low hearth, like a Lutyens detail. While living rough, he developed epilepsy, an attack of which would kill him in this room in 1843.

From the walls I could see the plain where Cortés had marched for three days, Skirting a saline area where they struggled to obtain fresh water. He wrote to the king that it was 'desert country which is uninhabitable because of its infertility and lack of water, and because of the extreme cold. God knows how much my people suffered from thirst and hunger, and especially from a hail and rainstorm that hit us there.' Even the local Natives suffered from

157

the cold, and numbers of the Caribbean ones died of exposure and hypothermia. No chronicler expresses remorse, or even regret.

The next places on the route were small market towns. The largest was Teziutlán, not easy to say but an improvement on the old name: Teziuhyotepetzintlán. I expected nothing to remain here from Cortés's time except the mountains. I was here to get a feel for the arc of his journey and its landscapes. The town was home to some political heavyweights, not all clean fighters. Maximino was the wild-man brother of a quiet and courteous President of Mexico in the 1940s, Manuel Ávila Camacho. Maximino fought as the highest rank of general in the revolutionary wars, then became the violent and ruthless political boss of the city of Puebla, south-east of Mexico City. He spent his time drinking, seducing, and blowing public money on whatever he fancied, including embezzling the funds to build this hotel. When his brother's term of office was drawing to a close, and with the presidency in the gift of the corrupt ruling party, he announced that if he was not made heir, he would kill his rival, Miguel Alemán. This seems to have been a boast too far for the Mexican fates, and on the eve of the party convention he died of a heart attack. His rival was elected as Mexico's 46th and first non-military president.

In Teziutlán's streets, cheap clothes at charity shop prices were for sale in barn-like halls where your receipt was demanded at the exit by men with well-used truncheons. Across the street, designer label clothes from Europe and the USA were sold at London prices. The square was hosting an informal Sunday market including a book stall featuring Adolf Hitler's *Mein Kampf*, a biography of him called *Painter, Soldier, Leader* which made it sound a rounded life, and *Germany Could Have Won*. More charming was the man my own age, on a park bench, who had a chicken tied by one leg to a cardboard box. 'I've come seven kilometres to sell her.'

'Any interest in her?'

He pursed his lips, managing to imply that if the punters did not snap it up that was their look-out. 'I want 100 pesos,' (5 pounds) 'but I'd take eighty.'

In the early morning, I bussed east with just a day pack, back to

158

Altotonga, a third the size of Teziutlán, but competing hard in the pointlessly large church stakes. The nave was approaching 200 feet long, the same as the wingspan of a Boeing 747 (should the town ever need to hide one). Before I reached the square below its main door, I knew they had just cut the grass, starved as I was of suburban smells. There was nothing from the time of the conquest so I bought cold water and started to hike back. I cut off a tedious modern hairpin by finding the old road, a winding basalt-paved lane across the neck of it, and walked 6 miles – all uphill – to Xalacingo, enjoying my returning strength. I paused for water on the bench of a bus shelter, at a village called Ciruelos, or plums. A sinewy man with 40 years of field labour behind him, and more to come, arrived with his wheelbarrow at the same time as the bus to Altotonga. He picked up two sacks, one of which he could only lift with quivering arms and leaden legs, and stowed them in the luggage compartment of the bus. He had only been able to get them both on the barrow by putting a larger baker's tray on top of it. The tray and wheelbarrow followed the sacks, market-bound. He skipped up to the driver, coppers in hand for his fare, plastic blue and white-striped sandals slapping the metal steps.

I came into Xalacingo along a narrow lane that squeezed between shops and church, through food stalls into the square. The church was painted in strong deep yellows and reds, which should not have worked, but it did. The side of it had a large sign on it: *Welcome Pilgrims*. Xalacingo is a farming town, and the prize product is chilli peppers. On the stalls they shone with that plastic gloss that really healthy chillies have. Despite its fame in Indian and oriental cooking it is an American plant, and chilli is a Nahuatl word, although the heartland of the mother plant was probably Bolivia. Portuguese traders and missionaries did not introduce it to Asia until the sixteenth century. The plant has high levels of vitamins B and C, magnesium and iron, and when early explorers refused to eat it because of the chilli heat, they often became ill.

The strength of chillies varies enormously, depending on the amount of the burn chemical, capsaicin, in them. Jalapeños barely register at around 5000 Scoville Heat Units (SHU). That means one unit of the plant has to be diluted with 5000 units of sugar syrup before its taste will be undetectable to a panel of punters. Thai bird's eye chillies, and their hotter relations *prik ki nu* chillies, which are common in supermarkets, come in at 50,000-100,000. The odd English name bird's eye chilli is the result of shunning the original Thai name, which not only sounds rude but means rat-shit chilli. Habaneros come in at 350,000 SHU. Some have names which would warn you off; I particularly like Naga viper, at 1.40 million SHU, or Trinidad scorpion butch, which can reach 2 million SHU. It has recently been discovered that one tarantula species has a venom that activates the same neural pathways as capsaicin.

There was some market gardening along the road in the last 7 miles back to Teziutlán. Men were bagging up 2-metre pear trees and aspens in soil as black as peat. One greenhouse shop was a sea of potted poinsettias, ready for Christmas decorations. Dodging the traffic reinforced my suspicion that walking more of Cortés's route was a nice idea that did not work.

I took supper in the hotel, persuading them to cook a Hereford steak that was what the French understand as rare: some blood, and perhaps a faint pulse. They brought it and were astonished when I said it was just right. I cleared the plate. I asked how to order a steak so rare; he said 'Ask for it English style.' It was the first time since leaving home I had eaten three cooked meals in a day. I am 5 feet 11. I weighed 9 stone and 8 pounds.

Next stop was Tlatlauquitépec. The road was tortuous, and, today, without views. The natural vegetation of this area is cloud forest, and we had the weather. An occasional lightening of the murk showed me the silhouettes of large pines: no colour, just grey on grey. 'Tlatlauquitépec!' the driver called. An old couple had been asking the driver for 5 minutes to make an informal stop for them, but the inspector was on board so rules were rules. I followed them, ghosting up the hill hoping they were going to the centre. Decisions like this make no sense but they often work. Fine drizzle was tangible against my cheeks. We arrived at a wall twenty feet high, painted to head height in the colour of anti-fouling paint, and mustard above. The founding of this establishment in 1531 dates back to the lifetime of Cortés. It was the Franciscan friary of Santa María de la Asunción, and I was standing in its former orchard. It is now a church to put other oversized churches to shame. The two towers which framed the west door disappeared into the cloud.

Tlatlauquitépec was getting the heritage treatment, but in an effective low-key way. In the square, where a concert-sized canvas roof was going up on twenty-foot poles, I found the Café Chocolate, where I chatted to Yolanda Jímenez Gonzáles. She wore a black and white striped jersey on a solid body, black leggings on slim legs, and had a plum knitted poncho with a powder-blue cashmere scarf thrown over it. Her fingernails were painted alternating pink and buff, her tousled collar-length hair could have been tidied by finger combing, but the strong eyes behind the bold black frames of her glasses suggested you would be brave to mention it. She would fit in on an arts committee anywhere in the world. She sat with the cafe owner, her sister. Outside the young walked hunched under hoodies, while older citizens had wound scarves round their chests and necks forming conical heads like chess bishops. Yolanda got up to smoke near enough to the door to pretend she was outside, and nodded at the tent. 'It's an outdoor theatre. We've got concerts and plays coming, everything. I'm the director. We are celebrating a year as a *Pueblo Magico*.' This was the brand name for the best of the historic towns like Coatepec and Xico.

'Has it helped you?'

'Oh yes! It's a lot easier to get the council thinking positively.' She reeled off a list of events that had been put on during the year.

Her sister was handsome, in her fifties, with lustrous eyes. They began discussing children, their own, then other people's, and what did she expect, three children by different fathers, and she doesn't know who is whose. She waved the local newspaper. 'That youngest will end up in here for all the wrong reasons.' The colour front page bore two mugshots of a sullen-faced youth, arrested for stealing mobiles from the TelCel shop in Teziutlán. Her red nails flashed against his green camouflage jacket. She was an empty nester watching chicks fall from the boughs.

The next part of my day's travelling involved two challenges. The first was to get two people to agree where the bus south left from. The second was to ask for a fare from Tlatlauquitépec to Ixtacamaxtitlán without swallowing my tongue.

The bus climbed to better weather on a high agricultural plain where prickly pear cactuses were grown in polytunnels for their fruit and edible leaves. I changed buses at the agricultural service town of Libres, where there were a few comfortably-off looking people and a great many more looking as if life were hard. I had to transfer to a *colectivo*, which made me feel Ixtacamaxtitlán might not be as big as I thought. It was the gateway to the heart of the mountainous region, and had been a thriving large city when the Spanish arrived. Somewhere around it, people argued where because no one knew, there had been a wall and gate across the road to divide off the land I was in from the fearsome Tlaxcala people.

17

How the Past Vanishes

The *colectivo* left Libres to weave round the spurs on the flanks of a green-sided valley. The bottom of the valley was as level as an old lake floor; the hills seem to rise out of green water. Villages were called Mirador and Bella Vista. There was one called Cañada where I noticed something that must have been before my eyes often, but had not registered: the church had no graveyard in its grounds. The burials were further down the hill.

After the Mexican Revolution, the 1917 constitution targeted five main elements of the Catholic Church's influence. Schools had to be secular, monasteries were outlawed, worship was confined to church buildings, religious institutions were banned from owning property, and church-owned schools and hospitals were nationalised. Priests and officials of the church lost many civil rights.

For eight years the measures were softened by weak enforcement, and reforms stagnated. Then an aggressively atheist president assumed the presidency: Plutarco Elías Calles, so virulently anti-Catholic that Scottish Freemasons awarded him a medal. Anti-clerical reforms were enforced. Resistance was especially fierce in five states to the west and south-west of Mexico City. Their rallying cry was Long Live Christ the King, and they became known as the *Cristeros*. Armed conflicts triggered a three-year long civil war in which the government persecuted and massacred *Cristeros*, often in front of their families. Violence continued into the 1930s. 90,000 people died, at least 40 priests were killed and 4000 expelled, until in 1934 there were only 334 licensed priests in Mexico. By 1935, seventeen states had not a single priest.

The Catholic writer Graham Greene came in 1937 to survey the

5. Main Cultural Groups in 1519

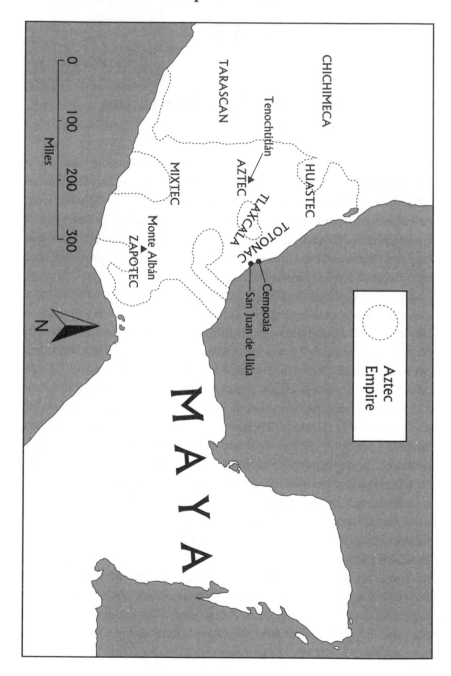

impact. He would base his novel *The Power and the Glory* on his experiences, but a year earlier he published *The Lawless Roads*, a non-fiction account of his journey. There was much injustice to report, but his bias saddens.

Greene knows his agenda before he arrives, does not refine it, and never explains the point of view of people he disagrees with. Not once in his book does he say why the elected government of Mexico enjoyed enough support to pursue these policies. It was because the Catholic Church cronied to the old monied elites, and was a servant of oppression and exploitation. The church owned huge swathes of the country, more than the local and state governments put together, and often badly underused it, depriving people of work. Given the choice of supporting a policy to protect the estates and privileges of the super rich, or foster education and a living wage among ordinary people, their priests told the labouring poor the landowners were their masters. These masters did not want teachers coming to the countryside to teach literacy, so they shot them dead.

When the Mexican Revolution came, it was driven by a ramshackle coalition of ideologies, but the slogan uniting Villa and Zapata was *Land and Liberty*. As the biggest landowner, the church opposed reform. When the fighting finished, the backlash against the church was as severe as it was unsurprising. The registering of births, performing marriages and burying the dead were made civic responsibilities, and burials now took place outside the churchyard, and still do.

Nearing the end of a long journey I saw the church locally nicknamed San Francisquito, little St Francis, perched on a conical hill with a ribbon of white road wound round it. It looked like a helter-skelter. There was an abandoned church in a field, a rare sight, then another. A third church came into view; a ceramic-tiled dome was corseted by flying buttresses in stately decay. The bus stopped, apparently in a rural lane, and we all got out. This was Ixtacamaxtitlán. The town smelled of the farmyard: the mellow odour of cow dung and the sour tang of pig manure. The asphalt road into town had given way to older basalt paving stones, worn and addled, settling my ankles at rogue angles. When people stop to stare at me, I know I have reached somewhere unspoiled and off the track. They gawped open-mouthed. The hubbub from farther up the street drew my eye to the stalls of a busy market set out under juniper and pine trees. I strolled up the hill, distracted by the bustle, then looked down to see I was about to plant my boot in a pile of crockery that had been stacked for sale in the middle of the road. A policewoman asked if she could help me. Mari-Carmen was 5 feet high. Girded with a utility belt pouched with radios, handcuffs, truncheon and other tools, she was built like a small asteroid. 'Of course we have a hotel!' she beamed, 'Follow me.'

'Is this a weekly market?'

'No, once every two months.' Not quite Brigadoon, but a symptom of a somnolent economy. Just off the square was a modern courtyard where she introduced me to the owner of Hotel de Razo, a lady with the deeply wrinkled skin of a lifelong smoker, and a manner that was simultaneously unctuous and unfriendly. All the rooms with an outlook were family rooms on the first floor; all the single rooms were on the ground floor. I said 'It's a lovely view from upstairs, would you do me a deal?'

'No.'

'I expect you are busy because of the market.' 'No.'

Cortés arrived here from Zautla where he had endured an uneasy stay. Its chief, Olintecle, was a substantial power in the region, and while he listened to the Spanish and their Cempoalan allies, he was not impressed by Cortés's talk-up of himself, his king, and his god, and he did not bend to the usual implied threat. Cortés asked if he was a vassal of Moctezuma. 'He showed surprise at my question, and asked who was not a vassal of Moctezuma, meaning that here he is king of the whole world.' Olintecle would not even hand over a few gold trinkets until the emperor said so. The usually cocky Cortés was advised by his Father Olmedo that attempts at religious conversion could wait a while, perhaps persuaded by the large racks of skulls of sacrificial victims placed round the town. Olintecle's reaction to a sermon against human sacrifice was to keep the gods happy with the sacrifice of another fifty people, a detail absent from Cortés's account.

Chiefs from the Cempoalans were sent ahead as ambassadors to the regional power, Tlaxcala. Meanwhile Cortés moved on to the next town, Ixtacamaxtitlán. It means Place of the White War God. 'On a very high hill is this chief's house,' he wrote, 'with a better fortress than any to be found in the middle of Spain, and fortified with better walls and barbicans and earthworks.' Having seen Medellín and Trujillo, I doubted it. It smacks of building up the opposition to flatter himself.

The Spanish stayed there three days to recuperate and await the return of the ambassadors sent to Tlaxcala. They did not come back. Cortés decided to press on, but soon came to a sign that conflict in the area was at a serious level. 'On leaving this valley I found a great barrier built of dry stone and as much as nine feet high, which ran right across the valley from one mountain range to another. It was some 20 paces wide and all along the top was a battlement a foot and a half thick to provide an advantageous position for battle; it had only one entrance, some ten paces wide.

'When I asked the reason for this wall they replied that it was the frontier of the province of Tlaxcala, whose inhabitants were Moctezuma's enemies and were always at war with him.' The location of this wall is either glossed over in histories, or statements are qualified by probablies and mays. The impeccable scholar Anthony Pagden has it as being 20 miles to the west, near the town of Tlaxco, and says traces of a wall have been found there. Hugh Thomas has it closer, at Atotonilco. But the chronicles say they came across it almost as soon as they left Ixtacamaxtitlán, where the road left the valley. Tlaxcalancingo, farther up this valley, fits the bill, but did it have a wall?

One of Ixtacamaxtitlán's cafes had set up a barbecue made from an old oil drum and was cooking chicken *al fresco*. The only clients were family. In small towns I found it harder to assess people. Middle-class couples huddled in layers of woollens, and ate in greasy spoon cafes, because there weren't enough of them to support a restaurant. The cafe owner looked like any other peasant woman who brought a chicken and some garden produce to market, but Elía Herrera and her friends and customers were a find. When I mentioned the walls, Elía said 'I have a book,' and came straight back with a hefty volume on the history of Ixtacamaxtitlán. Two of the photos had ironic titles: *Remains of the 'mythical wall'*.

'Where were the photos taken?'

Another customer, a young, very slim, and very pregnant woman called Irene Martínez said 'Tlaxcalancingo. I come from there, about twenty minutes up the hill. Those pictures are a couple of years old but the walls are still there. You need to speak to Areli, our tourist officer.' She then pointed to some mastodon fossils on a shelf. 'My brother's land at Tlaxcalancingo is full of them. My grandmother used to grind them to a paste and use it to make compresses for broken bones. She said it was also good when you were pregnant.' I did not ask how many mastodons had been sacrificed to bring her to term.

Elía chimed in: 'The author of the book lives at the top of the street, I'll take you when you've finished your chicken.' It was as though I had gatecrashed a seminar about my own project. We went up the side of the square to a shop where three men were talking. Elía introduced me simply: 'He wants to know everything about Ixtacamaxtitlán.'

A man with handsome, very straight, Hispanic features shook my hand. 'My brother is the author, I am Mario Martínez. He is away for a few days, but do you want to see the museum?'

'When is it open?'

He fished in his pocket, and held up a set of keys. 'Whenever you want.' Walking to the museum, Mario knew everyone, including the old women sitting on benches in the back of a pick-up truck, wrapped like desert mummies against cold and eternity. From behind the pick-up came a woman around thirty in smart western dress, with strong body confidence. She smiled broadly at us both. Mario said 'This is Areli from the tourist office. This is John, an illustrious client.'

She beamed at me as if she had been waiting all week for an illustrious client. 'Come and see me in the morning,' she pointed across the square to the town hall.

Mario and I continued to the museum, which is housed in the

Church of San Diego, dating from around 1531. It is a squat little building with lumpy designs moulded in stucco on the front, but it has the charm of something made as well as the jobbing builder knew how. En route we picked up a man who was built in the same way. He had a piratical beard as thick as a hedge. His left side was in the rudest of health, his right side had collapsed, including his face which had a sagging squint where his eye had been. He may have suffered a stroke but there was something else as well. He threw off random comments, and I could not tell whether they were for himself, or me, or passers-by.

The museum had some fine specimens, including a block of basalt intricately carved with a Huastec priest drawing an obsidian knife towards the throat of a victim. Objects like this sculpture, made by a coastal culture, showed that 2000 years ago this small town traded widely through much of central Mexico. The most intriguing piece proved the artists were keen observers not just of living animals but fossils, as a stone disc had been carved into the spiral of an ammonite.

Our piratical companion was waiting outside, and accompanied us back to the square, flinging out comments to the streets. As soon as Mario had said goodbye, the pirate launched into a summary of the boundaries of the Native cultures as they stood when Cortés arrived. He was correct in every detail. Abruptly he cut away from me on a diagonal across the square walking through the middle of a basketball game, with neither he nor they taking any notice.

I went back to the cafe to thank Elía and have a coffee. Irene was still there. She said, in a tone that brooked no argument, 'Of course the Natives buried almost all their treasure. The pyramids on the mountain have been razed to the ground but below them are tunnels ... ' I remembered as I watched her face, the same intensity in the eyes, far away to the south in Peru, a decade before. A man had clutched my sleeve in the hill town of Yanahuanca, and pointed out the peaks to the south-east. 'As a boy, I was playing with friends in a cave on that mountain when I saw a gleam in the dirt. Gold jewellery was packed into a hole that was I don't know how deep. It was Inca work of the highest quality. I covered it up and did not tell my friends.

I had to play with them all day, as we always did, so they did not suspect anything. I came home and told my father. We went up there looking for it, day after day, but I never found the place again.'

There is a need to believe that in some way they were not defeated. The Spanish did not get the money, the regalia. The old religion went on. Warriors sleep in caves waiting for the call. Dusk caught me by surprise. The mountains to the west of the town were close, and the sun disappeared not long after four. The day's warmth was in the sunlight, not the air. The amphitheatre of mountains to the west drained sheets of cold air right through the town. When I ate supper in an unheated cafe the owner turned off the fridge after taking out my beer. I asked 'Will no one else will drink beer?'

He laughed, 'Oh yes! But now the room is as cold as the fridge.'

The internet cafe was closed, and never opened, because no provider could get signals down into valley. I had no phone signal. Even now, the town is closed and isolated. One sound was missing. No street is empty until a dog howls in it. I wrote my diary sitting at the desk in my sleeping bag, and slept in it too.

Next morning I spent 90 minutes with Areli in the President's Office, which was a cement-floored open office with so little furniture it looked as if bailiffs had raided it. 'If you want to see the walls go to Tlaxcalancingo, take the Apizaco bus and ask for the Justice of the Peace or the Inspector.'

At seven the next morning the early light was softened by freezing mist and I hurried to the foot of the square where men and women hampered by layers of thick woollens lit braziers made from old dustbins, put up stalls and laid out fruit and vegetables. A *colectivo* waited with a board on the fascia saying Apizaco. I rushed over, climbed in, nodded *Buenos días* to an interior already half full of muffled bodies, and began to slide the door shut. The driver stilled my hand, 'We wait a little longer,' and switched off the engine, and with it the heater. When my ears had become brittle with cold, we bounced slowly down the potholes for 50 yards, and stopped for a group of ghosts, then halted another 15 yards along for a second group. I was probably the only one who wondered why they had not all walked to the square, if only to keep warm.

I could see little except huddled figures waiting by the roadside, some flagging down the bus with infinitesimal motions, others motionless, waiting for something else. We climbed. When Cortés reached the top of this valley, he was confronted by the wall. The sun punched a hole in the cloud, and a green sign read Tlaxcalancingo. We stopped at the first building. I decided to wait until we got to the centre. A minute later we had left the village. I had to stop the bus and walk back.

Mexican dogs had been torpid things: strangers to meat, or nourishment in general. Until now. The village was alive with dogs and they all came to bark at me. The village straddled the road in a loose scatter of homes and smallholdings. It stood on the shoulder of what seemed from below to be a mountain, but was again just the edge of a high plain over 7000 feet up. Looking back towards Ixtacamaxtitlán all I could see was the top 500 feet of the mountains. The valleys were long lakes of dense cloud. It was so still the maize was silent.

There was a modern chapel on a large flat base, far bigger than it needed. It might have been the base of an old pyramid. Irene at Ixtacamaxtitlán had said there were some in the area, but all reduced to a few courses above ground level. I was drawn up to fields above the village by the sight of grassy linear mounds, walking along a track where a timid pony watched me come, the nerve in one front leg trembling, the low sun blazing his mane. I climbed a mound by a pond; they were modern earthworks for irrigation. No sign of walls. On the way down I greeted a smallholder who came to his farm gate to chat. He was dressed in western clothes, and there was modern machinery round the yard.

'I'm looking for the old walls Cortés crossed here.'

'Oh! They are gone!' His speech was at odds with his appearance, blustery, inelegant. Perhaps he spoke an indigenous tongue as his first language.

'No, local people say they are here on this hill.'

'There they are, behind the school.'

They had come back quickly. 'Where? I've walked all over the hill.'

He pointed at the modern ponds.

'They are new.'

'Well then, there's nothing left after all.'

I am not sure who felt more confused. I crossed the road and climbed the hill which formed the other half of Tlaxcalancingo. At the top of the street was a man wrapped in a thick blanket, with another on his arm, giving off food smells. He looked as though he had sprung from the earth and was waiting for the gift of motion. If he did not know, no one would.

'I am not from round here, you need to ask the señor, there.'

'I have been told to see the Justice of the Peace or the Inspector.'

'He's one, his brother's the other.'

Señor Rómulo Torres López came out to see who was talking about him. He began a little defensively, even when I mentioned Areli, but he sat me down, and sent his daughter for something. He was, he told me, forty-eight years old and ran a small furniture workshop at the back. She returned with the same book Elía had shown me, and opened it at the photos of the 'mythical walls.'

'They are on that hill.' He pointed back to where I had walked.

'I've looked for an hour and found nothing, and the farmer said they have all gone.' He sighed and got up. He set off down the hill. I followed, feeling I had annoyed him. 'Where do you buy your wood?'

He perked up. 'All local. Mostly pine, there's only one kind here, but it's good wood, and tolerates heat and damp and drying.' He pointed to a juniper-like tree I had seen frequently. 'That's *sabino;* the wood is as fine as cedar. It's our national tree, and grows as big as anything in the world except the baobab. There's a *sabino* in Oaxaca that's nearly 40 feet in diameter; I mean just the trunk.'

At the food of the hill we picked up Modesto Martínez, a quiet man in a green polo shirt who heard I was from London, and said, 'On the internet I see France has been having a lot of bad weather; I am sorry to hear it.' I was touched by his concern, so it took me a while to realise he thought London was not just close to, but in France.

Rómulo led us across a shallow dip, then he turned along a field boundary where he stopped and pointed. A neat stream of stones ran away up the hill. 'Those are the mythical walls.' We tracked the line along the edge of the maize field. The wall then struck out in a smooth curve across an open meadow, to an enclosure: a perfect circle eighty feet across.

'It's odd,' I said, 'that the circle is so much better preserved than the other walls.'

Rómulo pursed his lips. 'When I was young, all the walls were so high.' He drew a level with his hand, high on his chest, 'I'm talking about the late 1960s, early 1970s, right?' Modesto nodded. 'We used to play on them.'

'What happened?'

'People quarried it to use themselves, or to sell. It was used to build homes, level ground, whatever. By the end of the 1980s it was at ground level, like now. The circle is here because it was used as a corral for livestock, so it was useful.'

'Didn't they know they were destroying something very old and valuable which they could not replace?'

'They do now. Archaeologists come asking about them. We usually don't say anything.' Grasshoppers sprang from our path. I pointed, 'I have forgotten the Spanish word for them.' Modesto said '*Chapulines,*' which did not ring a bell. Then it did: they were using the Aztec word, not the Spanish. When one language smothers another it is the homely words which often live on in everyday speech.

We followed the base of the wall to a small feature like a gatehouse, where it seemed to peter out. Backtracking, we came to a mound covered in scrub rising above the fields. Rómulo led the way, hauling himself up by the branch of tree with slender willow-like leaves, and fruit like red peppercorns. '*Pirul.*'

'Do you use it?'

'The wood is soft, no good.'

It looked familiar. 'There's a tree in Peru like this, they call it *molle.*'

'That's the one.'

The sap is antiseptic, and its twigs have been used since antiquity as toothbrushes.

The summit of the mound was pitted, and the tops of walls were visible. It was a small pyramid. I jumped in a pit and pulled up a stone, smooth on one side. They knew immediately what it was. 'From the wall; that's plaster.'

Faint traces of red paint still adhered. 'Has the pyramid been surveyed?'

'Pyramids.' He pointed to similar mounds scattered over the plateau. 'A little official, a lot of unofficial, but they didn't find much to rob, or they'd have dug deeper.'

Modesto intrigued me. At times he seemed simple; he had asked me 'Can your GPS see under the ground as well?' But he used the Spanish equivalent of the word autochthonous, and showed more curiosity about me than Rómulo.

The latter pointed west towards Mexico City. 'Do you see where the road goes behind the volcano? Look left, the old mule drivers went higher up, where the faint trail goes behind the volcano. They knew the ancient road, the one Cortés used. What about lunch?'

'I've got water and bananas.'

'Come and have lunch with my family.' I explained my eating problems. Modesto interrupted, 'You have had cancer and you are travelling alone?'

'I would rather something happened here, doing what I love, than hide from life. Alone is good, I prefer to be my own boss.'

Rómulo, the owner of a little factory, laughed. 'Can you eat noodles?'

The restaurants made bowls of thin tomato soup full of fine noodles. They were boring but were one of the few things I could continue eating until I was full. 'They are perfect.'

His house was a roomy cabin, and his extended family were mostly at home, including the school-age children, because the last Friday in the month was a management day for teachers. Four-year-old Yameli was the centre of attention. 'She has a happy personality,' I said. The adults winced. Rómulo said quietly, 'She is my son's daughter, his wife left him. Yameli still finds it difficult.'

An eight-year-old showed me pictures of animals of the world in her school book. When she reached the moose, I said I had met one, very close, in a forest in Newfoundland. I told her how big it was. Over the page was a painting of a *Tyrannosaurus rex*. I said I had walked underneath the skeleton of one, and described how huge its jaws were. She wriggled away from me along the sofa. 'You attract dangerous animals.'

The food came to the table. His wife had cooked noodle soup just for me. Looking round I saw that although he was a furniture maker, the walls of the home he had built for them were roughly shaped boards letting light and air come in. Nights must be cold.

I was very touched by their hospitality, and thanked them all for the meal and their company. Rómulo held on to my hand when we shook goodbye. 'We are proud you have come so far to see our past. You have studied hard. Take care, because you are alone.'

Alone. People always scent sadness in the fact of a lone traveller. Because I am grey-haired, they also see vulnerability. I do not feel alone with my own company. I engage more with local people, and they are more helpful to a lone traveller. A companion is a buffer, someone whom I would turn to first. I can take more risks, because no one else suffers the consequences. Being alone makes you reach for the strange in place of the familiar. I write better, because I think through everything, and write more notes, if only to pass time in a bus station or a hotel bed. I am more myself when travelling alone, and that is both more comfortable and more demanding. Travel also makes life seem more real: it challenges and refreshes tired thoughts.

I returned to the site and made a rough map of it, using my GPS. Then I sat down in the enclosure leaning against the pre-Columbian walls, writing my diary in the sun. The wall was described as varying width up to twenty paces. This was not such a monumental structure, but it was in exactly the right place. The most massive section of wall would have been that straddling the road, where the village now was, commanding the route down. Very likely, the village was made from that part of the wall. Other proposed locations, relying on the habitually sketchy geography of the chronicles, lack actual walls on the ground. The structures here had a strange layout, and I saw nothing like it elsewhere. Certainly it could have functioned as a defensive wall supported by strongrooms and gatehouses along it. The chronicle noted that it only crossed the valley floor. An army could easily outflank it but it was ample to block merchants. It may have been a joint effort by Mexico and Ixtacamaxtitlán to choke off Tlaxcala's trade route to the coast: an economic blockade.

The sky had been nearly cloudless all day. Now high cirrus was gathering in the north-west. To the north, across the main valley, was another segment of the plateau on which I stood. It was now obscured by a low bank of smokey yellow cloud that looked as if it had been poured over it. It began to slither down into the gullies of the escarpment below at some speed. It had been a good day, but it was time to go. At the roadside, a row of car tyres had been half-buried as a fence. I sat on one while chickens and turkeys ran in and out of the tyres and my legs. In the distance the wind came with greater swiftness through the standing maize, through the last of the green leaves. In the grass around, pairs of grasshoppers were locked together in angular Meccano intercourse, using up their fertility before the cold came.

I liked Ixtacamaxtitlán. I toured the town's churches, and spent Saturday sketching, snoozing by the river, and walking up a side valley outside the town. That night both restaurants closed and the only place to buy food was from a kiosk on the square. I had antibiotics so I gave it a try. She fried fresh finely chopped meats, sausages and onions to order, and served them in flatbread. I said, 'This is much better than the food in the restaurants.' She blushed, but nodded at her customers to make sure they realised what a good deal they were getting.

In the morning I took my leave of the competent but cheerless hotel, leaving for the seven o'clock bus. The other fifteen rooms were empty. If she had discounted an upstairs room halfway towards the single room price, she would have made half as much money again at no extra cost, and I would have been able to see something out of the window. I was closing the front door, thinking this, when a window opened above me. I was being too harsh. She was wishing me *Buen viaje*. Her voice rang out down the silent street. 'Where's the key?'

I was heading for Tlaxco. On the map it seemed the nearest town to Atotonilco big enough to have a hotel. Atotonilco was where Cortés emerged from the mountains onto the open plains leading towards his fable: Mexico. Tlaxco was big enough to have one very modest hotel, where the receptionist was also the cleaner and took time to sweep up some plaster which had fallen off the walls the night before. Outside the town, the land swept away west, a camouflage pattern of fields and copses, maize, grass and ploughed earth. In the far distance it seemed to rise and turn bluish, but the horizon was lost in stratus cloud.

Hotels that do not do plaster well seldom have internet. In a cyber-cafe I saw an email from a German friend from our student days, Marianne. We had been very close until I split up with my wife in 1993. Cath had conducted a years-long affair at work, and broken the marriage. Even her family blamed her. In twenty years I had spoken one word to her: 'No.' Marianne had taken the line that it was just one of those things, and now stayed at Cath's home when she came to Britain. She was surprised when I let our our friendship cool. Now she appeared in my life rarely, always without warning, and often slightly short of enough insight to avoid bruising me. I read her message.

Cath's breast cancer of ten years before had returned and spread. Cancer was something else we now had in common. When my diagnosis was at its bleakest, I had hoped in some way that the probability of dying soon could help me make peace with some of the bogeys in my past. It would be good if I could somehow use it to heal the lingering hurt of two broken relationships, use it to remind me that life and love are things more important than anything else. With this news, the sour residues of old anger melted away. I had loved her, and now, with Celia, I loved again. Compassion would help Cath, and maybe me.

Today was 1 December. In three days' time she would be fifty-nine. She is a fun and funny person. During one pre-Christmas meal on a cold night in Cardiff, an over-solicitous waiter greeted us. 'I hear it's snowing in Cwmbran.' She replied 'You've got good ears.' She is naive. As soon as she left me, and her new man saw commitment raise its head, he dumped her. She was now remarried to someone I had never met.

I wondered how she was coping. Her mother and sister had both had double mastectomies and not suffered again. Marianne had suggested I email Cath, and after consulting her, Marianne forwarded Cath's email address. I rang home and talked to Celia. Celia said, 'Do whatever you feel is right, but I think it would help her to know you had been through it, and were thinking of her.' I wrote a short email directly to Cath, wishing her well and repeating the advice all cancer sufferers receive about a positive attitude helping recovery.

I took a local bus to Atotonilco, historian Hugh Thomas's location for the walls. The bus turned off the main road to Tlaxcala into a pretty valley with small villages stuck tight to icing sugar churches. The dust-blown centre looked borrowed from a problem council estate. A white lorry trailer was parked without a tractor unit. Quiet couples sitting on concrete benches under an exposed sky did their best to make the square a human space. Two old men with beautiful straw hats sat smoking, their crossed hands resting on the heads of hand-made walking sticks ending in round heads like knuckle bones. I heard distant singing.

To the north and north-west the hills were more sparsely covered in scrub, harsher and drier. The Spanish had reached that ridge and looked down into this vale and known the cold of the mountains was behind them, and they were entering the powerful new state of Tlaxcala which they must either defeat, or recruit to their cause.

There was money in the town: smart houses and shiny US pick-ups that filed under my balcony all evening carrying Christmas trees back to their homes. Tonight Celia was going to a carol service at St Stephen Walbrook in the City. Tomorrow she was going to Borough Market in Southwark, to look for cheeses recommended by a Swiss friend. I was missing Christmas again. I walked to the top of the village where the road spread out into a farmyard with cows in sheds swinging piebald udders, and staring out at the rich maize stalks chopped and clamped into sugarloaf ricks. From a distance, the meadow before me had looked parched, but close up I could see it was an illusion caused by grey earth and grass-seed heads which were the colour of rare metals: polysyllables from unvisited parts of the periodic table.

No one had heard of any wall. Wherever it was, Cortés found it unmanned. He was on edge because two of his Native ambassadors to Tlaxcala had at last returned. They were late because they had been in jail, and had only escaped because their guards had been distracted by the preparations for war.

The ambassadors were still badly shaken, and frightened, when they reached the advancing Spanish and Cempoalans. The Tlaxcalans had taunted them 'Now we are going to kill those whom you call gods, and eat their flesh. Then we shall see if they are as brave as you proclaim. And we shall eat your flesh too, since you come here with treasons and lies from that traitor Moctezuma.' The Tlaxcalans had refused to believe the ambassadors' claims to be moving against Moctezuma.

Singing drifted to me again, across the unkind concrete edges of the square, where a procession was making its way behind a cross. Many of the women were bearing field bouquets just gathered, of a small white flower called *nubes*: clouds. It was Sunday. I took a pew at the back of the church and heard the hymns come closer. Soon there was scarcely a seat free. They were pure Native in descent; heads of shining black hair were bent to genuflect. I was the only man with thinning hair. A dog with a pelt like a black-backed jackal trotted in and, as no one chided it, slyly hid himself under a side pew. A few rows in front was a smartly dressed boy with a bristly new haircut and protuberant eyes, a perennially open mouth showing large buck teeth and a small aquiline nose. The tide of faces looked down for prayer; he stared at the chandelier. We looked forward for the recitation and response; he looked back to the door. We sat, he stood on the pew. His attention was always against the current.

I thought of Cath. Once, when we were staying with Marianne at the family's three hundred-year old picture-book farmhouse near Lake Constance, we had driven to a small country churchyard of great tranquility and peace. As we slid into our private reveries, Marianne reflected, 'I would like to be buried here.' Cath said, 'You should have brought a shovel.'

The bus bounced back. The procession was making its way a mile down the road to the cemetery. The jackal-marked dog was still with them. The women's umbrellas were raised against the sun, bouquets of clouds in their hands.

I checked my emails before bed. There was one from Marianne titled Urgent. Send nothing. Cath has had second thoughts. Her husband might be annoyed at our making contact. I suggested Marianne go into Cath's account and delete my message. Cath could truthfully say we had never been in touch. Outside my balcony the hotel's name flickered on an illuminated box sign. Too *film noir*. Much too pat.

18

Tlaxcala

In the air an eagle
Circles, shadowless as the God
Who made that country and drinks its blood.
BURGOS R S THOMAS

Dawn. Thin light. The land: built of different softnesses in grey. The sky: palest eggshell into whose fresh liquidities a trace of alizarin had filtered. The hills, whose blue had run into the base of the stratus last night rose into volcanoes the colour of faded terracotta, grainy with distance. On the left, a shallow cone, a quadrant of snow near the top. Its right flank descended to a col before rising again to another peak, ill-defined, a troubled, jagged ridge. The length of it was covered in thin snow that picked up rose madder reflections from the sunrise behind me. The ridge-topped mountain was Iztaccíhuatl, the cone was Popocatépetl. The col between was the Pass of Cortés. Iztaccíhuatl rose higher in my sky only because it was 6 miles nearer, but it is slightly lower than Popocatépetl's 17,802 feet.

Man writes meanings into landscapes. The Aztecs told that Iztaccíhuatl was a princess who fell in love with the warrior Popocatépetl. Her father agreed they could marry, but only when her hero came back from a war being waged in Oaxaca. Thinking Popocatépetl would not survive, he told her he had died in battle. Inconsolable, she killed herself. Popocatépetl returned alive, took her body in his arms, and laid her down in the countryside, and knelt by her side. The gods transformed them into immortal mountains and dusted them with snow. Her name means White

181

Woman. The disturbed skyline is said to look like a woman's body laid out under a sheet, like Magritte's *The Lovers* kissing through cloth, but the whole body, the whole mountain. From time to time Popocatépetl's anger explodes, and the mountain shakes and rains fire. It performed a particularly powerful series of eruptions when the Spanish arrived. The White Woman has not erupted since before the Ice Age.

Since I was a small child kneeling on the floor with an atlas, the name Popocatépetl had been magical to me. The fidgety, giggling syllables seemed just about to jump into a nursery rhyme or a spell. Now the spell was my skyline. I squeezed a chair onto the balcony and watched the light grow and change. In the mountains I had been re-reading Malcolm Lowry's *Under the Volcano*, and had finished it last night. The volcano is Popocatépetl. After the destructive drinking, during the twenty-four hours in which the novel is set, there is an ending without pity. Yet as the drunken ex-consul's shabby Eden collapses, you feel he sustained a belief in a bright paradise; it nourished him to know it was there, even if its gates did not open to him. That is a kind of hope, enough to sustain love. My last twenty-four hours had been a kind of coming together. I had come out of the mountains, seen the volcanoes standing astride Cortés's path to glory, my past had lurched out of the intangible world of the internet: my ex-wife was dying, pages of old calendars come and gone. In the night I had wept for Cath, over time passed, and loss, and careless destruction. She had started her affair when we had everything going for us, thinking she could have a happy home and something more. Happy, except we could not sustain a pregnancy. One loss, one vacuum, created another. My memories left me wide open to the emotions at the end of *Under the Volcano*, of feelings almost too unbearably tender to face. The plain stretched away to the volcanoes, one snow-lined, the other smouldering. They were often seen most clearly early in the morning, before cloud gathered and obscured them. Each morning: light, and hope. I learned to find them on the horizon by the faint disturbances in the clouds lying over them.

Tlaxcala was a powerful and stable federation whose four

constituent districts had continuous ruling lines going back seven generations into the fourteenth century. Other nations admired them more than they trusted them. They had history. They once encouraged the Cuextla people to join them in resisting the Aztecs, then stood aside and watched them be crushed. Tlaxcala had been a prosperous trading nation. Observing their growing power, the Aztecs throttled them economically, cutting them off from sources of luxury goods and basics such as salt.

Tlaxcala's main square was the most beautiful I had seen, with fine buildings on all sides. I ate brunch under one of the two colonnaded sides, facing ancient churches, and with the town hall, and its Diego Rivera murals, to my right. In 1528, when the town hall was half-built, they used the top of the first floor to stage the first plays ever performed in Nahuatl. Titles included *The Temptation of Christ*, *How San Francisco Preached to the Birds*, and *The Sacrifice of Abraham*. One imagines the fascination of the Natives as Isaac was presented, bound, on an altar, to be sacrificed by knife. A wholly familiar image, but instead of welcoming the blood, this new god stayed his servant's hand. When *The Conquest of Jerusalem* was staged, they built towers and siege engines. Hundreds of Tlaxcalans became extras, Moors or Christians, and the Holy City was taken once again, in another continent, and the Millennium came a step closer.

Between Atotonilco and here, Díaz and his comrades were reflecting on the Tlaxcalans' threats. The Cempoalans were certain the Tlaxcalans would fight. Díaz concluded: 'If it's like that, then forward, and may fortune be on our side.' Detailed tactics were agreed. If they were confronted with an army, 'the horsemen, in groups of three for mutual assistance, should charge and return at a trot, and should hold their lances rather short, and that when they broke through the Tlaxcalans' ranks they should aim at the enemies' faces and eyes, and give repeated thrusts, so as to prevent them from seizing their lances.'

The concern was that lances lodged in bodies, or which were aimed low and missed, could be torn out of the horsemen's hands. 'If however a lance should be seized, the horseman must use all his strength and put spurs to his horse. Then the leverage of the lance beneath his arm and the headlong rush of the horse would either enable the rider to tear it away or drag the Indian along with him.'

On 31 August 1519, they saw Tlaxcalan scouts, thirty Indians with plumed head-dresses, bearing shields, lances and two-handed flint broadswords. Cortés despatched a group of horsemen to seize some, but they only caught them after they had succeeded in alerting the main force. Far from surrendering, the scouts regrouped and attacked, killing two horses and wounding others. The Spanish buried the horses so the Natives could not assess their weak spots, but they could not bury knowledge; the enemy knew the horses could die.

The main Native army came into view, so numerous that the two Spanish friars were soon the busiest men in the expedition, hearing confessions. It would be their first battle since Frontera in the Yucatán. The cavalry drove into the Indian force and killed up to sixty men. Several of the captains of the crack Otomí forces were killed in the first volley fired from guns and crossbows, and fell with their standards: equivalent to a Roman legionary eagle falling. The Natives withdrew, but the Spanish did not pursue. They soon gathered some sobering facts. The people who had taken the field were not Tlaxcalans, but drawn from satellite communities. They had nevertheless put a large force in the field. Tlaxcala was much more powerful, and Tenochtitlán greater again. It was 31 August 1519. They camped, eking out their rations with small dogs from the nearest town.

In Tlaxcala there were conferences headed by Lord Xicoténcatl the younger and Maxixcatzín, a lord, and the military leader of the federation. Maxixcatzín favoured treating with the Spanish, and the influential merchant class agreed. The debates were subtle: they offered to pay compensation for the horses which had been killed to see what value the Spanish placed on them. Cortés's canny refusal left them in the dark.

The Spanish trusted no one. Their horses were left saddled and bitted all night but the contact did not come until they began to march the next morning. Díaz's numbers may be realistic when he described meeting two armies of 6,000 men. Cortés shouted, 'St James and at them': '[a]nd we rushed at them with such impetuosity that we killed and wounded many, including three captains. Then they began to retire towards some woods where more than 40,000 warriors, under the supreme commander Xicoténcatl, were lying in ambush, all wearing the red and white devices that were his badges and livery.'

The onset was furious and the Spanish made no headway. Pedro de Moron was a fine horseman, riding a piebald mare with white feet, which he had borrowed from Juan de Sedeño, who was incapacitated by wounds received the previous day. It was the animal used to arouse the stallion at the truce following the battle at Frontera. Moron was said to have the keenest sense of smell of any colonist, and could scent fires and habitations before any other soldier. The Tlaxcalans gripped his lance and brought him to a halt. A warrior brought his obsidian broadsword down on the horse's neck, and severed it with a single blow; the head was attached only by a flap of skin. Moron was wounded and falling when his comrades arrived, and beat a path back to their lines. Ten men were injured rescuing him. The mare's body was cut up by the Tlaxcalans, and exhibited. Her horseshoes were dedicated to temple gods. Díaz concludes 'As for Moron, I do not think I saw him again. He died of his wounds two days later.'

He was the only Spaniard to die. Fifteen were wounded. The Tlaxcalans withdrew in order, removing all their casualties: '[W]e never saw their dead.' Bernadino de Sahagún adds a dark postscript. In the night the Spanish guards were alerted to rustling noises, then snarling and growling. They 'watched the many wild animals that came down from those mountains to devour the corpses that covered the field. They suffered uneasiness, even fear, from the noise that those wild beasts made eating the corpses.'

The next day Díaz witnessed behaviour that would prefigure the final tragedy in Tenochtitlán. Cortés despatched two hundred foot-soldiers, seven horsemen and the Cempoalan fighters to patrol the area aggressively. He wanted to be seen to be unfazed. 'We captured about twenty men and women, whom we did not harm. But our cruel allies burned many houses and carried off fowls and dogs, and much other food.' Later depositions by Spanish soldiers would be blunter. Local people were mutilated; limbs, noses, ears and testicles were cut off, and it was not just the Native allies doing it. It was the first time Cortés had behaved brutally in Mexico, but the subjugation of Cuba, in which he energetically assisted, had employed terror. The Tlaxcalans had never suffered such savagery from their Aztec enemies. It risked setting Tlaxcala immovably against the Spanish.

The captives were fed, then released, along with two chiefs who had been captured in battle, to bear the message that the strangers wished only to pass through peaceably on their way to speak to Moctezuma. They received a reply from Xicoténcatl the son. His advocacy of resistance has made him a modern hero, but if followed, it might simply have led to the same result by different paths. He certainly did not muddy his message. 'We could go to the town where his father was and they would make peace by filling themselves with our flesh and honouring their god with our hearts and blood.' For the first time Díaz sounds weary, but he summons up sardonic humour: 'Still tired from the battles we had fought, we did not find this haughty message encouraging.' The messengers also told Cortés that Xicoténcatl had strengthened his forces. You read Díaz to know what it was to be a foot-soldier. Cortés makes you a fine speech; Díaz puts his arm round your shoulder.

On 5 September, every man, including the wounded, was summoned to battle order. 'What an opportunity for fine writing, the events of this most perilous and uncertain battle present! We were four hundred, of whom many were sick and wounded, and we stood in the middle of a plain six miles long, and perhaps as broad, swarming with Indian warriors. Moreover we knew they had come determined to leave none of us alive except those who were to be sacrificed to their idols.'

He describes ferocious hand-to-hand fighting, the butchery inflicted by the horsemen, and the attrition of the firearms. The Tlaxcalans used new tactics, attacking in groups rather the headlong assaults which had failed last time. In the previous encounter, one captain, the son of Chichimecatecle, been accused by Xicoténcatl of fighting badly, but refused to accept the criticism. Chichimecatecle's son cussedly stood aside and ordered a subordinate captain to do the same, so two of the five Native forces did not engage. Their local squabbles were still more dear to them than the threat of the aliens. Once again the Tlaxcalans conceded the field, but withdrew in good order. Sixty Spanish were wounded but only one killed. All the horses were wounded. Díaz took a stone to the head and an arrow in the thigh, but fought all day.

Díaz singled out Malinche for her unswerving courage. 'Although a Native woman she possessed such manly valour that although she heard every day that the Indians were going to kill us and eat our flesh with chillies, and though she had seen us surrounded in recent battles and knew that we were all wounded and sick, yet she betrayed no weakness but a courage greater than that of a woman.' He could have added 'and many men'. Malinche was at the forefront of all negotiations. She stood toe to toe with the Tlaxcalans during their embassies, and told them if they did not make peace the Spanish would 'kill them in their own city and destroy their country.' Her Spanish was improving rapidly, so she needed little help from Aguilar, whose Spanish had never returned to full fluency. We have glimpses of her speaking for herself, not just being a mouthpiece for Cortés. She heard the Cempoalan allies laughing at intelligence from two old men that the Tlaxcalans were planning a night attack. On her own initiative, she told Cortés. The Cempoalan allies had been spreading stories of the god-like powers of the Spanish, and their diet of human hearts. The wizards of Tlaxcala had been consulted and recommended attacking the Spanish at night when their divine powers were depleted. They did. Thanks to Malinche, the Spanish were expecting them. Back in Tlaxcala, heads rolled: wizards' heads.

A retinue arrived from Moctezuma, conveying his delight that the Spanish were attacking the terrible and untrustworthy Tlaxcalans. Cortés relished the deep antagonism between the two powerful states, and dipped into his reservoir of Latin homilies. *Omne regnum in se ipsum divisum desolabitur.* It comes from St Mark's Gospel: Every kingdom divided against itself will be brought to desolation.

While the Spanish might have been resilient on the battlefield, they had reached a stalemate, rations were short, and morale faltered. They also knew that if they fought alone, they would be beaten in battle; they had already lost forty-five men. Francisco de Solís from Santander later testified of their Cempoalan allies: 'If it had not been for them we should not have won.' He survived to father four daughters and thirteen sons. Dissident factions favoured abandoning the whole enterprise, complaining 'when a beast had finished its day's work, its saddle was taken off and it was given food and rest, but we carried our arms and wore our sandals by both day and night.' Cortés quoted some proverbs that Don Quixote's Sancho Panza might have been proud of, including 'You are seeking a cat with five feet,' but he closed with a favourite: 'The more the Moors the greater the spoils.'

In the Tlaxcalan camp, two defeats had shaken their will. We have accounts from the Native side of the impression made by the strange new fighting animals. They observed them very closely, in part to understand how to attack them. 'These stags, these horses, snort and bellow. They sweat a great deal, the sweat pours from their bodies in streams. The foam from their muzzles drips onto the ground. It spills out in fat drops, like the lather of soap.' Their impact is described as if it were an affront to the earth. 'They make a loud noise when they run; they make a great din, as if stones were raining on the earth. Then the ground is pitted and scarred where they set down their hooves. It opens wherever their hooves touch it.' Maxixcatzín and Xicoténcatl the elder both pressed for peace. They wanted to fight with the Spaniards not against them. Xicoténcatl the younger continued to urge war, but when over-ruled, he obeyed his father. This proud man went to beg for a peace he did not desire, to lay Tlaxcala at the disposal of the Spanish, and offer himself as one of the hostages securing the truce. They took the Cempoalans' descriptions of the Spanish as flesh-eating gods seriously enough to bring along some slave women for them to eat. Young Xicoténcatl complied grudgingly with this part of his orders, bringing 'four miserable-looking old women'.

In Tenochtitlán, Moctezuma's insecurity was fuelled. He sent more gifts, accompanied by speeches begging him not to trust his new friends. Moctezuma also issued an extraordinary command. The Aztec calendar ran to a fifty-two year cycle. At the end of it time had to be re-started in a spectacular ceremony known as The Binding of the Years, which featured the skull-headed god of death. The last one had been held in 1507. Moctezuma was thinking of repeating the ceremony with less than a quarter of the cycle run. That had previously been done only when droughts had threatened to trigger the collapse of the state. Moctezuma feared a cataclysm.

19

The Alliance Forged

A truce was negotiated at the fateful meeting on 18 September 1519. Not since 1492 had any Spaniard tried to forge an alliance with a Native ruler. Xicoténcatl the Elder was ninety-four and held up by two men who lifted his fallen eyelids so he could glimpse Cortés. Díaz describes the encounter touchingly. 'As Xicoténcatl the Elder was blind from old age, he felt Cortés all over his head and face and beard, and touched his body.' He was an extraordinary figure. In a time when old age began at forty, he lived from around 1425 to 1522. He was also a considerable poet. The relationship began as an alloy of sceptical trust and necessity. Cortés could be charming, and was a skilled diplomat, but he seems to have formed a genuine friendship with the two older leaders. Now he had stopped killing and mutilating them, Cortés found much in the Tlaxcalans to admire: 'they are such an orderly and intelligent people that the best in Africa cannot equal them,' he wrote to a friend. He mentions Africa because, despite Isabela's prohibition, he is assessing them as slaves.

Nevertheless, Cortés set guards outside his lodgings, and when the two chiefs remonstrated over this lack of trust, he mildly said it was their custom. They would stay twenty days. Xicoténcatl gave Cortés his daughter to marry, and gave four other noble virgins for his captains. Cortés passed his princess to Pedro de Alvarado, but used the gift as a pretext to demand conversions to Christianity; they could not marry pagans. Xicoténcatl's reply showed the ancient man's mettle. 'We have heard from you before, and certainly believe that your god and this great lady are very good. But remember that you have only just come to our land. In the course of time we shall do what is right. But can you ask us to give up our gods, whom our ancestors held to be gods for many years, worshipping them and paying our sacrifices? Even if we old men were to do so in order to please you, would not all our priests and our neighbours, our youths and children throughout the province, rise against us? Especially since the priests have already consulted the greatest of our gods, who has told them that if they omit to make sacrifices, and to perform all customary rights, he will destroy the whole province with famine, plague and war. Do not request this again, since we will not give up sacrifices, even at the cost of our lives.' Dwell on the words 'paying our sacrifices'. There is no bloodlust; it is a debt man owes the gods. When the previous age had ended and the fourth sun was extinguished, the god Quetzalcoatl went to hell to bring back the bones of the mankind and he gave his own blood to mix with them and bring back life. Mankind owes him this favour for all time. The Spanish backed off, not least because the friars did not want conversion at sword-point. They compromised on being given the use of a temple to cleanse and consecrate.

Two sources say Xicoténcatl also knew, because his god had spoken to his priests, that someone to rule over them was coming from the east. But both those accounts were written half a century after the event. If one looks at what was said and recorded at the time, and in the immediate aftermath of conquest, notions that gods were returning were considered but quickly dismissed. For one thing Mexicans bathed daily, their guests rarely, so the Spanish smelled too bad to be gods.

Cortés grilled the Tlaxcalans for knowledge of the Aztecs. Tenochtitlán was three or four days' march away; it was a great city with powerful warriors. Ambassadors arrived from Moctezuma and daily begged him to come to Tenochtitlán and escape these treacherous Tlaxcalans. It is said that four of the great lords of Tlaxcala were baptised during this stay, and just up a paved hill from Plaza Xicoténcatl is a large church, the former Monastery of San Francisco, one of the first four in the Americas. It has decorated roof beams, which lie so close together that the gaps are scarcely bigger than the beams. On them, simple carved geometrical patterns are highlighted in gold leaf. As you enter the south transept, at the foot of the left-hand wall, a massive stone font like a low, wide drinking cup stands on the plain stone-flagged floor. Here, says the inscription, Maxixcatzín, Xicoténcatl the younger, and the lords Tlahuexolotzín and Ziztlalpopocatl were baptised, and their sponsors were the godfathers of the Spanish conquistadors: Hernán Cortés, Pedro de Alvarado, Andrés de Tapia, Gonzalo de Sandoval, a young man who was a rising star, and Cristóbal de Olid: witnesses to this tortuous birth of Native Christianity. On the right is a fine carved wooden pulpit, raised high, with an octagonal sounding-board above. From here was preached, says the gold lettering in a small cartouche, the first sermon in the New World. A suitable text might have been Thou shallt not bear false witness, for there is no evidence the lords were baptised at that time.

Back down in Plaza Xicoténcatl was a Museum of Memory, and in it a fine replica of the Lienzo de Tlaxcala, a sheet of linen produced by a Native artist under the direction of the town council in 1552, to inform the Spanish King about the kingdom of Tlaxcala. The federation is well described because we have the work of two historians, one Spanish and one Native. The linen is a piece of graphic art with a main field showing the principal personages from each side arranged at a formal congregation around a central cross, with a series of panels along the base showing key meetings in detail. The principal figures on both sides are painted in cartoon form and named. It is skilfully done, but they are not portraits: each miniature bearded Spaniard looks the same, and the Natives in breech clouts and cloaks are interchangeable. Between the two, wearing a red cloak over a blue smock, stands Malinche, mediating between two worlds.

The old city of Tlaxcalan was called Tizatlán and was located in the suburbs, a few miles from today's Colonial centre, and reached in a *colectivo* which left from the market. Eventually. Following the driver's instructions I reached an area which could not seem to make its mind up whether to regenerate or just fall over. The streets were almost empty. The remaining inhabitants were the failures. There were no ruins, they were over here, no, there. I said hello to a seven-year-old boy who heard my accent and replied 'Hi!', then blushed and put his hand to his face, embarrassed at his forwardness. I instantly knew Davíd was one of those wise youths fate steers across the paths of lost travellers. 'You can walk with me, I am going to my friend's house, from there you can see the church, and the archaeological remains are thirty seconds past the church.' This was an improvement on the first old man I had asked who listened to my request and said, 'So, you have run out of petrol.' Davíd asked intelligent questions and we were soon chatting like old friends, about the usual things. I felt he needed to be told Liverpool had won the European Cup-Champions' League more than Manchester United. He was convinced I was making it up. When we reached his friend's house, he said 'It looks quiet, I think he's out. I'll visit my grandmother instead, she lives in the same direction you are going.' He just wanted to walk longer with the stranger. We turned a corner and he pointed across the valley to a hill topped with pine trees, through which a golden dome flashed as the wind tousled their canopies. 'That's the church. Safe journey. Wait—' He gave me an accurate summary of changing theories about the use of the site.

I gave him ten pesos, about fifty pence. 'Do not spend it sensibly. Buy sweets and comics.' He felt it in his hand, a solid shiny coin, then he gave it back. 'Some people just impose on you and pretend to help, then ask for money. I just wanted to help. My parents will ask me where I got it from and tell me it is wrong to help for money.'

I gave it back. 'They are right. But you never asked for money, and if you help, sometimes there is a tip.'

He grinned and walked away, glancing back at me from time to time, the hand with the coin pressed into a fist. The hill rising to the church was as steep as they come. The road then followed the contour, around the old green and white municipal offices, out onto a square which was unnaturally flat. In front of me was the church, which had been added to, but never quite in the same style, as if built by a child with a construction kit who began without reading the instructions. Inside the church was a feature which was still visible although it had been incorporated into the later extensions; it was a *capilla abierta* or open chapel. When baptisms of the Natives were carried out on an industrial scale in the wake of the conquest, churches could not be built fast enough. To ensure the Mass could be said to all, small chapels were built with one long side open, and with an additional wall each side fanning out like solid wings to a theatre stage. The service was conducted indoors but an unlimited space outside could be occupied by the congregation. It is extremely rare for them to survive later rebuilding. Here, a sixteenth-century chapel was built onto it, and the two thousand square feet of murals which remain are some of the oldest in Mexico, and of fine quality. At the other end of the square were some modest remains of pre-conquest structures, interesting because they display the use of brick in the walls, a technique only just coming into use at the time of the conquest, and known on only two other sites. There were altars with bright fragments of murals remaining. It was only when I went to the south side of the square that I understood what I was standing on. A rampart wall fell away twenty-five feet below my boots, one hundred yards clearly visible, and the original perhaps double that. This was the base of a Tlaxcala palace complex, where Xayacamach ruled and wrote poetry, until the sceptre passed to his much older brother, Xicoténcatl the Elder. These were the very suites of rooms where Cortés forged the alliance that won his victory. There was a sun shelter halfway along the top of the wall and a dig was under way. I met Arlette Soloveichik, a young archaeologist working for the government heritage agency INAH. She had a pretty, oval, face and enormous liquid eyes made even bigger with Goth make-up. I tried to talk while feeling I was losing my balance and falling into them. She said, 'I read English for work, but never speak it.'

'That's all right, I cope better with archaeology in Spanish than I do with a Mexican menu.'

She laughed. 'There's not much Spanish in there is there? It's all Native words. We are two weeks into a two-month dig to relieve six or seven metres of wall from damage done by tree roots. Half a metre down we found human skeletons.' She indicated over her shoulder.

'In a strange position?'

'Very strange indeed. They are so shallow there is no stratification in the soil.' She pointed to small clear freezer bags. They were full of fragments of pottery, simple and plain, the size of a fingernail. 'They may not help. Pottery changed so radically and rapidly after the conquest, with the first use of glazes, new minerals and additives. As for the bones, we have femurs and crania. It looks like a pair of people embedded in the tree roots.'

'May I take a photo?'

'Afraid not. We don't have clearance, because it could be a criminal case.' 'From any century?'

'Yes. The site has never really been investigated, just some digs in the 1970s to map the site. After the conquest Cortés and the Tlaxcalans ran a market here and goods from Philippines came here, so we could find anything.'

When I left the panorama over the valley had changed in a way it took a few seconds to identify. The horizon had cleared and there was a new presence: Matlalcuéyetl, the Lady of the Green Skirts, a goddess of rain and song. She is a stratovolcano, over 14,500 feet of her, with a ridge summit like Iztaccíhuatl. The Spanish, probably because they could not pronounce Matlalcuéyetl, renamed her La Malinche. Even as a volcano Malinche has a shifting name and identity. In the evening I called in at the Euzkadi shoe repair workshop off the square. Euzkadi is the Basque word for their homeland.

'Are you from the north of Spain?'

The cheerful owner shook his head. 'My family came from the Basque country generations ago.'

He was putting blocks of rubber on the heels of my sandals. The sandals were old and had taken on the shape of my feet. I could walk all day in them. I needed new ones, but deciding when to discard the old ones was like deciding when to put down an ageing dog.

'Did you see Malinche today?' he asked. 'There is something about that mountain. It can be very dangerous; people go missing. I have looked back in the newspapers, and twenty, including western climbers, disappeared for days, and were presumed lost. Then they came down the mountain, thin and weak, but they had survived.

Many reported having been found and cared for by a very old woman. She was so wrinkled it seemed impossible she could still be alive. It was Malinche who helped them.'

My next stop was Cholula. Watching Cortés forge his alliance in Tlaxcala, Moctezuma's envoys grew nervous. They urged him to move on to Cholula, where the people were a better sort, and more prosperous. They were also Aztec allies. Moctezuma became so agitated he even invited the Spanish to come to Tenochtitlán. The Tlaxcalans urged Cortés to continue via Huejotzingo, pointing out that this city had sent envoys to him while Cholula had not. The position was further complicated by Alvarado's Native mistress, baptised as María Luísa, confiding that her brother, who was one of four captains of the Tlaxcalans, was planning to attack the Spanish. Cortés took him aside and had him strangled.

Tlaxcalan spies reported that Cholula, on Moctezuma's orders, had prepared an ambush. The road ahead had been blocked and a new route prepared. Their spies had seen stones cached on rooftops, and streets were already being blocked to prevent escape. Or maybe Cortés invented this threat to justify what he did in Cholula. For it was there that Cortés showed that he was becoming indifferent to whether his methods were humane.

20

The Massacre at Cholula

Cortés was still managing the diplomacy well. Faced with having to offend either the Lord of Tenochtitlán or the Lord of Tlaxcala, he instead tested the water with Cholula by inviting them to send envoys. They did, but only low ranking ones. The Tlaxcalans were at his ear. 'See, they send nobodies because they are plotting!' Cortés decided to go where Moctezuma wished, Cholula, but he took Tlaxcalan troops with him for security. He had to ensure this important city did not remain an unknown quantity on his line of retreat.

Puebla's airport-sized bus station was on the city edge. The bus I arrived in was basic, but the local buses going west to Cholula were untouchables, exiled to a yard of potholes and ponds outside. It was a short trip, costing thirty-five pence, but we took a marvellously circuitous route. There was supposed to be countryside in between the two towns but I never saw it. We found every half-urbanised road and advanced like a toy robot, barging blindly around, and bouncing off in another direction. Sunshine picked out a gold and white church on a wooded hill. Something nagged at my memory, but would not come to mind. The bus crawled into the edge of a main square whose diagonally opposite corner was barely visible over three hundred yards away. I booked into a pleasant mini-suite in a hostel overlooking it. Although the rooms had, and needed, four small light fittings to illuminate them, there was only one bulb per room. I asked for more. The receptionist rolled out her lower lip. 'People steal them.' I started pining for the Colonial hotel across the square, with its courtyard restaurant, swimming pool, and light bulbs.

I was torn between rushing out to see the town, and reading my notes so I would understand what I was looking at. Scholarship won, mainly because I was so tired. Moving days took it out of me, as I had to carry my big pack. My average stay in a hotel for the first two months was less than two nights, so I was ceaselessly finding new places to sleep and eat and, in the towns, peace and quiet was a dream. In Cholula, the worst noise came from the optician's shop, whose speaker played pop music on the pavement below my room at a volume that would not have been out of place at a rave. Customers subjected to long eye tests could soon find they also needed hearing aids. It was a nice earner.

Cholula is the oldest continuously-inhabited city in all the Americas, founded around 1250 BC, watching the decline of the Olmecs, the then dominant power, the rise and fall of the Maya, seeing Teotihuacan flourish and fade. Then I came across the information that was nudging at the back of my mind when I had looked at the yellow church on a hill, and my jaw dropped. I ran out to look at it from the square. The Nahuatl name for the city was Tlachihualtépetl: The Mountain Made by Hand. The gold and white church of *Nuestra Señora de los Remedios* was not standing on a hill; the trees and grass had confused my eye. There was no hill. It was standing on a pyramid. I could discern distinct levels; it was made of six platforms, and extended by overbuilding. The final size of the base was 480 yards long by 415 yards wide, and it stood 180 feet high. The base dwarfs that of the Great Pyramid of Giza near Cairo, 160 by 152 yards, although Giza is much taller. Nevertheless, by volume Cholula is the largest pyramid in the world, nearly double the volume of Giza.

I arrived at the site at opening time, a little before the staff. There is a fine small museum full of the beautiful local pottery, the classic colour schemes being black with russet, and black with yellow ochre. It was fit for an emperor; Moctezuma would eat from no other tableware. At ten past nine a little man with the manner of a friendly but nervous rodent began opening the entry kiosk. The excitement of visiting the pyramid was instant, as I entered a tunnel that ran through the structure from side to side. Its sheer size meant that conventional archaeological exploration could go on for years and still only scratch the surface, so they drove tunnels through to provide sections. From 1931 to 1954, 5 miles of them were dug. I passed alone down an A-shaped stone corridor lit with yellow electric light. This outermost and newest phase was built in the ninth century AD. The archaeologists discovered a nest of pyramids, but they were not centred on the same spot. It may be that the ceremonial alignment changed to fulfil a new purpose, or that they now had more accurate readings for their original purpose. After an interval, I passed a side gallery in which a formal staircase could be glimpsed vanishing into darkness. I was time-travelling, passing through the facade of an earlier pyramid, the Temple of the Nine Stories, built between AD 350 and 450. The second oldest phase was begun in 200 AD, and the smallest and oldest 400 years before that.

The temple seems to have been a regional centre for pilgrimage, and a professionally organised tribute system. Cholula's prosperity flagged in the sixth century, and then foundered. The Great Temple was left unkempt, maybe for 200 years. Many of the elite moved out, some built mansions on the base of the great pyramid, its status exploited in debased coin. Between AD 800 and 900, human sacrifice increased greatly, usually a sign of insecurity. The only visible new structures from this period are in the north-west corner, where a mother was explaining the site to her son. I enjoyed her engagement; her pride in their history. We stood before an altar where the bodies of two human skeletons were found, aged six to seven years. I asked the boy's age. 'Eight,' said his mother quickly.

The Tlaxcalan historian Ixtlilxóchitl wrote that Quetzalcóatl came to Cholula in the seventh century AD to teach them to fast and worship the rain god. When the people ignored him he left, and a few days later one side of the great pyramid collapsed. At that same time we have archaeological evidence that the Courtyard of the Altars on the south side of the pyramid suffered violent profanation. The Quetzalcóatl story may be a mythologised memory of that period of iconoclasm. All these states set themselves up as supreme authorities on how to organise time, the year, the sowing and the harvest. So when crops failed, its rulers had set themselves up to be overthrown.

The lack of written records leaves many problems to intelligent speculation, an uncertain skill. Writing the cancer sections of this book illustrated to me the difficulties of explaining or even describing the past. I wrote them with every advantage, working from an intermittent diary I kept. I have the letters from the hospital calling me in for appointments, and Celia's notes from meetings with doctors and consultants. We talked them through and realised we had clear and definite memories which could not always be reconciled with each other, the paperwork, or photos with date and time signatures. There was always something that did not fit. That is my own history in a time of record, after a lapse of little more than half a year. At Cholula, and in many other places, and other times, I am trying to create a skeletal account of what happened 2000 years ago, from scrappy records and threadbare recorded narrative. Archaeologists writing about two millennia ago tend to write very conservatively. But historians write as if they know, while knowing they don't, because a narrative of caveats and qualifications is a poor read.

At the end of the two centuries of neglect, Cholula resumed devotions at the man-made mountain. But Mexico's underworld intervened. If you look for a line to demarcate the transition to Postclassic culture, there is a layer of ash running between the ceramic remains. In the ninth century Popocatépetl produced a pyroclastic eruption, which levelled the area north-east of the volcano. They may have had time to evacuate, but this type of eruption produces fine particles, each of which exudes gas, so it rides on a nearly friction-free cushion of lethal vapour. It was this type of eruption, of Mount Pelée in Martinique, which killed every soul on the island except a drunk in jail, below ground. Then Popocatépetl began a Plinian eruption, showering pumice everywhere, a foot deep, while clouds of ash towered into the sky. In Cholula I realised why there were so many huge churches in Mexico; they had to compete in majesty with Native structures. To illustrate how imposing Native pyramids were, Giza was the tallest building in the world for 3800 years, until the spire at Lincoln cathedral was completed in 1311. Cholula's more massive pyramid was not even the only monumental complex in town. A second cultural group came to the region, and Cholula was divided. The incoming Toltec-Chichimecans took over the great pyramid, while the previous occupants, the Olmecs-Xicallancas, built a new temple, which they dedicated to Quetzalcóatl, on what is now the main square. Each territory is still a separate parish to this day. In 1530, Quetzalcóatl's shrine was torn down to build the Templo de San Gabriel. San Gabriel was so extensive that old prints of it standing in poor repair, in fields at the edge of the city, look like views of Rome when the Grand Tour began, with shepherds and cowherds picking their way through the ancient ruins. It was the largest religious complex I saw in all Mexico, and it stood opposite the largest Native temple.

The Spanish wanted not only to compete with the existing religious buildings but appropriate them. Until a church could be built on the Great Pyramid, a large cross was planted on the summit to tame the old demons. I am biased against these attempts to sanitise a place sacred to black-taloned gods; they seem preposterous, like a vampire fiddling with prayer beads. In 1536 it was struck by lightning. Two more were erected. Same thing. The Franciscans dug beneath the burned stump and found snails: offerings to Quetzalcóatl.

In the evening I wandered through the Christmas fair, where a pop group called *Los Beatos* was playing Beatles songs. The group did not speak English but had learned the sounds of the lyrics. I was born in Liverpool, and was pushed up and down Penny Lane in my pram. Now Mexican ventriloquists sang my youth to me. It seemed impossible that music from my childhood was half a century old: as distant now as the end of the music hall was when I first heard *Love Me Do*. This music travelled and lived. All around me middle-aged couples tapped their feet and remembered old loves.

The sun was setting behind Iztaccíhuatl, and the low light showed how the hill on the edge of town formed the same silhouette as the giantess behind. Shadows rose up the sides of Popocatépetl, and touched the drapes of thin snow lying on the ribbed summit of Iztaccíhuatl, pressing the last of the light high into the sky above her prone body. *Los Beatos* greeted nightfall the opening chords of 'Here Comes the Sun', while fathers walked by with Christmas trees on their shoulders. A pocket-sized travelling funfair ground into action. Dust kicked up by running children mixed with thin blue smoke from food stalls and hazed the air. I thought of Malcolm Lowry living in Cuernavaca, 40 miles the other side of the two volcanoes, chronicling his own disintegration through the character of Geoffrey Firmin. He began the book in Mexico, and finished it in Canada, but first he lived it in Cuernavaca. And I thought about him now because of the best line to close the first chapter of a novel. He had climbed up a ravine with a funfair above him. 'Over the town, in the dark tempestuous night, backwards revolved the luminous wheel.'

When Cortés was still outside Cholula, he received a deputation of priests and captains. They apologised for not coming before; they had been afraid of venturing into the enemy territory of Tlaxcala. Cortés made his standard speech and the delegation agreed to swear vassalage to Charles V. As to changing their religion, Díaz recalled: 'They answered that we had hardly entered their country, yet we were already ordering them to forsake their gods, which they could not do.'

They were welcomed into the city, but asked to leave their Tlaxcalan allies outside. Cortés agreed, on condition that those bearers carrying Spanish possessions could enter. Cholula made the fatal concession; those goods included the cannon. Cortés wrote, 'The city is more beautiful to look at than any in Spain.' It was the second largest in Mesoamerica after Tenochtitlán, perhaps approaching 200,000. Cortés observed the city from the top of the great pyramid and counted 430 towers: temples, pyramids and other significant buildings.

I ate in a rooftop cafe overlooking the square. The tallest church spires had now lost all light. Although the crowns of the trees were barely stirring, someone had slipped a kite into the air. It was shaped and painted as a hawk, and nosed slowly from side to side, darting forward then falling back on the sliding air. The line thrummed, trembled; the bird was bait to catch the wind, a chill current from the west that brought the night into the city.

Cortés was ushered into a palace so large the whole Spanish force was lodged in it. A supper of turkey was given to all, including the allies from Tlaxcala, Cempoala and Ixtacamaxtitlán. The initial hospitality did nothing to allay Cortés's fears, and the subsequent three days, during which little food arrived and they received few visits from their hosts, only raised his suspicions. No person of rank called on them. The secular ruler, Tlaquiach, excused himself as too ill. Meanwhile the Aztec ambassadors had reverted to their primary tactic of excuses: the road to Tenochtitlán was poor, Moctezuma would die of shock at his first sight of the Spanish. Their Cholulan allies added local colour; Moctezuma's palace was full of alligators, pumas and jaguars, which he would set loose to kill and eat them.

Vigilant though the Spanish always were, Cempoalans and Tlaxcalans were more adept at spying. They found that the men of Cholula were plotting with the Aztecs and suborning the Cuban Natives still with Cortés. They found pits full of spikes in the roads, skilfully covered over. The Cholulans had built breastworks on the edge of the flat roofs, and amassed heaps of stones for slinging and throwing. Storehouses were filling with poles on which ropes and leather collars were attached. They were used to restrain prisoners. Women and children were being evacuated to the surrounding hills. The plot was confirmed thanks to the matchmaking wiles of an old noble woman of Cholula who came secretly to Malinche. She was married to a captain, who had just received rich gifts from Moctezuma, reminders of loyalty, together with orders to attack the Spanish. The woman confided, 'I can see you are a rich noble woman and I do not want you to be killed with the rest of them. Moctezuma's army is just outside the city, and will hide in the ravines to the west. When you leave, the army of Cholula will drive the Spanish into their arms. You must hide with me, and when it is over, you can marry my son.' Tlaxcalan spies brought more news. 'There is no time to lose, they have already sacrificed five young boys and five girls to the war god to ensure success.'

Cortés persuaded the religious leader to summon Tlaquiach, who admitted he was under orders from Moctezuma not to provision them. When he had gone, Cortés had Malinche fetch the senior priest and a colleague. He promised them anonymity if they would explain what was going on. They did not like the Aztecs and had only recently been subsumed into empire. Their loyalties were divided. They admitted Moctezuma already had half his army hidden in the city, and the other half in the ravines. They betrayed Moctezuma's increasingly confused mental state. 'They said that their lord Moctezuma had known we were coming to Cholula, and that every day he was of many minds, unable to decide what to do about it. Sometimes he sent them instructions that if we arrived they were to pay us great honour and guide us on to Mexico; and at other times he said that he did not want us to come to his city; and now the gods Tezcatlipoca and Huitzilopochtli had proposed to him that we should be killed at Cholula or brought bound to Mexico.'

The Spanish captains met in council, and decided on a pre-emptive attack. Cortés continued to play the diplomatic game with Moctezuma. He assured the Aztec ambassadors – a permanent presence now they had left Tlaxcalan territory – that he trusted Moctezuma not to be behind this outrageous plot. Then he confined them to quarters. He sent word to Tlaquiach that they were leaving in the morning, and asked for porters and food. Gómara, inventing what he could not know, wrote, 'At this last request they smiled and said to themselves: "Why do these men want to eat, when they themselves will soon be eaten, served up with chilli? Indeed, if Moctezuma, who wants them for his own table, would not have been angry with us, we would have eaten them ourselves by this time!"'

Cortés also said he would say farewell in the courtyard of the temple to Quetzalcóatl, which happened to have high walls and only one gate. Díaz, who is usually sensitive to the Natives, wrote of how 'we should give the Indians the beating they deserved.' Fear had trumped his scruples.

In the morning, far more porters were provided than had been asked for. Cortés assumed it was to help with the ambush. He had arranged for his allies to wear a flower in their hair so the Spanish could recognise them at a glance. Cortés mounted his horse, Malinche at his side. The large court filled with people. It was said one hudred lords of the city were there. He saw the two priests who had informed him of the Aztec presence, and tipped them off to leave the courtyard. Then he spoke to his Cholula hosts and asked why they had not accepted his friendship. The signal was a musket shot. Spaniards shut the doors and began to kill every living person in the square. Then they worked their way through the surrounding streets for five hours, killing and killing. The people of Cholula were not given a beating; they were massacred. Gómara recorded: 'They [the Spanish] were dripping with blood and walked over nothing but dead bodies.' The Tlaxcalans defeated the Aztec force outside the city then entered, killing, looting and taking prisoners. When the Spanish were tired of killing, the Tlaxcalans were not: they went on killing. Late in the day survivors crawled out from under the heaps of bodies. They were killed. The number of the dead was between 5,000 and 10,000.

Violence permeated everyday life, including the punishments of the law. Here is an account of an English legal punishment of the time.

'In such a case the prisoner is laid in a low dark room in the prison, all naked but his privy members, his back upon the bare ground, his arms and legs stretched with cords, and fastened to the several quarters of the room. This done, he has a great weight of iron and stone laid upon him. His diet, till he dies, is of three morsels of barley bread without drink the next day; and if he lives beyond it, he has nothing daily, but as much foul water as he can drink.'

The victim found out who his real friends were; they stood on the frame to put him out of his misery.

The 'case' referred to is not for a serious crime, but for failing to enter a plea. The comparison is not meant to condone the violence meted out by the conquistadors, but to show it was not unusual, let alone beyond understanding.

Cholula was a not a military battle; it was a civilian massacre. Cortés attempted to justify it by saying he needed to *atemorizar* a treacherous people. It means terrorise. No Spaniard wanted to speak about it afterwards. Díaz offers feeble excuses, of how they found wooden cages in which prisoners were being fattened for sacrifice, and set them free. Yet Cortés let his allies take home prisoners for sacrifice in Tlaxcala. The day after, Cortés wrote insouciantly: '[T]he whole city was reoccupied and full of women and children, all unafraid, as though nothing had happened.' It is eerily reminiscent of Gabriel García Marquez's description of troops firing on striking banana workers in Colombia in 1928. The bodies and site were cleared. Next day, it had never happened.

It is only recently that Western societies have regarded all injury and death as abhorrent. We sanctify the body, the individual and human rights; other societies have sanctified the soul and god's laws. This massacre would not have seemed unthinkable, if it broke the will of pagans to resist Catholicism. Cortés's final achievement, the conquest of lands of fabulous richness for his king, and untold souls for Christ, would excuse his means. But the action left a stain on his reputation. He had also learned that he could not control the murderous enmity of the different local cultures once it was unleashed.

His men had been suffering from danger, privation, illness, and unfamiliar and, recently, unsalted food. There were regular petitions to go back to the Caribbean. Something had built up inside them, and that darkness had been released in bloodletting. Then they delivered a lecture on the evils of human sacrifice. Were they any better? Were they looking at savages and seeing themselves? The Spanish did not leave. Cortés lectured the remaining city leaders and 'told them to give up robbery and their customary bestialities'. The Tlaxcalans sought out the salt they had been deprived of so long by the Aztecs. Cortés's long-standing allies from the coast now bowed out. The Cempoalans had cold feet over getting any nearer to Moctezuma, having imprisoned his tax collectors and ceased sending tribute. Now that Cortés had the much more powerful state of Tlaxcala on side, with a power-base in the heartlands, he could afford to thank the Cempoalans and let them go.

Four blocks up from the square is the old, rough, busy road to Mexico City, signposted to Huejotzingo. Gómara says they passed through Huejotzingo and a place called San Martín de Texmulacan.

At the bus stop a woman with a clear plastic bag bulging with cakes said, 'I am going to Huejotzingo too; you can be my travelling companion,' and handed me a muffin overflowing its case like a sugary mushroom. The bus conductor approached, and she held out two muffins. 'They are worth more than the fare, I don't have any money until I sell something.'

'I have to give my boss cash, so you give me cash.'

This went on some time. He won. She then felt the brim of my hat which was on my lap. 'It's good quality.'

'Now I need the cowboy boots to go with it.'

She reached down and felt my shins and ankles, returning to dwell on my knee, which reminded her of a recipe for bad knees; sugar was involved. She chattered on in seamless paragraphs. 'Did you not have problems there?' She felt round the nearest knee with great thoroughness. 'My mother had bad knees and this remedy sorted them out.'

'How old is she?'

'Seventy-five. She's otherwise in good health. Her mother lived to be 110.'

I did not think that I would unless she let go of my knee. Her grip loosened, but before I could breathe a sigh of relief, it re-attached, to my thigh. She mentioned hot cakes but I was not sure if we were still talking about baking. I risked a look at her face. Her eyes were closing, her grip softened. My thigh was not exciting enough to keep her awake.

The rowdy main street of Huejotzingo opened in front of us: a two-storey ragbag of buildings whose main square was being dug up. The town was dominated by San Francisco, another convent with a size complex. The perimeter wall was no higher than a good prison needs, and the chapel looked like Colditz. I entered a smaller church where the altar was decorated with Christmas candles and a small nativity scene set in a nest of greenery. From its heart a toy electrical device piped out Yuletide tunes. The selection had been carelessly chosen, as the carols were interspersed with *Rudolph the Red-Nosed Reindeer* and *Santa Claus is Coming to Town*.

There was nothing to be gleaned here so I moved on to

Texmelucan, where there was less. It was a noisy, traffic-choked town with one pleasant square. Leaving town on the bus back to Cholula we passed a yard where lorry engines stood rusting on blocks. The fan on one turned in the wind; the blades still beating after the power was stilled.

21

Through the Volcanoes

Time for a momentous move. If visibility were good I would today have my first sight of Mexico City, but before I entered the city, I was going to divert to places which would help me make sense of what happened in Tenochtitlán in 1519. I had met a chef who came from the town on the other side of the volcanoes, Amecameca. He told me to take a *colectivo* to the highest village on this side, Xalitzintla, then a bus over the pass between the volcanoes.

It was a crisp, cloudless morning as I crossed the empty square just after seven, the shadow of a church tower pointing me up the street. In minutes I was in a *collectivo* bouncing across the plain, straight towards the peaks of Popocatépetl and Iztaccíhuatl. It was so flat, the water in the irrigation ditches barely stirred as it slaked the fields of maize and vegetables. A triangular trail of pale brown vapour hung in the sky above the snow on Popocatépetl. The bus began to climb, crops gave way to scrub. We detoured into the village of San Nicolás where the asphalt road became rough paving, then dirt. We squeezed through the houses of Xalitzintla and into the main square, which attacked all five senses. A three-piece funfair which folded onto a single lorry hit the eyes with party colours. Polystyrene food trays chattered to and fro on a wind whose dust left a bitter savour in my mouth. Ears were assaulted by rockets announcing the procession led by a teenage band, including a white sousaphone player walking shotgun at the back. I watched it from my seat on a rough stone wall for which my skinny backside provided no padding. Smell completed the suite of the senses when the sun hit the dog shit.

A spry and cheerful man neatly dressed in a cream shirt, brown gilet and a sombrero like my own sat by me. 81-year-old Tomás Jímenez might have passed for being in his sixties, except his lower lip drooped, revealing teeth worn to spindles. 'I've had a check-up with the doctor; everything is okay, and the stomach is good enough for a little drink now and again.' He extended his thumb and little finger to mime pouring. 'There's not much to do round here except field work, which will fill your belly, but you won't grow fat. There's some fruit, apples in season, but the season's all finished. The young want other things, every house has to have a television. Some of them turn to drugs, and that's that. Where are you going?'

'Amecameca.'

'Across the Paso de Cortés!'

'There are buses from here, aren't there?' I hovered between a statement and a question, because I had watched all the buses turn around and go back to Cholula. It seemed the kind of town where nothing at all happened. Not even buses.

'Yes, but not at the moment.'

I looked up the street at a single-decker bus. 'How about that one?' 'It's going on a *peregrinación* but they might take you.'

I thought he meant it went a long way round, but I had forgotten the other meaning for the word. A lorry driver offered me a lift to the saddle of the pass, but he was not going down to Amecameca. I thought 12,000 feet was not the place to test Mexican attitudes to hitchhikers. Tomás tipped his hat and continued with his morning stroll. Above me, now a physical presence, like someone who stands too close in a room, the bare ash and rock cone of Popocatépetl squatted, smouldered and fumed. On 30 April 1996, five climbers reached the rim but never came down. Their bodies were found two days later, killed by volcanic ash. When 2000 began, there were still small glaciers on it, but the cone became more active and they shrank. On the advice of vulcanologists, 41,000 people were evacuated. Popocatépetl broke into its most violent eruption for 1200 years, and the activity has continued to this day: climbing is forbidden.

After an hour had passed, I walked up to the single-decker, which was surrounded by families, and teenagers on good road cycles. The bus was spotlessly clean, down to its shining steel wheel-nuts. On the back of each cyclist's tracksuit were the initials VoG. Signs on the bus reminded me of the other meaning of *peregrinación*: it was a cycling *pilgrimage* to the Basilica of the Virgin of Guadalupe. A mother said, 'My two boys are cycling to Mexico City for an overnight vigil before the Virgin's festival tomorrow. We'll follow in the bus. We'll be happy to give you a lift – no! there's no need to pay!' I sat and waited. I waited some more, and wondered how anyone knew when an event began. If Mexican sex is like their logistics, the foreplay must be exquisite.

The Virgin of Guadalupe is the most powerful religious figure in Mexico, more important than Jesus or God. She is an incarnation of Mary associated with a miraculous vision on Saturday 9 December 1531. A Native convert, Juan Diego, left his village to hear Mass in Tlatelolco, and pray for the health of his sick uncle. Passing the base of the hill of Tepeyac, like Tlatelolco, long since swallowed by Mexico City, he heard a burst of birdsong and saw a light on the hill. A voice called him by name, and he saw a girl of 14 years of age standing on a golden mist. He knew it was the Virgin Mary, and she asked him to ensure a church dedicated to her was built on that site. The young man went to the Bishop of Mexico City, Juan de Zumárraga, who was an enlightened man. He sent Juan Diego back to the hill for a sign to prove the lady's identity. She appeared again and said his uncle was cured. Finding his uncle well, Juan Diego returned to the bishop. The cure was dismissed as chance. He was sent back, now torn between his desire to obey the Virgin, and fear of arousing the bishop's anger. The Virgin appeared again, and told him to gather Castile roses from the top of the Tepeyac Hill. He sighed because the flowers were foreign, rare, and out of season. But he climbed to the peak, and among the barren rocks, found Castile roses in full bloom. The Virgin instructed him to gather the roses in his cloak and take them to the archbishop, where he nervously requested an audience, and spread his cloak on the floor. The flowers spilled out, and on the cloak was an image of the Virgin.

In 1810 the Virgin of Guadelupe blazed the banners of the first rebels against Spanish rule, and a century later adorned the flags of

Zapata in the Mexican Revolution. The Nobel prize-winning Mexican poet Octavio Paz wrote that 'the Mexican people, after more than two centuries of experiments, have faith only in the Virgin of Guadalupe and the National Lottery.' Bishop Zumárraga never wrote a syllable about the event or mentioned meeting anyone called Juan Diego: odd for a man committing to huge expenditure. In 1556, there was an enquiry into the miracle of twenty-five years before, and Juan Diego was not mentioned. In fact no document mentions him until a century after the event. Abruptly, in 1995, the Jesuit Father Xavier Escalada, author of an encyclopaedia of the legend, produced a codex on traditional deerskin paper, which gave an illustrated account of the vision, and the life of Juan Diego. It had never been seen or catalogued before, but it bore the signatures of the one of the greatest scholars of Aztec life, Bernadino de Sahagún, and the priest Antonio Valeriano. Sahagún's signature is odd because he was not enthusiastic about the Virgin; he complained she was familiarly called *Tonantzín*, Our Mother, not Mother of God, so, he worried, she might be a gate opening the path back to idolatry. In 2002, eager to promote new saints in the areas where Catholics were many, but saints few, the Vatican made Juan Diego a saint. Scholars have concluded the timely discovery of the codex was 'rather like finding a picture of Saint Paul on the road to Damascus, drawn by St Luke and signed by St Peter'.

At the end of their devotional ride, the cyclists and their supporters would kneel in sight of the original cloak, which is suspended in a low oxygen atmosphere behind bullet-proof glass in a new tent-shaped basilica on Tepeyac Hill that can house 50,000 people. It is the most visited Marian shrine in the world; during two days, over six million visitors will file past Diego's cloak. Its state of preservation is exceptional; the only areas that show significant ageing are repairs. Permission has never been given to subject it to modern testing. Maybe the oxygen of science would kill it, but hope lives on without oxygen. Tepeyac hill had been a holy site for centuries before the conquest, sacred to the mother goddess Tonantzín. Her temple was burned down by the Spanish, before she was reborn in a form acceptable to the Spanish as the dark-skinned

Virgin. She taps a vein deep in the Mexican soul. Carlos Fuentes, the touchstone essayist of Mexico said, '[Y]ou cannot truly be considered a Mexican unless you believe in the Virgin of Guadalupe.' She gives succour and power to a gender without any power outside the home, and precious little in it.

It was the only bus going over the mountain. For the moment, with a 40-pound pack on my back, I believed in the Virgin. With one exception, everyone on the bus assured me they were going to Amecameca. The passengers swore we would be in Amecameca in 3–4 hours. The exception was the driver. I took the front seat and, as the bus stood, engine idling, waiting to go, saw the speedometer surge to 40 kph. Just think how fast we would go when moving. The cyclists left. 15 minutes later we followed. Pines leaned over the dusty grey lane which no longer cut the long curves of modern engineering but drove straight up the mountain. This was the old road. We were soon passing young people pushing their cycles. Their leader, a forty-something with the confidence of the school games teacher who now plays all his sport against boys, sat in the fold-down seat by our front door and shouted 'If you can't ride it, milk it,' at anyone not in the saddle. To perform this role, he had dressed in a team tracksuit and spanking white trainers on their first outing.

Alongside the road the bushes and the rich mix of plants dwindled until there were just pines and other evergreens. Wiry white grass grew in spiky clumps, eventually forming a solid floor to the understory: an army of sea-urchins marching downhill. In the road cuttings, layers of volcanic ash were exposed: black and red, like Cholula pottery. The mass of Popocatépetl swelled to fill our view to the left, and as we neared the Paso de Cortés the road twisted into tight bends only a little longer than the bus, until we reached the shallow, wide saddle of the col, where the road uncoiled onto a bare altiplano landscape, seen through needles of ice-crystals forming in the corners of the windows.

Cortés set out from Cholula assisted by one thousand Tlaxcalan porters, but no soldiers. Once again, he wanted to pose as an ambassador, not as the head of an invading coalition. He despatched ten scouts under Diego de Ordaz to take a closer look at activity on

Popocatépetl, which was still smouldering following a violent eruption in 1509. Ordaz was a literate captain who left a lively body of correspondence. We know he was forty-one when he set off that morning, tall, with strong features and a short black beard. He was a good swordsman, but not much of a rider, had a slight stammer, and a speech impediment that made some words hard to pronounce. Ordaz ascended Popocatépetl and reached the rim, but explosions drove him down. He had seen sulphur deposits which, with saltpetre and charcoal, could be used to make the Spanish self-sufficient in gunpowder.

Camping near Huejotzingo, where the baker with hot cakes and wandering hands plied her trade, Cortés was visited by minor local chiefs and priests who warned him the road ahead divided. The road which passed round the side of the volcanoes was swept and cleared. The other, the road we had climbed, was blocked by trees, making it impossible for horses. That was the one they must take, for the clean road led to an Aztec ambush. What the Aztecs could move, the Spanish could remove. Díaz says that half a century later some of those trunks still lay at the roadside. When they reached the top of the pass, it began to snow and the ground was soon coated.

Our bus rolled over the watershed and down a smooth asphalt road between pines towering above lush ground cover starred with yellow flowers. Then it stopped in a forest clearing. 'Picnic!' They began lighting wood fires for barbecues.

I smiled thinly. They were being very kind, but asking when they would depart was like consulting a talking doll: I got a different answer every time every time I pressed the button. The average guess was four hours.

I walked to the silent road and put my thumb out every time a vehicle passed. This did not cause a repetitive strain injury. I began walking. After an hour I sat on the verge ready to dig in my pack for the bananas that had been brought as snack but were now lunch. Before I finished opening the pack, I had company; a long brown snout with a white tip was testing the air from the shadow of a bush. A pair of eyes appeared with white spectacle patterns in the fur around them. It was a white-nosed coati, a mammal the size of a dog, which has a head like a bear with a pointed nose. I sat perfectly still, but it was not shy, and walked straight towards me. My camera was on my belt, and I delightedly took pictures from close range as it leaped forward, head first into my bag, and ran off with my bananas. A short chase ensued. Final score: coati one, writer, two; a fair division, given my greater bodyweight.

At some point on this road Moctezuma made his last attempt to delay the Spanish. Necromancers were summoned from across Tenochtitlán and commanded, with dire threats, to prevent them entering the city. Climbing towards Amecameca, they met someone walking down, as I was now. It was Quetzalcóatl's dark twin, Tezcatlipoca, or Smoking Mirror, the plotter who brought human sacrifice and downfall to Tula. Native sources say, 'He appeared to be drunk and his chest was bound with eight turns of hemp rope. As they grew closer they saw he was indeed intoxicated, not by drink, but rage. He berated them: "Why are you returning here again? What is Moctezuma trying to accomplish? Has he realised too late they are determined to strip him of his kingdom and all he has, including his honour, because of the great tyrannies he has committed against his vassals? He has not reigned as a lord, but as a tyrant and traitor. You can accomplish nothing. Turn and look towards Mexico, and you will see what will befall it before long."

'Then they turned towards Mexico and saw it devoured by flames: temples and other places of worship, all the seminaries, all the dwellings of the nobility and common people; there was presented to them the war that would end with the destruction of Mexico. Upon seeing this, the necromancers' and sorcerers' spirits melted like wax, and a lump in their throats made them speechless.

'Upon hearing these tales of misfortune, Moctezuma became greatly saddened and crestfallen; seated on his throne, he could not speak, he lost his speech. "What are we to do, since the gods and their friends oppose us and our enemies prosper? We must not flee, nor show cowardice, and let us not imagine that the Mexican glory is going to perish here. We are now resolved to die in the defence of our homeland."'

From this road the Spanish might have glimpsed their first view of Tenochtitlán, which occupied an island linked to the lake shore by causeways, its temples and palaces rising above the well-ordered streets and canals. As I continued walking, I could not see a city; I could see a sea. Cloud was pooled up in the Valley of Mexico, a smooth layer of pale grey cloud, tinged yellow-brown by pollution, above the modern metropolis. It is likely the Spanish saw the same sea, for not one account mentions a sight of Tenochtitlán from the heights of Popocatépetl. The onset of night kept the Spanish on the mountain, and though they ate well, the cold pinched. In the morning they walked down to Amecameca. I was coming out of the forest into the agricultural land, when a pickup truck stopped.

'Amecameca?' I asked.

A businessman and his young teenage son made space on the bench front seat. 'Holiday?'

'I am writing a book.'

'You are heading for the right place. Amecameca means The Place Where Papers Matter,' he said, 'but what does that mean?'

Cortés rested here; I needed a bed for the night. I passed a low Colonial building with bars on the windows and doors, which announced itself as *Amecameca Neurotics' Mutual Support Group*. They were busy enough to meet four nights a week to share fear, mania, irritability, anxiety, anguish, depression and loneliness. It might be a good place to meet other travel writers. Next session, tonight: six till eight.

The square was framed by low two-storey buildings. On one side the silos of a sugar mill looked over the roofs while opposite them stood a church in the whimsical style known as early Liquorice Allsorts. Underneath its tower, well-positioned to hear the electric chimes which had replaced the bells, was the Hotel San Carlos. A plain, clean room cost six pounds a night. Amecameca is not a pretty town, but it is bustling and friendly and fun to look round, with a market that sprawls over the square and off into the side lanes like a souk. However restaurants closed as fast as I could find them. A crowd gathered where a pedestrian lay trapped on the ground between two taxis. When I came back later the tarmac had been hosed. At nine the market stalls came down, leaving the garbage on the road for street dogs to quarrel over. A skewbald bitch licked at some nameless spillage while a black brute bit her neck and humped her vigorously.

I was awake and packing before the 6am firework explosions celebrating The Virgin's quiet, pure life were augmented by the church's electric chimes, which sounded like a 500-watt doorbell. Amecameca's streets were empty and clean as I hurried for the early bus to Tepotzlán. In Mexico City, the cycling pilgrims were ending their all-night vigil for the Virgin.

As the bus passed along the flanks of Popocatépetl, I watched the sunrise swell behind it, illuminating the radial ribs of the volcanic cone, leaving the hollows between holding soft mists in their dark folds. The lower slopes changed from Payne's grey to green, and the right side of the mountain flared with the first sunlight.

Within hours, my ears were popping as we crested the hills around Mexico City, then began to coast down through the curves. I glimpsed a panorama to my right. Lingering on my retina was a view I knew, but had never seen: the unchanged line of the hills rising above the plain that was once a lake, familiar from early prints of the Aztec capital: Tenochtitlán. Another glimpse: light pinpricks from a thousand windows and windscreens, pools of smog, yellowish-grey. Down we flew on a modern toll-road.

As Cortés descended, envoys arrived bearing gold. The bilingual *Florentine Codex's* Spanish narrative, written for consumption at home, says 'they were pleased and greatly rejoiced over the gold.' The original Nahuatl account is rude and mocking. 'For gold was what they greatly thirsted for; they were gluttonous for it, starved for it, piggishly wanting it.'

The Spanish arrived at the lake shore among the satellite towns of Tenochtitlán, with the fire-smoke of the capital on the horizon. At the modern toll booths, times mingled in my head and I pictured Cortés held up there while Aztec officials leafed through papers, trying to find historical precedents for what to charge a horse. I was entering Mexico City to take a bus south. There were places I needed to understand before the Climax of Tenochtitlán. Besides, it was Christmas.

Part 3

Ransacking the Dream

22

Acapulco

In Britain, Christmas on your own can be difficult: families shut their doors and so does every business. When I travel to write, I find it best to keep working. This would not a terrible chore as I needed to visit Acapulco. After the mountains, the Pacific coast heat was welcome, even though it was thickened by humidity. I found an apartment in the Hotel Etel Suites, and was greeted by Etel, a short blonde woman with a ladies-who-do-lunch hairdo and a bright smile. In her right hand were the keys, and in her left a bottle of cold beer with the top loosened. The hotel is set high on a headland in the old town. From my terrace I surveyed the Pacific coast in one direction, and the harbour in the other, and prepared to suffer.

Acapulco was the chic resort of the 1950s. Hollywood stars John Wayne, Lana Turner and Johnny Weismuller owned places here, regular visitors included Frank Sinatra and the Rat Pack, Elizabeth Taylor married Mike Todd in Acapulco, John and Jacqueline Kennedy honeymooned here, and the mad and skeletal billionaire aviator, Howard Hughes, spent his last days at the Acapulco Princess Hotel, before dying on a flight back to Beverley Hills, with which Acapulco is still twinned. In 1963, when Elvis Presley signed for a film called *Fun in ...* , it had to be *Acapulco*. In the seventies, the beautiful and the damned moved on, drug dealers moved in, and swish tourism migrated to the other end of the bay.

From my terrace, the prospect west was the view to the Philippines. Sail due west along the latitude of 17°, keeping the sunset before you each night, and 4000 miles later you are 15 miles south of Manila. On moonless nights, there is only starlight; your ship has no lights because no other vessel is in the ocean. The blackness ahead is final, and you move into it at the pace of a trotting dog, in a ponderous galleon made of teak in the Philippines to Spanish designs. On cloudy nights you align the ship with the wind and waves and hold her there, consulting a simple dry box-compass when you can.

The wealth that came out of Mexico was almost entirely in the form of bullion, and what did not cross the Atlantic to Spain came west to Acapulco. The Acapulco-Manila trade was established by Miguel López, who took Andrés de Urdaneta as navigator, a friar whose life makes Indiana Jones look like a recluse. His adventures included an eleven-year circumnavigation of the world. They fulfilled Christopher Columbus's silk route dream of reaching the East by sailing west, but the Americas forced them to do it as two trades. In 250 years the Spanish made around a hundred return voyages, each of about ninety days, following the route pioneered by López and Urdaneta, going directly to Manila to stay in the trade winds, and returning as far as 45° north to catch westerly winds and east-bound currents. The first traders in Indian and the Orient had suffered a shock to their considerable pride. They had no trade goods that the civilisations of the east coveted. Spain and the other trading nations had to pay in bullion. The trains of silver and gold that Columbus intended to use to fund the liberation of Jerusalem, and consummate God's experiment with mankind, went through the Spanish economy like an express train through a country station.

Of the estimated 4 billion pesos produced during the period, 2.5 billion was shipped to Europe, of which 500 million was re-traded round Africa to Asia. Of the remaining 1.5 billion, 650 million went directly to Asia from Acapulco. Little stayed in Spain. Money was blown on military campaigns and imports, spent, never invested, and spent faster than it came in. By 1665 the debts of the Spanish crown were 30 million pesos short-term and 300 million long-term.

In the heart of Acapulco, I was woken on Christmas Eve by cockerels. For the first time in three months I had the use of a kitchen, and I needed groceries, which I bought in friendly small stores. The old town now attracts ordinary Mexican holidaymakers, who spend Christmas on the beach. The headland on which my hotel stood curved round sharply to enclose a small bay. On the shore opposite its tip, commanding the entrance, is Fort San Diego. The shore has been extended seawards about seventy yards since 1614 when Fort San Diego was first built, on a low hill, tight to the shore. So few vessels visited the port that San Diego was never garrisoned by more than eighteen men, and then only when the treasure galleons were in: at most two arrivals and two departures a year. Yet no pirates ever took the fort; the Pacific was too big and empty to find your prey. In 1776 the fort was flattened, but by an earthquake. The rebuilt San Diego is now a museum housing some of the treasures which cost the wealth of the mines, the labour of Natives in conditions no better than slavery, and two crossings of the world's largest ocean at an average speed of five knots. Here are the oriental fans, ivory trinket boxes, *cloisonné* vases, porcelain and japanware. As savvy then as now, Chinese merchants were happy to commission from their suppliers faux-oriental goods which appealed to Europeans more than the real thing: the household goods equivalent of chicken tikka masala.

In the dusk, I watched the cliff divers, young men and teenage boys, cord-thin and muscular, who dive in a cove known as the Quebrada. The cliffs slope outward, into a narrow inlet, little more than a gully. Paying crowds gather on the opposite side, or drink at terrace tables at the head of the inlet, and watch the boys fly. First they dived from lower ledges, then, aided by ropes fixed to the cliff, they scrambled to higher and more perilous perches. They must spring outwards, committing totally to the dive, or they will hit the rocks, head first. The last diver worked himself onto an outcrop right at the top. At first his trajectory seemed that of a normal dive, then, a third of the way down, he seemed to be snatched downwards at terrible speed, before smacking into the water. After a moment of silence, his head appeared and a sinewy arm waved. Applause rose like clattering pigeons. On the terraces, attention returned to cocktails.

At seven on Christmas morning I walked to Tlacopanocha cove in the old harbour, thinking to have it to myself. There were already families pitched out along the beach as if they had been there all night. Perhaps they had. I slipped into the sea, which even to my skinny body felt almost too warm. Others had acclimatised. A fourteen-year-old girl stood waist deep, hugging herself, waiting for courage, muttering, 'It's so cold.'

As I dried myself, the towel snagged on a toenail loosened by the chemotherapy. I carefully lifted it off, and disposed of another scar.

I Skyped Celia, who was in Chicago having a white Christmas with her daughter's family. They beamed as they filed past waving and calling Merry Christmas. She showed me the view from the 49th floor over frozen Lake Michigan: no swimming, just ice fishing.

Tomorrow: Cuernavaca and death under a volcano.

23

Cuernavaca

The bus approached Cuernavaca past hedgerow trees which looked as though their branches had snatched handkerchiefs out of the wind. My neighbour, a man with almost no gap between his aquiline Maya nose and his top lip, saw me looking, and said, '*Cazahuate*. One name for it is poor man's snow. The country people use it for medicine: everything from hair falling out to scorpion bites.'

The heart of the city is little touched by its rapid expansion in the last half century. Its moderate altitude gives it a pleasant climate all year, and Cuernavaca became a twentieth-century playground. The Hotel Posada Antigua has a narrow tropical garden with rooms in steps down a slope. I sat on the small terrace with views across a valley not quite steep enough to be a ravine. The houses below were mostly lost in the rich greenery which rose to a ridge less than half a mile away where grander villas marked the line of Calle Humboldt. On it, Malcolm Lowry rented the house he made the setting for *Under the Volcano*. A lancet between the boles of the hotel's trees revealed a disturbance in the line of the cloud lying snug to the horizon where Popocatépetl was hidden on its hunkers, always threatening to rise. Forty miles away, its presence intruded.

I lunched on rabbit stew in a Zapata-themed restaurant. Two dozen portraits of him lined the walls, one in the style of Picasso, the next Van Gogh, then Munch, even Mondrian, and, more plausibly, Diego Rivera. Cuernavaca's centre comprises two offset squares, touching at one corner. The larger, lower one is the Plaza de Armas. The facades mix competent Colonial public buildings with undistinguished 1960s and 70s blocks. I walked between jugglers, clowns, candyfloss stalls, lottery ticket sellers, then, underneath the raised rifle of Emiliano Zapata, riding high on a plinth, I stopped dead, faced with a building which occupied most of the lower side of the square. It was as large as a castle, with castellated walls and few windows. The original centre section looked domestic, in a palatial kind of way. It had later been hugely extended. Where the land fell away at the rear it was four storeys high. This was Cortés's main residence, begun in the 1520s. On a grey day, it would look grim, but the evening light softened it. In its courtyards, deep down, I glimpsed the foundations of pre-Columbian buildings, torn down, but haunting their successors from troubled graves.

The former house of the American artist Robert Brady is a sizeable mansion below the cathedral. It was turned into a museum merely by putting up a few lengths of red plush rope suspended between stanchions; it was already an orderly jay's nest of art and collectibles. He was born into a wealthy Iowan family who made their money in transport. His parents funded art studies in Chicago and Philadelphia, before he moved to Venice and befriended his neighbour, Peggy Guggenheim, who acquired her money when her father went down with the *Titanic*. He moved to Cuernavaca at the start of the sixties when Mexico became popular with American and European A-listers such as jazzman Charlie Mingus, artist Marcel Duchamps, and Woolworth's heiress Barbara Hutton, whose fortune in modern currency would make her a billionaire. It was Duchamps who advised Guggenheim to buy art, saying, 'It's the investment of the future.' She collected Picassos, Pollocks and Dalis at 1930s prices. The visitor who obsessed Brady was the exotic singer and dancer Josephine Baker. Born in St Louis, Missouri, she made her name in Paris where she danced nearly nude in the company of her pet, Chiquita, who often added excitement by wandering into the orchestra pit. Chiquita was a cheetah. She spent two months a year as Brady's house guest, although his library tells you about his own sexual orientation: Jean Genet, Oscar Wilde, Gore Vidal, Noel Coward, Truman Capote, Tennessee Williams and Christopher Isherwood. On the evidence of the museum, Brady's own artwork was patchy and there were only two fine pieces, both of the flamboyant women in his life: Peggy Guggenheim and Josephine

Baker. He himself was a peacock. The most worn piece of carpet in his bedroom is the spot where he could see himself in all three wall mirrors at once. His own collecting was top notch: Frida Kahlos, of course, and all manner of jazz prints, masks and pottery from around the world. He collected by appearance, and would place an African mask alongside a Polynesian, so you would think they came from neighbouring islands.

Brady also owned a copy of *Under the Volcano*, which the guide, Sergio González, allowed me to handle, but when I began to open it I heard the dry glue of the spine crack. Sergio was handsome and dashing enough to model for an Aztec prince. I told him I was going to find the places featured in the novel. Without a moment's pause he began, 'The Calle Nicaragua of the book is now Calle Humboldt, just behind the Cortés Palace. Iguana Green's Cafe is one of the mescal bars where he drank,' and he continued until my day was planned.

I said, 'I can pay you back with one small piece of information.' I took him to a Paul Colin lithograph from 1925 advertising a Paris nightclub called the Tabarin. 'I have seen one other copy of this poster and it was in Antarctica, in a British base built in World War Two as a campaign of deception. The scheme was hatched in that night club, and the whole operation was code-named Tabarin.'

He threw back his head and laughed, 'You are a writer, yes?' 'Yes.'

'Only a writer or a spy loves clues and secrets so much.'

I lunched in Iguana Green's: the kind of backpacker place where tourists sign the walls. I thought of Lowry, mixing, in my mind, the author and his creation, Geoffrey Firmin. A man appeared at the door with a professionally painted clown's face. Two springs came from his hat and wobbled. So did his legs. A waiter turned him away. A musician was admitted. On a small harp he played Hugo Blanco's delicately mournful Columbian rumba, *Grinding Coffee* using a slow tempo that turned a dance into delicate lament.

Just above the café were wrought-iron gates marking the entrance to a public garden, at one time very private, once the gates of the richest man in Mexico, then later, of the Emperor of Mexico, a royal line of one, lasting three years. The estate was the creation of José de la Borda, born around 1700 in either France or Aragon, the uncertainty arising from his father's service in the army of Louis XIV. Aged seventeen, la Borda followed his brother to Mexico to work a silver mine at La Lajuela near Taxco, between Mexico City and Acapulco. His brother sank another mine west of Mexico City at a tiny settlement called Tlalpujahua. It produced great wealth, and when his brother died four years later, José found himself the owner of a silver mine or two. He delved deeper in La Lajuela and found deposits even bigger than the original find. When that ran out he found another one, which produced for nine years. Under his touch, money flowed out of the ground. He was immensely rich, but spent wantonly on projects, including this property in Cuernavaca, which is still, even after the bulk of it was demolished, big enough to house an art gallery and offices. His lavish reconstruction of Santa Prisca church at Taxco almost bankrupted him. Aged sixty, his property mortgaged, the mines ran out, and debts were falling due.

La Borda was not the kind of man to find a bench in a tavern and bore everyone with yarns of who he used to be. He spent much of the last of his money financing a trip to the state of Zacatecas. The first mine did no better than break even. His last throw of the dice was Esperanza mine: Hope. It proved so rich that he made a second fortune as big as the first. A contemporary portrait shows no sign of a dynamic personality. There's a pinched face on a man with a long nose, small mouth, and receding chin. Head and hands emerge from an enormous coat finished down the chest and cuffs in gold brocade. He looks like a hungry tortoise who might slip out of his shell. He was worth 40 million Pesos when the Peso was on a par with the US dollar. Converted to modern purchasing power, that is over a trillion dollars. He must have been the richest man in the world. His son Manuel became a priest, as José's father had wanted him, José, to be.

But money could not buy a doctor who could cure the poisoning caused by the mercury used in refining, and he retired to Cuernavaca aged sixty-six. This property was so huge he could walk round the whole city block on the balcony of his palace. He enjoyed this for only two years before Manuel stood over him to administer the last rites.

Manuel loved botany, and he planted the structure of the gardens as they are today, collecting plants from around the tropics and semi-tropics. A lake was added, and fountains, the largest as big as an Olympic swimming pool. I toured the grounds with local historian Hugo Malbuena. 'Most of what is left is Spanish Colonial. When the Emperor Maximilian came to Mexico ... '

When he came it was an exercise in arrogant futility, in the worst kind of greedy, competitive colonialism. In 1864 Mexico had a president it could be proud of, Benito Juárez, a man of indigenous stock, from the Zapotec culture of Oaxaca. His parents died when he was three years old and, until he was twelve, he was an illiterate shepherd who spoke no Spanish. Then he walked the forty miles to join his sister in the care of Antonio Salanueva, a bookbinder in Oaxaca. The house is a modest single-storey property opposite the cathedral, running back into a secluded courtyard, in the Calle García Vigil. Salanueva's old binding machines and presses are still there. The artisan saw a sharp and determined boy, and paid for him to be educated. He studied law and went into politics, proving honest, dogged, and as Maximilian would find out, ruthless when he needed to be.

Juárez drove through reforms to make Mexico a modern constitutional democracy. He abolished privileged courts for the military and aristocracy, and subjected church, army and state to the control of the law. It beggars belief how reactionary and corrupt it had been before, most recently under President Santa Anna. The conservatives opposed reform with every imaginable manoeuvre for three years and then, when they failed, petitioned a European regime to invade. It was more important to maintain their privilege than preserve the independence of the republic. The successful groom, invited over to rape the bride, was Napoleon III of France, nephew of the great general. He was married to a Spanish noblewoman, the Empress Eugénie de Montijo, whose personal project was for France to re-establish a Latin empire in the Americas to check the swelling power of the USA. Napoleon III picked a Habsburg to take up the Crown on France's behalf: His Imperial and Royal Highness, The Serene Prince and Lord, Ferdinand Maximilian

Joseph, Archduke and Imperial Prince of Austria, Royal Prince of Hungary and Bohemia, Prince of Lorraine, Count of Habsburg, Governor of Trieste, and that closing vanity, etc. Paintings and photographs show him sporting a centre parting in black hair brushed flat, while his whiskers flare wide and woolly. Both forms of portrait show an earnest but irresolute face. In some he looks insecure. He was brother to the Austrian emperor Franz Joseph, but his politics were very different from that autocrat, who had helped crush the liberal uprisings across Europe in 1848. Maximilian was a liberal sympathetic to just the kind of reforms Benito Juárez had pushed through, and which his would-be hosts, the conservatives, had tried to suppress.

Maximilian's wife was Charlotte, daughter of King Leopold I of the Belgians. In a painting by court painter Franz Winterhalter, she has the same heart-shaped face and doe eyes as portraits of the young Queen Victoria. Photographs and daguerrotypes show a heavier jaw and neat but sullen features. The long exposures of early photographs often deadened expression, but there is no spark of life in her eyes or lips. It reminds me of the face of a friend, when she is approaching a period of depression, and her vivacity disappears behind a paste mask.

Charlotte persuaded him that this was their chance to rule in a manner that would be a lesson to Franz Joseph, instead of serving his brother's reactionary monarchy. This sincere desire to exercise power benignly would turn what was just another colonial project into a short, sad drama. For the royal couple it was a complete tragedy.

They arrived to popular acclaim, and set themselves up in the palace at Chapultépec Castle in Mexico City. The bedroom was so ridden with bedbugs they slept on the billiard tables. For a country retreat, they were recommended Cortés's old mansion fortress on the square of Cuernavaca, but after one night there they declared it impossible, and took the more agreeable la Borda mansion.

My guide, Hugo, took me through their chambers, which are comfortable, but not grand. 'Charlotte wanted to be known by the Spanish version of her name, Carlota. This was his bedroom, through here, Maximilian had a secret passage into the chapel at side of altar.' So did Philip II of Spain at El Escorial palace, and the Roman Emperor Constantine at Hagia Sophia in Constantinople. This is pomp not piety. It says: I have special access to God.

Hugo continued, 'Maximilian's principles were not so severe as to prevent him having mistresses. He had a long affair with a Native beauty whose nickname was simply *La India Bonita*, The Beautiful Indian. Priorities were strictly observed. The closest room was his billiards room, he was addicted to it, and the next, the bedroom of his second favourite pastime, his wife. When they were here, Maximilian and Carlota entertained with European grandeur and sophistication, with parties every weekend, including operas and concerts.'

After assessing the situation in Mexico, Maximilian declared his wish to support the new liberal reforms, and one wonders why this came as a surprise to the blinkered conservatives. Benito Juárez watched with a jaundiced eye. He had seen Mexico's fortunes frittered away by strongmen and internal strife, and fettered by reactionary practices and institutions. He had fought to set Mexico on a path of reform guaranteed by law and institutions. He was not going to suffer a monarch promising to protect those goals through decree; it was a contradiction in terms.

Maximilian and Carlota tried sincerely to be reasonable, but offended both sides. Cynically, Napoleon III abandoned them. While Carlota was in Europe, lobbying for support, Maximilian was captured and sentenced to death. European heads of state pleaded for mercy, but Juaréz went through with it. Those same Europeans had supported the invasion of his country. Many Mexicans had died defending the republic; he wanted to send a message to other would-be colonisers. Maximilian accepted his fate with dignity, saying, 'I forgive everyone, and I ask everyone to forgive me. May my blood which is about to be shed be for the good of the country. *Viva Mexico, viva la independencia.*' He gave each rifleman gold, asking to be shot cleanly in the chest so his face would not be disfigured and upset his mother. But one hit him in the eye, and the embalmer had to replace it. There was no call for blue glass eyes in the town of Querétaro, where he was executed. He was fitted with a black one. Edouard Manet painted the execution five times, as a criticism of Napoleon III's shameless abandonment of an ally. Juárez, after a period of public display to ensure the death was accepted and believed, granted the body respectful treatment. It was taken home for burial in Vienna, with one black Mexican eye and one blue Austrian eye. He was thirty-four.

Carlota, still only twenty-seven years old, lost her mind, and was confined in an apartment for the rest of her life, dying aged eighty-six in 1927. She never understood Maximilian had died, and wrote to him for nearly sixty years. Her huge wealth fell under the control of her brother, the future Leopold II of the Belgians. She was betrayed a second time as her money was used to fuel his shameful genocidal exploitation of the Congo as a personal fiefdom, the most despicable of all colonial regimes, excoriated in Joseph Conrad's novella *Heart of Darkness*.

In *Under the Volcano*, which unfolds in twenty-four hours on the Day of the Dead, the Consul's wife and brother rode through the estate of Maximilian and Carlota. Lowry's complex structure of allusions makes it the Garden of Earthly Delights. Late in the day I walked along the side of Cortés's hulking palace, down the hill to traffic lights where the traffic poured blue exhaust gases onto the walls of a small hotel called *Bajo el Volcan*: Under the Volcano. A ceramic plaque marks it as *Casa de Malcom Lowry*. He would have laughed at them misspelling his name, and woven it into the book. In the centre of the plaque is a bouquet of lilies, tenderly apposite. I followed Calle Humboldt towards a bridge. When the consul's wife and brother finish their horse ride, they pass over the ravine that the consul calls the Malebolge, the eighth circle of Hell in Dante, and home for eternity to counterfeiters, hypocrites, grafters, seducers, sorcerers and simonists. Its presence haunts the Consul's final day as he criss-crosses the city.

> *Upon the right I saw new misery*
> *I saw new tortures and new torturers*
> *Filling the first of Malebolge's moats (Inferno Canto XVIII)*

It is here that the novel's denouement is enacted, in a swift few lines, shocking as a slash to the face.

The houses on Calle Humboldt are mostly fine affairs behind old trees, high walls and electronic gates. From the bridge I could see some of the properties around Lowry's old home. Their fronts might be smart, but the backs were brutal. For security there were no windows on the lower storeys. Prison-high walls and fences separated their curtilages from the ravine, so the dirty river picked its way through boulders fouled with garbage at the foot of cane-choked slopes in a space which belonged to no one, and which no one could access. Nothing bigger than a rat could move through the vegetation with ease. Even the pariah dogs that shadowed the consul when he walked out would not go there. I made my way up a narrow road to escape into the square, on the opposite side of the Cortés Palace, with a troubled feeling of having escaped a threat.

In the warm night, I sat at the table outside my room, and made plans to pass again through Mexico City and visit sites to the north that were vital in the development not just of the Aztecs, but of civilisation in all Mesoamerica.

The sky had the finest gradient of colour from grainy blue in the zenith, falling through faintest pink to a violet tinge in the east. The farthest hill was a grey Chinese wash cut across the sky's delicate texture and colour. Lights came out in close clusters: spiders' eyes ready for the darkness. I wrote my diary and used my iPad to play live radio from Britain: Classic FM. A full moon lit the garden, Jupiter at her side. I was tracking time through full moons. November's had fought to come through the cloud above my riverside balcony in Xico. October had been the Yucatan jungle. My September full moon had flown over the ruined Roman aqueduct of Mérida in Extremadura. Tonight I remembered tenderly how much weaker I had been then, feeding almost entirely on food substitutes. Celia had been at my side beneath the Mérida moon.

It was approaching four in the morning in Britain. I emailed a message to Nick Bailey at Classic FM, saying where I was, and asking for something with a New World connection. In five minutes

I heard my words on the radio, and he played Bernstein's *Candide*. Now, we are all connected. Celia slept on. I completed my diary and watched baby bats fly circles against the face of the moon.

24

I Am Probably Going to Die Soon

Aspiration: inspiration, the act of breathing, a breath, a sigh. Steadfast desire for something above one. More needles in the neck. I wait for the results, and think about the side effects of chemotherapy. I need not fear treatment that makes my hair fall out. The Harrison genes are already on the case.

Saturday again, back in the pub with Tony. 'This type of cancer is indolent, so not discovering it early doesn't matter: it's treatable, and nine out of ten survive. You are young for a throat cancer sufferer, you're fit, and have no other health problems; there's no reason why you won't be one of the nine and live another thirty years. Nine out of ten cancers do not metastasise to other organs. Of course, I don't need to explain statistics to you – if you are the one in ten, you are not ten per cent dead, you're a hundred per cent dead.'

I hold on to the word indolent.

Then, being two intelligent men faced with a life-threatening problem, we talk about football. Chemotherapy means being attached to a drip all week for 23 hours 40 minutes a day. During my first session I read, and open myself to the material, as the daily trivia fall away. My mackintosh against life has fallen off, and I can feel the rain fresh on my skin. I start Dante's *Divine Comedy*, something I have promised myself I would study since reading T S Eliot in my teens. I love the opening book *Inferno* or *Hell*. The wicked and their punishments are great fun. The first circle of hell is limbo, which just means the edge. That is all I am suffering at this stage, the edge. When I have had enough of *Hell*, I re-read Seamus Heaney's *The Naturalist*. His meaning is newly transparent to me, and I hear the music without interference. There is no special beauty in my life, no sights or hints of a deeper truth, except to see daily life made more urgent, and to feel the value of it because it is held on a short lease. Accepting that death may be close clears the dross from my mind. A window cleaner's blade has made the glass vanish, so that the pale reflections and refractions that complicate vision are not there any more. It is more powerful than the other ways I have experienced this: walking, wilderness, and isolation. And it's simple, just death, crouching on his scrawny haunches the way long-distance walkers can, with their loose hamstrings.

One afternoon I review my life. Fear is under control. I find I am content and almost happy. If I was to have cancer, it has at least happened after I have spent fifteen years doing what I love most: travelling and writing. I have a partner I love and trust absolutely. A pension will soon arrive, on my sixtieth birthday. Cancer is awful, but I am starting in a good place.

My appearance will change rapidly. The less you look like other people, the farther you feel from them. When I catch sight of myself unexpectedly in a shop mirror, I wonder why that grey man is following me. Sitting on the bog, I run a hand through my pubic hair. A whole hank falls out at the roots in a crisp bouquet. In two days the hair on my head starts falling, in smaller, finer sprays. I have already made my mind up what I will do when this happens. I had seen the head of my neighbour in the next bed to me at Charing Cross. In the mirror Patrick's hair would to him have seemed unchanged, but at the back a hank hung from the crown, and below it there was only bare skin, greyer than his other skin, with a very smooth texture; skin which has had hair on it never wrinkles. The newly-exposed skin wasn't quite bare, as there was a thin, woolly fuzz of new hair growing through, fine and disordered. I cut mine back to the skull. That way, I am controlling it. I buy an arty round cap from a craft fair, and a gaudy headband from an outdoor shop.

One night I wake from light sleep at four in the morning to find Patrick standing beside my island, in the shallows. Because we are all newly-discovered islands, our position is not yet fixed, and we appear where we are not supposed to be, like Jonathan Swift's flying island of Laputa, in *Gulliver's Travels*. His brain has been rescanned that afternoon, and they have found more tumours, inoperable ones. He begins without preamble. 'Four months they've given me. I thought it would be quick, but four months. Jesus!' He plans to return to Ireland as soon as he is well enough to travel, and make his peace with all his family.

He that dies pays all debts.

The chemotherapy chemicals don't just destroy tumours. They are dangerous to the skin if spilled, and could damage the flooring. To stop it trashing the veins into which it is dripped, I have an operation under local anaesthetic to insert a tube in a vein in my chest, which they can access by a small port. Before he begins the consultant pauses, scalpel raised, looking at the monitoring display. 'You're very nervous – your blood pressure and pulse just rose.'

I explain the science. 'You're going to cut a hole in me and it will hurt.'

Afterwards, the infusion port appears as a raised pad the size of a five pence piece but the tube either side is invisible under the flesh.

The chemical brew also attacks my bone marrow. The white corpuscles in my blood which carry antibodies now fall to levels so low that any infection could be dangerous. I must not inhale on the Tube. The mouth is one of the dirtiest places in the body and even with continual cleaning, and sterilising rinses, mine fills with ulcers. My entire lower lip is a cold sore for six weeks. Even though I am using cocaine-based mouthwashes, eating becomes agony. It takes ten minutes spent weeping with pain to recover from each mouthful of cereal. A tube is inserted into the front of my stomach and I learn to inject food drinks into it if eating becomes possible. Despite assurances that this is a minor procedure, as the anaesthetic wears off, the tube in me hurts so much I cannot speak to ask for painkillers; I just groan and point. I promise myself I will keep eating come what may, and will never use this disgusting device. The hole in my stomach is poorly cut and leaks, so one minute after I take a drink, it spills, mingled with brown stomach juices, over my belly.

This is more degrading than pain, which at least has a clean dignity about it, a Captain Scott kind of aseptic misery.

The feeding tube and infusion port add one final isolation: I cannot hold Celia close without pressing on the tube and the chest wound. We fashion A-frame hugs like executives wanting to signal mateyness, but avoiding trouser contact.

I wake dreading breakfast and watch the dawn light up the distant London Eye, catching the uppermost pods, making shining discs of them, like the out-of-focus highlights in a Vermeer. Other wards offer sights of the Harrods Depository, famous once a year in Boat Race commentaries, and the ornate cast-iron towers of Hammersmith Bridge, disappearing, despite their clumpy mass, into the clutter of the riverside.

I lose all my body fat, and my muscles waste. Loose folds of skin hang from inside my upper arms. Between treatments I hunt at the back of the wardrobe for jeans which last fitted a decade ago. Some of them are still too tight, and I wonder when I ever wore them, or if I put them in a 90° wash with the sheets. Ridges appear at the base of my fingernails and some of my toenails. They may fall out, warns the advice. Fingertips become less sensitive and motor-neurone skills decrease. Buttons become tricksy puzzles. The skin on my fingers is so dry I can drop the same piece of paper three or four times in a minute. The Macmillan Cancer Support leaflet lists other signs and wonders: you will be more sensitive to the sun; it is inadvisable to father a child while on Docetaxel; you may lose the ability to hear certain high-pitched sounds; you may suffer from hearing sounds that aren't there; you may notice changes in the way your heart works, and increased production of tears.

There are rests between sessions of chemotherapy for the healthy parts of my body to recover. I feel the cold acutely, wear fleeces indoors, double my bedding, sleep clutching scalding hot-water bottles, and the heating is never turned off. It is a very raw way of feeling my vulnerability. Mammals, when alive, are warm. I am cold, life is escorting me forwards, tottering, with a tenuous, formal grip: two bony fingers on my elbow.

After the first week of chemotherapy, I come out of hospital the night before my sixtieth birthday. I wake early, dress warmly, and take a mug of coffee into Hyde Park at seven. Five days ago, my father reached ninety and a small party had been arranged. I had spent the year hoping he would make it, and we could have a joint 150th birthday party. He had gone to the party while I had been six stories high looking at the Thames, steadying myself with a drip-frame like a mobile hat-rack. He had complained that I had not come. He was no sooner told about my illness than it was gone. At no time in the months when I might have died does he contact me, or ask my brothers to wish me well. In his Alzheimer's world, when other people left his vision they no longer existed, vanishing from reality, leaving him to rule alone. At his court the phantoms bowed.

Hyde Park is a Royal Park, and under Prince Charles's influence the grass beneath the trees is managed as a wild-flower meadow. They are taking a late hay crop, and the ground is scattered with tightly-wound cylinders of grass, an incongruously rural sight in the heart of London. Something digs into my wrist. I am still wearing my plastic hospital wristband which identifies me by name, number and allergies. Tagged on my parole. When I am reclaimed by Charing Cross I go to a different ward and more worried faces on new islands. The small wards are called bays and are lettered not numbered. Inevitably, on the third visit, I am put on eBay.

25

Footy and Tiddy Oggies

I wanted to visit a source of the obsidian blades that were the Sheffield steel of Mesoamerica. The Pachuca obsidian is very special; it is gold-green in colour, indicating a very pure mineral. I could not trace anyone who worked it the traditional way, but I discovered two things. Obsidian is still used for specialist surgery. There were also other, irresistible, reasons to go to Pachuca.

This industrial city is both fifty miles north-east of the centre of Mexico City and a world away. The roads continuing beyond it do so half-heartedly and dwindle out in the hills. The bus's entry to the town was through a modern commercial and industrial area with shiny car dealerships and the John Deere tractor franchise. The old centre is lined with shops selling Cornish pasties. In 1824, four ships in Falmouth docks, south-west England, were hurriedly loading engineering equipment; the manufacturers had run late. Cornwall was the centre of world expertise in copper and tin mining, and home to Richard Trevithick, inventor of the world's first high-pressure steam engine and the steam locomotive. These were the first steam engines to go to Mexico, and would be used to pump water from the mines, crush and dry ore, and move material and men up and down the shaft. With the equipment, and 120 men, came Cornish pasties, the staple food of Cornish miners. It is one of the world's great simple meals. The secret is raw ingredients, meat and a few root vegetables, which cook in the pastry during baking. The Cornish also brought tennis, golf, football and Methodism.

I went to school in Cornwall, and adore pasties; the Cornish still use the old phrase for them: tiddy oggies. My first bite of a Mexican pasty, at the *Kiko Paste* chain, was impressive. It was an authentic mix, with good shortcrust pastry. On the second bite the chilli kicked in, and I ate the rest with my eyes streaming. But I ate it. I felt an enormous sense of relief at having a new food I could swallow. They had diversified into new fillings. Refried bean pasties, potato and chicken, chicken with red or green chilli sauce, sausage and bean, were all just about understandable, but loitering at the foot of the menu were the heresies: potato and tuna, chocolate, and Hawaiian. Desert was a nice rice pudding pasty. I could hear Trevithick turning in his grave on a steam-powered rotisserie.

Cornwall is a place with a cast-iron identity, and the centres of mining towns like Camborne and Redruth have not changed, because granite buildings do not fall down. The architecture is plain because the stone is too obdurate to prettify. You are lucky if you can get a drill in the wall to put up shelves. In Pachuca, near the old market, is a Methodist church with semi-circular Roman arches in pink and white stone, and castellated tops to its walls, that could have stood quietly in the main street of any of the towns that sit on the granite bosses which make up the mining areas of Cornwall. It was arresting and poignant to see such familiar architecture so far from home.

Around the corner I came up against a decidedly Spanish building built like a fortress: a financial fortress. Like Antigua, the failed site of Veracruz, it was one of ten eventual collection points in the whole of Spain's New World empire for the royal fifth. The building's strength reflects the wealth extracted from the veins of metal running like nerves through the mountains around the city.

In the street alongside the Royal Strong House I waited next morning for an ageing *colectivo* to gather enough passengers to leave for the small hill town of Real del Monte, where the mining migrated, following the seams. The stores were not yet open, but many passengers had been shopping in the market and were returning home. The *colectivo* started up and we weaved through the quiet streets.

Next to me was Fabián, a spare, spry man in his late seventies, with a thin moustache along his top lip like RAF wings. A warm smile lit his face when I told him I had grown up Cornwall.

'I started work in 1952 and worked for thirty-four years.'

It was the year I was born. Looking at his build, like a jockey, and remembering not every mine worker heaves a pick and shovel, I asked him what he did.

'Underground, dangerous.'

He did not say hard, which I had expected. 'How are your lungs, and your joints?' The mining museum showed X-rays of workers' lungs; opaque shadows occluded the delicate traceries of the healthy tissue.

'I am lucky, still fit.' He pointed down at two large bags full of empty plastic containers of all sizes. 'I make my own wine, I don't come into Pachuca unless I have to. Real del Monte is my home, a very tranquil place. Mountain air, not like here.'

'Yes,' he continued. 'It got safer during my time, more safety conscious. I remember though,' – he laughed and I saw that all the lines in his skin were laughter lines – 'they sacked one man for smoking marijuana. It wasn't illegal then, but they said it was dangerous. Not as dangerous as working in a mine in the first place.'

Ex-miners I met in Wales who were now working as guides at coal-mine museums expressed satisfaction at excelling at a tough trade, and sadness for the loss of the camaraderie of the pit. 'Do you miss it?'

'No,' and his laughter lines vanished. 'Thirty-four years was enough.'

We slowed down by a very odd-shaped plaza they called the square. 'This is our stop.' On the steeply sloping pavement my feet were below his, but I still towered over him. His smile disappeared again. He looked moved. 'I am so pleased you have come all this way to understand our work here. '*!Que le vaya bien!*' He squeezed my arm and his eyes were moist. He let me take his picture when I asked, but he could not put the smile back.

'I would like to know how to work obsidian. Does anyone still do that?'

'Only with grinders and cutters, not the old flaking.'

'Do you have time to show me around? I would like to be guided by a miner. I'll pay you, and buy you a beer.'

242

He shook his head. 'I have things to do, I own a little land that I work. I am back home now. Nothing bothers me here.' He was lonely, but he would not feel sorry for himself.

He pointed to pines on the top of a small hill. 'That's the English cemetery, don't miss that!'

I moved to Cornwall aged twelve, when my father's work took him to Redruth. We romanced the life we would have, but just how special it was hit me on the first night. When we arrived in darkness, in the chill of March, we saw, at the bottom of the guest house garden, the telescopic tower of a Cornish mine-engine's chimney. The lower storeys were granite, the upper, bricks. It pointed at the sky: a gun barrel shooting the sailing moon. The owner of the B&B turned out to be Squadron Leader Johnny. I will omit his surname, because at dinner he reminisced. 'Tommy, I can remember so much about our time together, but I can't recall the last time I saw you.'

When I turned eighteen, my father was the only parent who was welcomed by my friends to share a pint. He was cool. He also lifted a curfew on his memory. 'Do you remember Squadron Leader Johnny in Redruth?' Dad was scathing about men who took their ranks into civvy street. 'The reason I didn't answer his question was that I remembered exactly where I had last seen him. He was outside a Cairo brothel, lying in the road. We thought he was dead, but he was just dead drunk. We expected that he had been robbed of everything, but nothing had gone, not even the coins in his pockets. He had collapsed alone in the street, and every footpad who passed assumed he had already been stripped.'

Where the odd-shaped square ended, and below the cemetery hill, was the Dolores mine. Its chimney took me back to that childhood night in Redruth, and cliff-top tin mines like Botallack, Geevor and Levant, and showery skies at the end of a spring day, knelled by a hidden blackbird pealing bright lemon pips of sound into the dusk.

A small museum was being built, not to memorialise mining but football. The first football matches ever played in Mexico were played here on Sundays by Cornish miners in 1900. They played only thirty-five minutes each way, probably in deference to the altitude and miners' lungs.

I climbed narrow back lanes between stone walls, thinking of my first day at work at my father's Redruth office in 1968. I was sixteen, and tongue-tied with people I did not know. I found it even harder to talk to my father here, where he was an inspector of taxes with his own office. At lunchtime we walked through hot narrow lanes, in searing light bouncing off white granite gemmed with platelets of mica. An old man was pulling new potatoes from the sides of dry earth ridges without lifting the plant. He greeted my father and they chatted easily for a while. Dad must have featured in the man's day, passing by at ten past one. I can pull back the memory with ease. We talk about memory bringing back a time to us, but it has never gone away. One time is all time. My father waited until we were out of earshot and said, 'I don't know why they latch onto me; they sense something in me.' He never really had time for other people. He could be charming when he wanted to, but it was a skill, not heartfelt. He had begun flying missions for the RAF in the war, aged eighteen. His mother confided in me that he was never the same when he returned, having flown seventy-four missions, which should have been enough to guarantee being killed. But he was skilled, intelligent, and careful. And lucky. She said, 'When they came home, they were all old for their age. But with Tommy, there was something else.'

Something he kept from others, so it could not hurt them, or perhaps something he managed, to protect himself, like the workmen wrapping their machetes in cloth. Don't let anyone get too close. It can be taken away. A few years ago, with the sixty-fifth anniversary of the end of the war approaching, I had visited him to find his RAF missions logbook open on the table. Staring into a distance far beyond the walls of his flat, he said, 'Fifty-five thousand men in Bomber Command died, and their average age was twenty-two. It made me think of the closest scrape we had, men injured, the plane damaged, and fuel lost. He read the details from the log. The entry finished with the words: *A close call*.

'At the time I was twenty-two years old.' His time had come, yet he was not taken.

'Blessed are those who die in the Lord' said the plaque in the cemetery wall. The needles on the pines were fine and took the wind softly. The rust-coloured mat of fallen needles in dappled shade damped all sound from my footfalls. Robert Noble, late of St Hilary, a parish in the far west of Cornwall on the road to Penzance. From its hills, you can see both coasts. He died at Velasco, twenty miles east of here on 3 May 1875, aged forty-two. His son James had died aged four months, two years before. The son, Robert, whom he left a suckling infant, was dead within two months more. Nearby lay a relative of one of the founding men, Richard Rule and his six-month-old son, clay warmed by God in Camborne. Nearby were other Cornish names: Scobles and Pengellys, and William Stonewall of Bolenowe, a hamlet only seven miles from my former home, but so small I had never heard of it. William died at the mine aged twenty-six; his neighbour in the earth: William Trelease.

From crevices in the wall around the cemetery, and from the corners of the sunnier graves grew a small white flower which flourishes in Cornwall, where it is called white rock. They did not forget their own roots. The Wesleyan Chapel in Redruth was built with the help of remittances sent back by these miners.

On the other side of the valley is an abandoned mine where the empty wooden *pulquerías* still stood outside the padlocked gates to the mine yard to catch dry mouths while their money was still weighing heavily in their pockets. True *pulque* is a thick, milky, alcoholic distillation from the sap of maguey cactus, and before the conquest had been a sumptuary drink, like chocolate, permitted only to nobles and priests unless you were old and ill, or pregnant. Surprisingly for an alcoholic medicine, it is effective: full of vitamins and iron. When modern breweries began competing for business, it was persuasive to point out that *pulque* fermentation was often hastened by slipping a muslin bag of animal manure into the brew.

Just beyond the other side of the town in the twist of a narrow green valley lay the Acosta mine, a silver and gold mine active for forty years. If I narrowed my eyes I could imagine myself on a still, hot day in West Penwith near Land's End, climbing walls pierced by arched windows more severe than those in the Methodist church. The mine engine's chimney of dressed stone topped by brick was identical to the one in the garden of my childhood guest house. The information panels had pictures of Botallack, Levant, and a disused boiler made at the Williams' Perran Foundry, in Perranarworthal, just outside Falmouth.

An adit tunnel was still open. I walked on the level, going 500 yards into the mountain. The roof was a brick arch but the walls were living rock, slowly creeping closer together under the press of the mass of stone above. I was over eight hundred feet below the surface. At different times, a hundred and sixteen mines wormed their way though the mountain, nibbling its wealth. From the end of the Second World War prices fell and the seams grew thinner. Token activity at Acosta produces only four ounces of silver and a few scraps of gold from each ton of ore.

Lunch was easy: it was just a question of whether to buy at *Pastes El Colibri* (the hummingbird), or one of the ten other pasty shops named after utterly un-Cornish things. I had one more sight to see before closing time. In 2012 Real del Monte opened the world's first pasty museum. Cornwall has not got one. Staff were winding down at the end of the day, and the other visitors were heading for the cafe. I was taken straight to the kitchen, and set to work making a pasty. They were incredulous when I said I knew. When word got round that someone who had lived in Cornwall had arrived, the staff converged on me. One young guide, Raúl Salvador Ruíz Rangel, was going to Redruth for their mining festival next year. He was already excited. We walked around, swapping stories. Beneath a photo of the Levant mine on the cliffs leading to Land's End, I told them about the disaster there in 1900, when, due to negligence, the vertical beam on which the men entered and left the mine sheared off. Thirty-one men died. Raúl said, 'We had the same, a cage had plummeted down the shaft. Twenty-seven men died, two walked away unharmed. Thrown into the air, they had landed on the cushions of their workmates' bodies.

I waited for the bus, looking down the valley towards Pachuca as street lights came blinking out of the dusk. The *colectivo* deposited me near the older, smaller square, where the Native town had been before the conquest. The mine owners made fortunes; the current town hall is the former house of Francis Rule: *El Rey de Plata*. Two musicians dressed head to foot in black cowboy clothes stood leaning on either side of an arch in the colonnade, one silent, worrying at his hands, the other singing and playing the guitar for the crowds thronging the warm night.

26

eBay

Some patients arrive in dumb shock. They were being scanned for something harmless and a shadow or a light appeared where it should not. Most cancers are found when looking for something else. Some arrivals barely talk to their family, but stare in wild accusation at the high ceiling, which has to stand in for the world and its cruelty. One muscular South African in his early thirties, built like a rugby flank forward, is visited only by his mother. His voice is always on the edge of tears. I hear fragments. 'I imagine this as the rest of my life, with puss oozing out of my arse.'

She consoles, 'It's not like a tumour, cancer, paralysis or anything. In a few days you'll be fine.' Their sentences do not join up. She abruptly asks, 'Is it a boil or an abscess?'

He soundlessly shakes his head from side to side. 'They haven't got a tube for it.'

He has to wait for it to heal. Meanwhile he wears a huge absorbent nappy and fulminates with disgust at his own body.

Nurses come to my bed. 'How are you?'

How do they think I feel? My body is growing something to starve and choke me. The woman I love may lose her man, otherwise healthy, aged just sixty, for the second time in six years. I am frightened and have no religion. Weetabix with banana tastes like brake-pads soaked in battery acid with a side portion of radiator hose. That is how I feel.

Then I think about Patrick at four in the morning. 'Not so bad, how about yourself?'

A pretty nurse asks me about my bowel movements and warns that the drugs may either cause diarrhoea or constipation. There are many things we could discuss if I were young and well, but we discuss the fact that I struggle to crap things which have the shape and size of ceremonial mace-heads and the texture of mahogany pineapples.

Whatever I say they must raise another bag of chemicals, and set the timer on the dispenser. I watch the clock run down imperceptibly: the flight details on a long-haul flight to the other side of night.

I pull out Dante, a long-haul book. I have progressed with him from *Hell* to *Purgatory*. In Dante's cosmology the Southern Ocean was empty except for the mountain island of Purgatory. I have spent nearly a year of my life sailing the Antarctic waters of the Southern Ocean, so I feel an affinity with Purgatory, especially its uncertain location. Purgatory isn't in the Bible; the notion of it developed in the Late Middle Ages. It had been seen as a soft version of Hell but Dante reinvented it as the ascent of a mountain, a process and a progress, whereas Hell is an unchanging state. Purgatory is a more encouraging allegory for a soul in my condition.

When I am too tired to read I listen to music. Usually I play all kinds of music, but my taste now is only for classical. Classic FM is reassuring, playing only music I know. And repetitive. I soon loathe Margherita Taylor's voice introducing Smooth Classics each night as though history's greatest composers and musicians were contributing to a branch of aromatherapy. Radio 3 provides a broader reach, but sometimes I fall asleep to Mozart only to be woken in the small hours by something loud and atonal played on dustbins.

Opposite my island is another rectangle of snow inhabited by Edmund the Happy Scotsman. He wants to go home because the Weetabix there is easier to eat, and he will be all right if only they let him go home. He has lost two stone so far. Whenever I speak he grimaces and turns his face away. I try not to cajole him into optimism since his wife, who is Polish-Irish, sits for four hours a day at his side and has made no progress. *He receives comfort like cold porridge.* Besides, his treatment is more advanced than mine. I may soon be as he is now. I next see him four months later in an outpatients' clinic. If he has reached this stage, he will survive. The look of misery on his face is unabated. Unhappiness is a commitment he will honour to the death, however long he is made to wait. His wife turns the page of a magazine, smiles at an obese nurse. I am introduced to her as my nutritionist. At least she likes her work.

Edmund's island empties and is taken over by a Rastafarian around thirty years old who looks as fit as anyone you could find. He has liver cancer and a fourteen-year-old son who he is determined will not grow up without a father. He even talks, though these islands are normally wholly isolated. He fetches me a newspaper, because he has been brought in to rest, and is not attached to drips and stands. I like him very much. It is not likely he will survive this year. Another man, with intensely dark blue-black skin spends two nights in the corner bed, letting out farts that smell like rotting vegetation pulled from a cesspit. Even the nurses wrinkle their noses.

Misery acquaints a man with strange bedfellows.

Many snore. One lets out small cries every few breaths, like a wounded gull. In a private room across the ward a Chinese woman wails, ceaselessly, piteously, but is judged not to need anything, and is left.

Be not afeard: the isle is full of noises, sounds and sweet airs, that give delight and hurt not.

But burrow into the soul, like storm petrels tunnelling the turf above cliffs where waves burst their cold hearts in white spray.

Over the months I plot the ridges rising up my fingernails until the nails lose purchase and fall out. They grow at the same speed that continental plates drift apart. When they fall out after six months, I know that there is a strip of land a centimetre or so wide all across the centre of Iceland that did not exist when I began treatment.

The winter that now begins belongs in Iceland. The snow is persistent, the cold relentless. I keep irregular hours and am awake for stretches of the night, and sleep a lot in the afternoons, knocked out by the morphine patches. When at home, I sleep in the spare room, which is small and snug, and comfortingly lined to the ceiling with poetry books, plays and autobiographies. For the first week when I wake up alone I first wonder what Celia and I have argued about. I pull out Dante. I have reached *Paradise*, and the tedium of virtue.

On Christmas Eve I struggle to complete a small bland meal. I have been to Charing Cross Hospital as an outpatient for more chemotherapy. My mouth ulcers are not as bad as they were after the first session, but my body has been worn down. There is a large raw ulcer in the middle of my tongue that I cannot miss no matter how I eat. I pour a nutritional drink and take all morning to swallow it through the swellings, as the flesh surrounding the lump of the tumour has been enlarged by the reaction to the treatment. I am so poorly nourished I feel faint, and my balance is not reliable. I give in and use the stomach rig to feed for the first time. I have lost so much weight my shoes are too large. Internal features become prominent: ribs, veins and tendons stick out; my sternum is trying to escape. The port in my chest to feed the chemicals into my blood now stands proud of my flesh. I look like a Richard Rodgers building. The outpatients department closes for Christmas Day. I cook lunch for Celia and her daughter's family then retire to the kitchen to inject my milk. Feeding and taking all my tablets and medicines takes about an hour, then I sleep, and wake to do it again. On Boxing Day I return to Charing Cross. The medicines are not controlling my nausea any more. I am vomiting raw stomach acid into the ulcers in my throat. My knees can seize up, leaving me unable to move without rocking myself into motion. Awake at odd hours, I receive cheerful, if incoherent, emails from my friend Tan pointing me to curious strands of the world wide web.

On New Year's Eve Celia watches me in my bed at home, neither eating nor drinking. 'I'm driving you to Accident and Emergency at Charing Cross.' I try to object but cannot speak, which rather proves her point. I am barely strong enough to stay on the waiting-room chair. They admit me as an emergency, dehydrated and with my blood in a mess from inadequate nutrition. Busy with admissions procedures, they forget to feed me all day. If I am too ill to keep to the timetable, the treatment may be less effective. This may also be expressed as I am less likely to survive. On the 2 January Tan dies. There will be a post-mortem, but his body just seems to have given in to multiple assaults. One of the last times I saw him he had been in hospital, surrounded by batteries of *Sun* readers. He had let out one of the giggles that sat so oddly in a big, tall man. Life's a game, good to see you. God bless you, from one atheist to another. I come out of hospital two days before the funeral, and lie at home, far too ill to travel but nevertheless suffused with pointless guilt.

Radiotherapy begins. Dante and Heaney have gone. I read P. G. Wodehouse and struggle to remember the story.

For each treatment, I have to put a piece of angular plastic in my bone-dry, ulcerous mouth to hold my tongue in place. It is like the device they use to mark the position of a snooker ball when it is lifted to be cleaned. There is a groove for my teeth; the mouth must be presented to the radiation in exactly the same position each time, with a tolerance of just a few millimetres. I gag, try again, gag, try again. Sit up, take a drink, breathe deeply, gag. They talk patiently to me, wet the plastic. I do not want to let them down. I put it in and gag. I do not want to suspend the treatment until I feel better. I resist the urge to gag, not by fighting it, but by stopping thought. I put it in and lie down.

They clamp a lime-green plastic webbing mask over my head and shoulders. The mask was moulded, wet and pliable, to my face ten days before treatment began, left to set, and put in storage, waiting. They clamp it so tightly to my face that my eyelashes can barely brush past to close my eyes. Twenty minutes without moving, without thinking about the plastic in my mouth. Every day, again and again. But while I am being treated, days have purpose, and fear is on hold. As I become used to death's proximity, a plastic sheen begins to form over my sensibilities, and form another carapace.

My last bout of chemotherapy runs parallel to the radiotherapy. I leave the chemo-ward at lunchtime to have the radiotherapy, then return. I have seen what radiotherapy does to throat cancer patients and been appalled. Now it happens to me. The burns on my neck do not recover by the next day. Thick scabs begin to form all across my neck and onto my shoulders. They fall off, leaving open wounds which have to be covered in cling-film so they don't stick to the radiotherapy mask. I can barely swallow through the tiny gap remaining on the left side of my throat, and have to grind up my tablets and inject them into my stomach tube. I can't keep down the anti-nausea tablets, and so a vicious circle begins. I need three bags of blood to try to keep my own blood healthy enough to do its work. My diary goes silent again.

I drag myself out to walk the icy paths of Hyde Park, with layers of fleeces and coats, like a John le Carré Cold War spy looking for safe caches to leave messages, to arrange a rendezvous with the chill incubus crouching in the back of my throat. A cussed desire to beat it drives me on. I still have not missed a single hospital appointment.

The chemicals – this one is cisplatin – are loaded onto the stand after two staff have checked that the code and the patient are matched. First it is wrapped in a creosote-coloured bag to signal its danger to people who aren't already at risk of dying. Downstairs, my lime-green alter ego waits on a shelf, interleaved with others, a row of busts: the plastic philosophers: a limited edition. Each lunchtime, in the interlude between bags of chemicals, I travel down six floors in the lift and walk across the hospital to meet my plastic self and put him on. Like an Aztec sacrifice victim, I put on a new skin and become the god, am treated well, until the time comes. I sit in the middle of the bench, swivel and lie down, raise my knees for the leg support. The small hole for my mouth is located over the plastic wedge in my mouth. They ask if I am all right. I answer with my thumbs. The machine is set in motion. I pretend I am not there.

When it is over, they remove the mask and return it to the shelf where it may dream of a life that might have been, as webbing on a yacht, carving cool waters.

The chemotherapy lasts a week, but day after day the radiation continues. The nurses are endlessly patient as they help me to peel my shirt out of the neck wound. I lie down, insert the tongue gag, clamp down the mask, and let the machine run its computer-guided path, burning me from a string of finely calculated angles. One

January morning at 9am it is the thirtieth time, the last. I look at the smooth android face of the mask, sixty years younger than me, unscarred by the radiation. I put it under my arm to take home. I feel a grim companionship with it, like an old friend you'd like to kill.

When the radiation sessions finish, I see Dr Basak the registrar who has administered all the programmes and been on the end of my temper when I was in the pits, fighting to get medicine delivered and administered on time, to keep a handle on the pharmacy of over thirty drugs which I was using at one time or another, pacing the painkillers, treading on the edge of addiction. Two days later, I was back as an emergency admission, ten kilos lighter, my ribs like a poor man's fence, skin grey, eyelids like snail-skin. Dr Basak said, 'You looked so weak after the last radiotherapy session, I nearly took you straight to a ward.' I shrugged.

And what strength I have's my own, Which is most faint:

27

The Birth of Quetzalcóatl

Not far from Pachuca is the small town of Tula. The cathedral and my Colonial period hotel were the only stylish buildings in a town that has the slightly hopeless air of submission of some north Kent towns, bombed by the Luftwaffe and rebuilt with matching malice in the style of budget brutalism. But a thousand years ago Tula was a style centre, and a powerful religious hub, dominating the region before the rise of the Aztecs. Probably.

The head of the plumed serpent Quetzalcóatl bursts through the facade of the temple at Teotihuacán.

Tula's ancient culture was Toltec, and so admired by the Aztecs that the word came to mean 'of high craft'. Tula and its Toltec population were to the Aztecs what Rome was to Renaissance Europe, a model of wisdom and virtue they would set on a pedestal and imitate, but which in their own minds they could never surpass. Harvard historian Davíd Carrasco has even said: 'The Aztec sense of place depended on replicating the *time* of Quetzalcóatl's Tula, where agricultural abundance, artistic excellence, military prowess, and a harmony with the gods was achieved.' In short, for the Aztecs, Tula was their Golden Age.

The culture grew in the vacuum left by the fall of Teotihuacán, which would be my final destination before entering Mexico City. The Toltecs flourished for a period of two hundred years, beginning around 950 AD, and Tula is believed to have been its capital, although some scholars argue that the remnants of Teotihuacán were adopted and adapted for the purpose. Folk traditions say its founders had migrated here from the north-west, in a period when changes in climate undermined their nomadic pastoral life. Rustic and relatively uncultured when they arrived in central Mexico, they were sneered at as Chichimecs, literally people who came from the land of sucking: an unweaned people, wet behind the ears. Aztec history was written both to dramatise and transform their own Chichimec origins. They were desperate to bill themselves as the heirs to Tula's Toltecs.

The first Tula pottery dates from around 700 AD and is similar in style to ceramics from the north-west, confirming the folk traditions. But pottery from a century later, together with linguistic clues, reveals a second migration from a quite different direction, which would give rise to the key myth of the Spanish conquest: the return of a god from the east. The second wave came from a place at the very foot of the gulf of Mexico, called Nonoalco: which means 'Where Language Changes'. That is, they were not Nahuatl speakers. They brought with them a god named Quetzalcóatl. In the central highlands his home became Tula. In Tenochtitlán, Quetzalcóatl was a lesser god. The Aztecs would have been interested in the prospect of a god returning, but not paralysed; they were not expecting a messiah.

Tula became a large city of 60,000 souls, with a lesser population living in the surrounding countryside; this created a society in which the majority of its people were city dwellers. Britain did not pass that benchmark of urbanisation until 1851. When Tula was at its zenith, building the array of temples, plazas and administrative buildings I now overlooked, London was a small trading town of just 10,000 inhabitants. Across the street, the cathedral was silhouetted against a sky in which the sunset's glare was being swallowed by sheets of mine-dark clouds powering out of the west. Grackles gathered to raise bedlam in the trees until the palm fronds danced against the last of the sun.

In the morning, I walked through the empty streets, recently pedestrianised at vast expense, to the suspension footbridge over the river, where many planks, which locally cost a pound each, were rotten. The river mud at the edges of the dirty grey water sent up nauseous clouds of fetid air. Upstream, so much water is taken for industry and irrigation that the river no longer flushes clean.

I climbed to the old city, which straddles a step in the plateau above. After passing central Mexico's largest ball court, the first building I came across was a five-tiered step pyramid temple. The walls of the first step were twenty feet high, supporting a frieze carved from the limestone on which Tula stands, harsh visions of eagles, jaguars and coyotes gulping down human hearts. Not even the dead were spared; serpents devoured skeletons and skulls. The frieze was framed at its top and bottom by two borders of zigzag designs. A fretwork stone-and-stucco coxcomb ran along the top of the wall.

The temple was dedicated to Quetzalcóatl in his role as the Morning Star, or Venus, and it may be easier to stay with our name rather than the Aztec: *Tlahuizcalpantecuhtli*. At first, the Spanish thought the Native peoples worshipped a crowded pandemonium, but came to realize there were few gods, but they appeared in many manifestations. The planet Venus offers one example. The Aztecs knew it was the same object moving between the dusk and dawn sky, but regarded the evening star as Quetzalcóatl and the Morning Star as Xolotl, the dog-headed monster. This duality made him the god of twins, so women struggling to conceive would pray to him. Multiple births associated him with fertility. Fertility connected him with rain, and heavy rains followed the high winds of tropical storms, so he was also Ehécatl, the wind god. In all the cultures of the region, the planet Venus was male and dangerous. The Maya had known since the third century AD that its wanderings across the stars followed a 584-day cycle, and believed its passages between night and morning portended drought, danger and war.

Turning the corner, a view of the main plaza on the lower level began to emerge, 140 yards square. To my right stood a forest of columns, called the Burnt Palace, because of a layer of ash on top of the ruins. In here was found, in mint condition, a chac mool, a coffin-shaped mass of stone carved to show a figure reclining on his back, calves nearly upright, knees extended a touch forward at one end, and shoulders canted back at the same degree at the other. The thighs, stomach and chest form a platform; the head is turned at ninety degrees to stare at the onlooker like Manet's Olympia – an urbane gaze, redolent with superbia. Like the odalisque, something is suggested. With Olympia it is sex: with the chac mool, death. On this slab people died, stretched on their backs in an arc, their hands, feet and head forced down by priests, and their taut upper abdomen sliced open by an obsidian blade plunged below the sternum and ripped down. The priest's hand reached up for the heart to tear it out, and held it up steaming. The statue's worldly stare was the last glimpse of time for the victims. They met its unblinking eyes only once. Why did priests kill people?

In Mesoamerica the daily world was frightening. The weather is capricious. Climatic data record an average that seldom happens. Spring rains, needed to generate growth, might come late or not at all. If the autumn frosts began early the maize would not ripen, and all but the rich starved. Between 1450 and 1455 the harvest failed every year in central Mexico, and people sold their children to coastal peoples for a handful of maize. Hurricanes could devastate coastal provinces: in 2007 the winds of Hurricane Dean reached 240 miles per hour. Earthquakes bring mountains down on top of the towns, while volcanic eruptions may cover the land in burning ashes. There are toxic plants, snakes, reptiles frogs; pumas and jaguars may devour you. The main force of Mesoamerican religions is directed at this world, not the next, and its aim is to keep the sun alive and working. No religion, no sun: end of universe.

This fragility is all the more terrifying because the sun has already failed four times, bringing earlier universes to an end. Here is the story, told by anonymous Aztec authors writing after the conquest to explain their cosmography.

The first sun was called 4-Water, and it ended when everything was carried off by water and people became dragonfly larvae and fish.

The second sun was the jaguar sun, 4-Jaguar. Giants lived under this sun, wishing each other 'May you not fall.' For those who fell, fell for ever. At its end, the heavens collapsed, the sun stalled in the zenith, all grew dark and then the people were devoured by jaguars.

The sign of the third sun was 4-Rain. In this sun it rained fire and stones and lava boiled. The people were consumed by fire.

The sign of the fourth sun was 4-Wind: under this sun everything was carried off by the wind. Men were turned into monkeys, and afterwards the monkey-men lived scattered through the forests.

We now live under the fifth and final sun. Its symbol is 4-Motion. The ancients say that under this sun the earth will move, there will be famine, and we shall all perish.

If the sun is to be kept in its course, it must be fed by the most precious of things, the blood of men. The fifth sun was born on a hill north of Mexico City, and I was on my way there. At Teotihuacan the gods sacrificed themselves to bring life to earth again and we owe them the same in return.

In 2002 the Royal Academy ran an exhibition on the Aztecs, and one reviewer wondered whether bloodthirsty savages merited the name civilisation or indeed an exhibition. It seemed to surprise the reviewer that religion could involve pain and killing. Other writers have been quicker to catch on. Lucretius (99-55 BC) wrote in *The Nature of Things* that religion is invariably cruel and the quintessential image of religion is a parent sacrificing a child. He was thinking of Agamemnon sacrificing Iphigenia to obtain fair winds for his expedition to Troy. A Jew might think of Abraham's willingness to sacrifice Isaac, and a Christian of Jesus's self-sacrifice on a cross. The Christian scholar, Lactantius, tutor to the son of the Emperor Constantine, wrote: 'God cares about humans, and the sign of that care was anger. God was enraged at man; anger was the characteristic manifestation of his love. God wanted to smite him over and over again, with spectacular unrelenting violence.' We tend only to see the violence in other people's religions, particularly those of civilisations we perceive as less advanced than our own. Aztec religion, like the older forms from which it was descended, placed sacrifice centre-stage in its rituals, and not through love of death, but love of life, and a fear that death and chaos should win.

From Tula's plaza I could climb the Temple of Venus-Quetzalcóatl, up steps as steep as a ladder, which gave views to all horizons. My only company on the flat summit was a squad of warriors twenty feet high, atlantes, male statues as columns, which once held up the roof of a temple. The carving is still crisp and clear; they stand fresh and ready for action. Built in four sections, with heads larger than nature, their kit and regalia are carved in every detail because their dress tells you what they do, what they are. Hiding from the noon sun in a warrior's long shadow, I gulped water.

Quetzalcóatl is an old god. It is possible he was conceived in the ancient Olmec lands south-east of Veracruz where, around 900 BC, hands carved a feathered snake rearing up behind a shaman. From this heartland, the idea travelled east to the Maya, and north to Tula, and the Toltecs, then the Aztecs.

As a serpent, Quetzalcóatl can pass through the earth and bring upwards the revitalising powers and matter of the dead. His feathers connect him with the sky, where he collects clouds to bring the rain that makes the seeds grow. At Tula, and the Maya metropolis of Chichén Itzá, I saw columns decorated with a plumed serpent, each pillar signifying a bond linking earth to heaven. By bringing these worlds together he creates fertility and rebirth. He is, like the ancient gods of the Middle East and Egypt, from which Christianity descends, a vegetation god in the same traditions as the myths of the Holy Grail. The most striking sculpture of Quetzalcóatl as a plumed serpent is a piece little known in Mexico, because it is kept in the Vatican

260

Museum. Granular red stone is carved into a snake curled on itself to make a pillar, as rough and tactile as coarse Manilla cable. The head seems to know it is hated for its fierce ugliness, and squats in a nest in the top of the coil. It has a powerful air of something accustomed to being hunted, which has decided to be what its enemies wish.

Quetzalcóatl is a tireless traveller in the realm of the dead. He dared to go there in the timeless chaos following the destruction of the world at the end of the fourth sun, to demand the bones of a man and woman. He played music to madden the Lords of the Underworld who govern their realm in darkness and silence, and tricked the bones from them. Needing warm liquid to mix them back to life, he cut his own penis to draw the life-giving blood. Man and woman owe their existence to his daring and sacrifice.

In this age, humankind's birth is therefore associated with a power that moves between levels of the universe. To pass through solid earth, Quetzalcóatl fragmented himself continuously, which is why his feathers are quetzal plumes, whose iridescent patterns continuously disappear and reappear.

At some point an actual historical ruler of Tula called Nacxitl Topíltzin, who adopted the name Quetzalcóatl, became bound up with the god's biography. The story is confused. One codex describes Quetzalcóatl as if he were a god who ruled the city from a private shrine in a palace, where he taught the true religion of the divine duality which created the world, and he banned the sacrifice of humans. It was the Golden Age, when huge maize cobs were so abundant they were left on the ground, and cotton grew in colours and did not need to be dyed. The birds sang more beautiful melodies than today and chocolate tasted better. No one was poor and sorrow was banished.

Then brother gods appeared, devils like Tezcatlipoca, Smoking Mirror. They mocked Quetzalcóatl, telling him he must demand human sacrifice. When he refused, Tezcatlipoca appeared with a gift wrapped in a cloth. Quetzalcóatl held it in front of him and slipped off the cloth. It was a mirror. Because he was a god, he did not expect to see his own face, but he did, and was confronted by features weighed down by the years:

His eyelids were swollen, his eyes were sunken in their sockets
And his face was bloated! He hardly looked like a man!

He had aged, he had a destiny, and could be overthrown, and die. The wizard persuaded him to take pulque to cure his ageing. A second tempter brought rich clothing and ornaments to cover his ugliness. Quetzalcóatl succumbed to vanity and was delighted with his apparel. He threw off his austere life and arranged a feast, where he became drunk with his sister and they had sex. In the morning, he lamented, 'Ah, that I could remain here, but how can I? My body has become clay! I have only anxiety and the desires of a slave.' Wracked with remorse, he quit the city of Tula, which, as the devils had planned, fell into devil worship, human sacrifice and decline.

As in the religious myths of the Middle East and Egypt, the prosperity of the land and the country was bound up with that of the ruler, and when he became a broken god, the land fell with him, into decay and ruin. T. S. Eliot reworked the Middle Eastern versions of these myths and symbols when creating his poem *The Wasteland*.

Quetzalcóatl reached the coast and sailed east on a magical raft of serpents. A Mexican text written before the conquest laments:

Never can your name be lost, for your people will be weeping.
The turquoise house, the serpent house,
you built them here in Tula where you came to rule.

One day, in the year 1-Reed, he would return. In their calendar, this year only came around every 52 years. He would return over the sea so boundless its distant horizon merged with heaven. He would return for what was his. Quetzalcóatl was bearded and associated with the colours turquoise and black. Cortés would appear, bearded, dressed in black because it was Good Friday, in floating houses, craft never seen before, flying the pale blue flag of his family. He would arrive in 1519, the year known in the Aztec calendar as 1-Reed. Would Moctezuma be mindful of these symbols? He was religious and superstitious, and his mother came from Tula, home of the cult of Quetzalcóatl.

It is a compelling story, one which is repeated as a core truth of the Spanish conquest. It explains why a powerful military state was overcome by a small group of mercenaries. The Aztecs' own beliefs duped them into a fatal passivity. There is one problem with it. It's not true. As the historian Professor John Elliot (an expert on relations between Spain and the New World) remarked, no one could find evidence of any tradition expecting the return of Quetzalcóatl before the 1540s. Cortés never mentions the name in his letters to the king. It was a construction which surfaced a generation after the arrival of the Spanish, to try to reconcile, in Aztec circular time, how this alien and calamitous intrusion into their history could happen without precedent or warning.

The oldest fully developed versions of a plumed serpent are at Teotihuacán. If, for the Aztecs, the Toltecs were Romans, Teotihuacán was what Egypt had been to the Romans, a place of barely imaginable antiquity, almost outside time. When the Aztecs found mammoth bones near Teotihuacán, they knew they belonged to the giants who built the city.

It was around 200 BC that Teotihuacán took shape on a gently sloping plain twenty-five miles to the north-east of the future Tenochtitlán, and grew into a city of up to 50,000 inhabitants. By 100 AD its people, whose origins are uncertain, had completed the Pyramid of the Sun, with a footprint equal to that of the Great Pyramid of Cheops at Giza. Fifty years later they began an astoundingly innovative Temple to Quetzalcóatl. Teotihuacán reached its apogee between 350 and 650 AD, when the population peaked at nearly 200,000. It is worth pausing to think of this, as some Western scholars are now making free with stories of the supposed collapse of civilisations, to sell warnings about the present day. Which current Western power can boast of their country enjoying 300 years of dominance and prosperity?

Teotihuacán's fourth and final phase, beginning in 650 AD, lasted about a century, until its palaces and temples were trashed and burned in riotous fury. It was a time of droughts, and the number of child skeletons showing signs of malnutrition increased cruelly in this period. The destruction may record an uprising against religious and secular rulers who had failed them by losing the gods' good will. A weakened Teotihuacán may even have been toppled by invaders.

Teotihuacán was not an empire built on military power. Its art does not glamorise warriors, or promote the elites of warrior, priest and ruler, as art did in Tula and Tenochtitlán. Ironically it was becoming more militarised at the time of its fall. Its influence was through trade and art. In the phrase of historian Nigel Davies, its cultural fingerprints are all over the archaeological record, north, almost to the USA, and south to Guatemala and beyond. Unlike Tenochtitlán, with its system of forced tribute, Teotihuacán engaged in reciprocal trade: their orange pottery and obsidian are dispersed all over Mesoamerica.

I arrived at the Hotel Quinto Sol, the Fifth Sun, and two large cold rooms painted purple and mauve. Unlike all the others in the hotel, my balcony turned its back on the lawns and swimming pool and overlooked the car park and the highway slip-road into town. This was so absurd I spent the evening on the balcony, drinking beer and watching the desultory traffic enter and leave under a concrete gantry painted with words of welcome. A small lorry with some of its chassis lights broken parked opposite. The remaining bulbs made the pattern of the Plough in blowsy red giants.

In the morning, particoloured teardrops of hot-air balloons rose over one of the largest archaeological sites in Mexico. I took a taxi to the north of the remains and began to explore its eleven square miles. Although it is Mexico's most visited site, for over an hour I was alone. The balloons hung in the slow air, following a drift my skin could barely feel.

The dominant feature of the site is the straight line axis of the Avenue of the Dead. One-and-a-third miles are still lined with great public buildings, with the Pyramid of the Moon at its head, and it originally continued a farther two miles, but these were ripped up to build a road.

A year before, in hospital, I had smiled at the black humour of a city whose main thoroughfare was named as if it were a necropolis. Three centuries before Christ, the philosopher Epicurus wrote: 'Against other things it is possible to obtain security, but when it comes to death we human beings all live in an unwalled city.' Lying in bed, thinking I had only a few months to live, I did not clutch at religion, but I did think about it. Mankind has always sought a way of dealing with yearnings for there to be something more. The shallowest level of belief is the false scent of Fate among the randomness: everything happens for a reason. It's the last wreckage people are left to swim with when their faith sinks: there must be something, mustn't there? Committing to a religion is a comfort because it provides rules and structure. Atheism means coping with the resignation, even despair, of a universe without meaning and a messy world that shows no interest in our welfare.

The great historian of religion, the Romanian Mircea Eliade, argued that when humans begin to structure religion, nothing can happen without an orientation. 'If the world is to be lived in, it must be founded ... [.] The discovery or a projection of a fixed point, the centre, is equivalent to the creation of the world.' Laying out a city's core spaces is a message to gods and man. It both recognises divine order and repeats it as an act of worship and confirmation. It is part of the battle for good against evil. The untouched landscape is like the universe before creation, without form or meaning, where people cannot function. A grid of meaning must be laid down before we can begin to manage fear.

The Greeks did this, believing Zeus had revealed the centre of the world to be the omphalos stone at Delphi. A stone with similar meaning lay in Jerusalem beneath the Ark of the Covenant in the Temple. Teotihuacán's founders did the same.

Buildings fixing the world in place often align with the points of the compass, but, in Mesoamerican eyes, more important things went on in the heavens. Sometime after 100 AD, Teotihuacán's elite learned how to measure time and pin down the start and end of the solar year, so they would know the season of the rains was close, know the time to sow, and the time to reap. The discovery was so profound that the centre of Teotihuacán was torn down and rebuilt around the Avenue of the Dead, which is orientated at the curious angle of 15° 28´ east of north. Why, and was it their discovery, or were they told about it?

Monte Albán was an ancient city near modern Oaxaca (pronounced Wah-ha-kah). When I later headed east to begin my journey home, I made a detour to this hearth of the Zapotec people. By the early Christian era, Monte Albán was a city-state with well-developed social structures and a sophisticated calendar. Over Mesoamerica the traditional solar year of a little over 365 days was recognised and used. But in tandem with it, so the pair operated like intermeshed cogs, was a shorter ritual year comprising 13 months of 20 days. Once the two calendars were set running, each on Day One, it would be 52 years before the cogs returned to their starting position. The ritual calendar may be likened to an astrological clock running in parallel to the regular one. Your destiny and luck for life were strongly influenced by the day on which you were born, but like Calvinists discussing predetermination they argued over how much. The reason for calibrating the ritual calendar to run for 260 days has been uncertain, and speculation has included that it records the average time of human development in the womb, from the first missed period to birth. I approached Monte Albán with an academic paper under my arm which I believe provides the solution.

Foreground: the Observatory in the main plaza, Monte Alban.

It was a recondite article published by Damon Peeler and Marcus Winter in an occasional series published by Mexico's national heritage agencies. Looking for patterns in the size and orientation of ball courts, the authors noticed an error in the published measurements for those at Monte Albán. The large and small courts were listed as the same size. Peeler and Winter measured them again, and found the ratio of the length of the small court to the large was 0.71355, which does not at first seem too exciting, but this precise figure is coded into other features, including the most curious building on the site: The Observatory. Why?

To reach Monte Albán from Oaxaca, I had hoped to hire one of the local novelties, a three-wheel motor taxi; quirky, and fun, they also undercut car taxis. There were none about, so I climbed into another Nissan Tsuru, with a driver who, as we bounced up the hairpins, left me exceptionally well-informed about the high death rates among moto-taxi passengers.

The city occupies a shallow saddle rising a little at each end. The Zapotecans levelled the centre by hand, creating a space like an elongated football pitch over three hundred yards long, with pyramids rising on the mounds at either end, and grand buildings framing the central plaza. The faint drone of insects hung low over the desiccated yellow grass. Steel-blue martins with white rumps scissored the air.

A cluster of buildings in the centre follows the rectangular shape of the master plan, but between them and the southern pyramid mound is the maverick. When the sun stands directly above it, terrible scenes spring into three dimensions on its sides, bas reliefs of conquest, dead eyes swinging in decapitated heads. The Observatory, unlike any of its grander companions, is a pentagon shaped like an arrowhead, and it points north-east, an insolent 45° out of alignment with the grid-iron. Many astronomical alignments have been proposed to explain it, including the rising of the first magnitude star Capella. Whatever the explanation, if you extend the lines of the arrowhead's blades and base to form an isosceles triangle, the ratio of the sides to the base is also that odd decimal 0.71355.

When the ratio is expressed as a fraction, the meaning becomes clear. It is 260 divided by 365: the number of days in a ritual calendar year, divided by the days in a solar year. The secret of why all Mesoamerica chose 260 days as the length of the ritual year lies here at Monte Albán. The two astronomical events which nailed the fixed point of their solar calendar were the zenith and nadir passages of the sun. The first is the arrival of the sun precisely overhead at noon. The second is its unobservable opposite, the time when calculation tells you the sun is precisely beneath your feet at midnight. The Zapotecans observed where on the horizon the sun

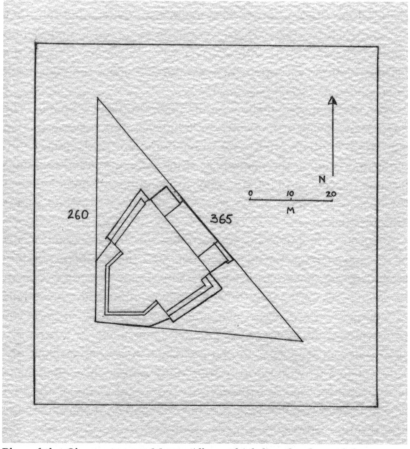

Plan of the Observatory at Monte Alban which has the days of the calendar year and astronomical calendar coded into the architecture.

rose on those days. The angle between those points changes with the observer's latitude: at Monte Albán it is 35° 28´. If you draw a right-angled triangle with a smallest angle of 35° 28´, the ratio between the two sides which join at the right angle is 260:365. The Mesoamerican calendar originated on this hill, and with it the astrological religion adopted throughout the middle Americas. The famous Mayan calendar is not their original work, but adapted from that of Monte Albán.

The quality of their observations was superb, even by modern standards. The Maya calendar had, by 700 AD, calculated a year as 365.24200 days. In the twenty-first century it is measured at 365.24219, just 16 seconds longer. The Julian calendar we use in everyday daily life is more than eleven minutes less accurate than the Maya.

There is a human trace of these anonymous scholars. The article's authors, Peeler and Winter, wondered whether there had been contact between Monte Albán and Teotihuacán. Had the Zapotecs taken their knowledge north to Teotihuacán? Peeler and Winter walked west from the Avenue of the Dead and used the location of the extant temples as markers for the zenith and nadir sunrises at this new latitude. Nearly three miles away they found the point where an observer could line up the Pyramid of the Moon and the Temple of the Plumed Serpents to watch the zenith and the nadir sunrises. They dug and found nothing. After exhausting the various combinations of temple alignments, one of the pair made a suggestion. What if the visiting Zapotec maguses did not know their sacred alignment varied with latitude, and they had repeated the calibration used at Monte Albán? They measured out the Monte Albán formula, and redrew. The angle between was exactly 35° 28´. They dug and found peculiar clay frog figurines, and clay bowls with a distinctive looping line inscribed in the base. Only one culture made them: the Zapotec. Here, within the great city, was an enclave of around 800 immigrants, the foreigner astronomers who made sense of the city for their hosts. On this spot, they made the observations, and set up an altar. Even when the temples were enlarged, and moved a little to one side, the Zapotecs set up a new altar at the new intersection of sight-lines, repeating the error of latitude, but providing the archaeologists with a double confirmation of their thesis. To make the geometry work, the Avenue of the Dead had to be offset to 15° 28´ east of north, the exact orientation we see today.

Other numbers embedded in the architecture and layout of Monte Albán and Teotihuacán include 584, the number of days the planet Venus takes to complete a cycle of movement across the background of the stars. The ratio of the distance from the Temple of the Plumed Serpent to the two pyramids is 365 to 584. Remarkably, if the 584-day cycle of Venus is set running on the same day as the other calendars, it coincides with them again after precisely two 52-year grand cycles. These sacred numbers underpinned the natural universe, and were brought down from the heavens, like Newton's Laws uniting celestial and terrestrial gravity, to shape humanity's footprint on the earth.

I climbed the Pyramid of the Moon and stood on a salient from the facade which looks down the Avenue of the Dead. It was like a runway, the only features breaking its line being low flights of steps hidden from my view at this range. On the left-hand side was the Temple of the Sun. I took stock before beginning to climb it. Despite the sprawling width of the long straight avenue, the pyramid's bulk was overpowering. It is the world's third largest pyramid, behind Cholula and Cheops. Despite erosion and some demolition by the Spanish, it is still 200 feet high and each side of the base measures 660 feet. This was the centre of the works rebuilt to inscribe the city with their new knowledge of time. So far, 260 victims of human sacrifice have been found, their blood dedicating the new stones to the sacred. Its modern name was given by the Aztecs. In Nahuatl, Teotihuacán means The Place Where Gods are Born. Alignments and carvings tell us something about the city, but they speak selectively, and are sometimes silent. We do not know its own inhabitants' name for it. We do not even know what language its citizens spoke.

The heat built as midday approached. At the summit came a welcome breeze, but the land below baked, and each view disappeared into the roiling haze.

The earliest and most elaborate Plumed Serpents at Teotihuacan are those on the Old Temple of Quetzalcóatl around 200 AD. All four facades were once decorated with Plumed Serpents swimming in a sea replete with precious conch shells. Another important characteristic in Quetzalcóatl's extensive duties was to send, to each of the earth's cardinal points, its cargo of destiny, mined in the underworld. In this role he is regarded as the creator of the calendar, creating temporal order.

In the sloping panels of the Temple of Quetzalcóatl, towards the south of the Avenue of the Dead, the undulating serpent emerges from the earth, carrying on its body a headdress featuring the emblem of the earth monster, the first sign of the calendar, and an indicator of the beginning of organised time. With the end of mythic time; our modern lives begin. In the vertical sections of the facade each head emerges from a ring of feathers like a petal necklace. The effect is startling, as if the snake monsters had burst through the surface of a stone sea to glare at you.

In the rooms of a small temple attached to the palace were fine wall paintings with a vivid green parrot still ruffling the plaster, stooping to spill water from its yellow beak onto the flowers beneath, germinating crops with rain, bringing the new spring: an allegory for rule and a ruler's responsibilities, identifying the health of the ruler with the state of the nation. To exercise this function using their most modern science, Teotihuacan's own heart was torn out and rebuilt. Around the palace courtyards, more flowers, and conch shells ornamented with feathers, decorated the pillars. Beauty lived side by side with the frozen stone snarl of the Plumed Serpent, and the groans and screams of sacrifice.

As I walked back to the hotel down the long avenue, I stepped around conical heaps of earth from which tiny paths snaked out through the grass, the ground worn bald for the first two yards by brown ants returning from foraging, challenged by guards, disappearing into the nest's single black eye.

6. Cortes's Approach to Tenochtitlán in 1519 and Subsequent Flight

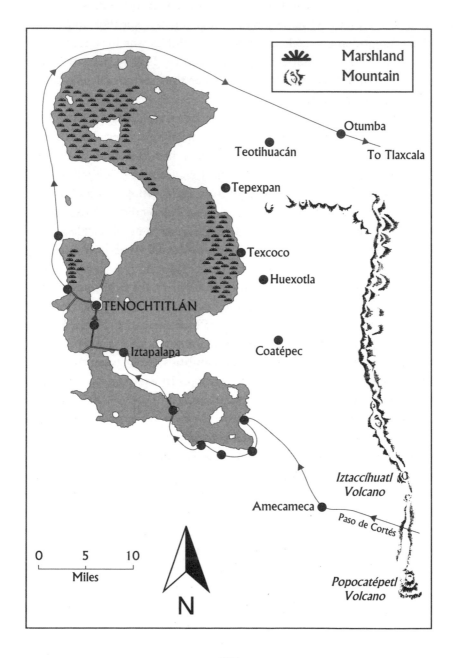

28

Things Never Dreamed of Before

Who could conquer Tenochtitlán?
Who could shake the foundation of heaven?
AZTEC SONG FRAGMENT

So far, like Cortés, we have seen Moctezuma only through the words of others: some of them enemies, some servants, but none of them neutral. His behaviour, to a twenty-first century European observer, appears mystifying, but we should not conclude that he himself was confused. The informants of Sahagún who describe his apparently erratic policy to the approaching Spanish, were not ministers, nobility or high priests, they were the civil servants and scholars who spoke later, knowing Moctezuma had lost the war: wise after the event. None of them had ever enjoyed the ear of the palace elite.

The supreme ruler of Tenochtitlán was called the *tlatoani,* or great speaker. He was chosen from among the elite; and while bloodlines mattered, primogeniture was not followed. Each *tlatoani* was a descendant of the first one, but on his death the elite would choose the next blood-relative on merit. In theory any noble could be chosen, but in practice only the previous ruler's son, brother, grandson or nephew was ever elected. Moctezuma's father Axayácatl had been *tlatoani*, and Axayácatl's two brothers ruled for two decades before Moctezuma was elected in 1502. He was then aged about thirty-four. Cortés believed in knowing his enemy, the better to defeat him. Along his route he had asked local rulers what kind of man Moctezuma was.

Physically he was 'lean, with a fine straight figure'. In another description he is a 'mature man, not corpulent, but slim and slender, on the thin side'.

274

Two sides to his character soon emerge. He was a successful general, and the war which, by custom, he fought on becoming emperor was considered one of the most effective ever. He subdued the rebellious coastal state of Teuctépec, and captured 2300 warriors, who were taken to Tenochtitlán and sacrificed at the Templo Mayor.

He was a conservative about life at the court, and was prickly about status. The modest degree of meritocracy recently introduced for court appointments was abolished, and he made it a policy that the king must never appear in public unless the occasion was extremely important. His new sumptuary laws forbade non-nobles to wear gold, cotton or shoes, and banned anyone from looking him in the face. Cortés, in statements designed to be reassuring, had insisted he must come to Tenochtitlán himself, because he wanted to look Moctezuma in the face and talk to him. Unwittingly this must have been read as a threat to the ruler's dignity.

Moctezuma was religious, and often made the twenty-five-mile pilgrimage on foot to Teotihuacán to meditate among the ruins, like a Dark Ages Saxon ruminating among the temples of Roman Bath. It was a place of ancient wisdom, where inspiration might come. He went there at least once while pondering what should be done about Cortés.

On the road the Spanish heard that an ambassador of Moctezuma was travelling to meet them. The stakes were rising. A palanquin appeared, sparkling in silver and gold, gorgeous with green feathers. From it stepped Cacama, a nephew of Moctezuma. He did not trust the Spanish one little bit, but he had advised Moctezuma to welcome them, as any other course would look like weakness. Moctezuma's brother Cuitláhuac offered contrary advice: 'I pray to our gods that you will not let the strangers into your house. They will cast you out of it and overthrow your rule, and when you try to recover what you have lost, it will be too late.' It is unfair to condemn Moctezuma as a ditherer; at this point, there was no consensus about what to do.

Cacama greeted Cortés: 'We have come to place ourselves at your service and to give you all that you may need for yourself and your companions.' Moctezuma, was, unfortunately, ill, and apologised for not coming in person. Cacama escorted the Spanish to the small town of Mixquic, on the southern shore of the interlinked lakes around Tenochtitlán. There they saw a city of great towers built out into the water like a New World Venice, which the officer Andrés de Tapia described as 'the most beautiful city which we had until then seen'. From it extended another wonder, a stone causeway crossing northwards across an arm of the lake, to manage the waters and keep undrinkable brackish water away from the sweet.

This area, around Xochimilco, which means 'place of the field of flowers', is now the only place to see a survival of the inventive agriculture which kept the citizens of the city of Tenochtitlán fed. The metro leaves Mexico City's main square and flies on an elevated section south through respectable but uninspired suburbs.

It terminates at a small market where I boarded a two-carriage tram that ran at street level, chugging in and out of the traffic, leaving behind the modern city centre, past the towering Estadio Aztec football ground, and into the suburbs. Although seats were vacant, a skinny girl with the look of Amy Winehouse about her, piled hair and a pierced septum, stood at the head of the carriage, where she would be seen. Listening to her ear buds, she sucked the round head of a red lollipop, staring expressionlessly into space. Tattooed on the top of her left breast was a swallow in flight.

A walk through narrow streets ended in a canal-side that looked for a second like a part of old China. Gaudy wooden barges touted for business from Mexico City day-trippers. I hired one and, given my arms were still more like a ballerina's than a stevedore's, a man to punt it. It was Sunday and the canals were choked with boats full of families unpacking picnics and cool-boxes of beer. The low banks gave views over flat market gardens, where for 700 years fruit and vegetables have been grown to fill the city's maw. There were fields of yarrows and a Mexican vegetable called *choyote*, the size and shape of a sweet pepper, but with a bristly skin. Raw they are tough; cooked, they look and taste as if they have been through a heavy programme in the washing machine. Thickets of bamboo had been left, and an occasional Peruvian pepper tree, useless as timber, their rough bark weeping sap.

The Aztecs arrived in central Mexico from the increasingly arid north. Legend preserved the name of their far-off home as Aztlan, which means place of the heron, but perhaps, with its images of fish-rich waters, coined to conjure an idyll, like Avalon, the Isle of Apples, in Arthurian myth. They were latecomers in the waves of migration to softer lands, and found all the good land already occupied; the people of Xochimilco were themselves descendants of earlier migrants. The Aztecs settled briefly, but were driven on by the war god Huitzilopochtli. He told them they were destined to found a homeland based on conquest; only this would fulfil their destiny. They arrived at Chapultépec, a steep hill on the western shore of the lake, now a green lung west of the city centre. The land was held by another group from the early migrations, the Tepanec. When the Aztecs refused to accept the Tepanec as overlords, they were driven out. They begged to stay at the place Cortés went next: Culhuacan, whose people contemptuously showed them the worst land left: the marshes. The beggars could not be choosers. They began to catch birds and reptiles while they reclaimed land to plant crops. Snakes and lizards, even larvae from the lake, went into the pot. One of the delicacies they enjoyed was yellow axolotl, the strange amphibian with external gills. Axolotls – the word is pure Nahuatl – were only ever found in two sites, both on Xochimilco's waterways. Surveys conducted over the last fifteen years began finding 6000 animals per square kilometre, falling to 100 five years ago, and none in 2013, although workers searched for four months. We passed an Axolotl Education and Support Centre. It may never work with wild animals again. The Mexica served the Culhuacan state as mercenaries. The Culhua were of Toltec origin, and the Aztecs saw an opportunity to associate themselves with gentry. They asked for the daughter of Culhuacan's king in marriage. He agreed, and she was brought to their marshes with great ceremony. From then on, the Mexica would also talk of themselves as Culhua, hence the coastal Natives crying 'Colua!', and pointing inland.

The King of Culhuacan had not understood what kind of marriage

277

was being proposed. His daughter was married to the Aztec god, Huitzilopochtli, in a ceremony which climaxed in her being sacrificially killed, and then flayed, before the priest danced in her skin. Her father was then invited to see his daughter in her new and honoured state. War was declared, the Aztecs were driven into marshes on the north west shore, where, on an island in the lake, they saw the sign long promised by Huitzilopochtli, an eagle seizing a serpent in its beak, claws grasping the paddle leaves of a prickly pear richly hung with scarlet fruit the shape of human hearts. Here they rebuilt Aztlan, their Avalon. A wooden temple thanked Huitzilopochtli. This would grow into the Templo Mayor, which dominated the growing city. They were subject to another Tepanec city, Azcapotzalco, to whom they paid military service, fighting their wars. They dredged channels through the lake shallows and piled up the rich silt behind hurdles set in the shore, and grew crops on the reclaimed land they called *chinampas*. My barge-sized punt, called a *trajinera*, took me through the last relics of this system. With no pack animals to move goods to market, the city relied on human porterage. Taking produce across the lake in canoes, paddling into the heart of the city, solved their haulage problems. Today, under the willow trees and pollards with ridged grey bark, I was besieged by punts selling toy guitars, toffee apples, and roasted maize. Everyone called everyone else *joven*, young 'un. Whole barges were filled beam-to-beam with mariachi bands, complete with marimbas and xylophones. One featured a singer who was an eye-catching Frida Kahlo lookalike.

The difficulties of the lakeshore site stimulated enterprise, and by 1375, as the mists of mythologised tradition burned away, and events entered datable history, the Aztecs were civilised enough to once again ask the king of Culhuacan for a daughter in marriage. The resultant son, Acamapichtli became the first Aztec king. From different marriages, the heirs of Acamapichtli became emperors of Tenochtitlán, and Kings of Texcoco, the poet-kings with whom Cortés would forge the alliance that brought down the Aztec empire.

On 8 November 1519, the Spanish awoke in the town of Iztapalapa, in houses whose masonry Cortés considered to be 'as good as the best in Spain'. Around the houses, flower beds and vegetable gardens intermingled with orchards and fishponds. As they set out, Malinche was close by his side. She would have cut a petite figure, the average height of women in Native societies was four feet ten inches, but as a slave she had performed physical work so she would not have been frail. Her Spanish had improved to the point where she no longer needed help to translate directly from Nahuatl. She would therefore be centre stage in all the negotiations that followed, and although there were times where enemies in both wings wished to undermine her, no one questioned her fidelity or loyalty to the various men she was traded to, as a chattel or wife. Reading Cortés, you see he knew her value to him, but not her worth. He refers to his translator very briefly, but did not put her name to paper until 1526, five years after the fall of Tenochtitlán. Díaz knew: '[w]ithout Doña Marina we could not have understood the language of New Spain and Mexico.'

Cortés's journey had become eerie. Feeling unable to repel these aggressive ambassadors, Moctezuma signalled his displeasure by ordering everyone living in the countryside along the route to Tenochtitlán to stay indoors. As they marched the deserted roads, tension grew. Seeing the layout of the lake cities, the Spanish became concerned that if Moctezuma chose, such causeways could be severed, isolating them. Their lodgings at Iztapalapa were close to the Hill of the Star, where every fifty-two years, as the clocks of the two calendars came together, and time stuttered, the dangerous cluster of three days outside time arrived before the next cycle began. The priests stood waiting in an intense darkness, every fire and light in the empire having been extinguished. Priests and nobles watched for Alcyon, the brightest star in the Pleiades, to reach the meridian line, to be assured that the universe had not stalled, and was ready to begin breathing again; the priests would then cut the heart from a living victim and raise it steaming to the sky. A fire would be lit in the chest cavity, and distributed to key points in the city, from where every householder would come with a rush light to carry the new sacred fire back to their hearth. Moctezuma had performed this rite in 1507.

The Spanish had brought their own time. They arrived on the shores of Mexico and claimed it not just in the name of the Emperor Charles V, but in the name of Jesus Christ. The past was swept away, and history began again, and Mexica time would be measured from the date of his birth. The time the Aztecs knew was ending: the declarations had been made, and now Cortés arrived at the head of an army to enforce it. All the events which the Aztecs credited as being crucial to their world view, had happened in mythic time, in the period outwith time before the gods created man; it was a higher reality. Their religious ceremonies were vehicles to take them back to that time. Now the Christians arrived, with a god who had appeared on earth. This was the first time in the history of any religion that a god had been appeared in historic time.

It was almost nine months since they had sailed from Cuba. Now at last they could see the myth made real, the land of gold which was always over the next hill, the city too powerful to fall, the emperor who ruled all the world known to him. Pyramid temples, whose walls of whitewashed stucco rose blindingly above the one and two-storey palaces of the centre, were reflected in the lake across five miles of glassy indolence. When they looked at their day's march, they saw that a second dyke ran ten miles north, protecting Tenochtitlán from flooding. Bernal Díaz's pages describing his first sight of Tenochtitlán are the most famous lines in all the accounts of conquest in the New World. It was, like the rest of his account, written in old age. Although he is often patronised for his lack of style, he has a greater gift. He is able to look back on himself as a young man and recapture the sense of wonder, and the flush of optimism in his warm veins, and write of it with the wisdom of maturity. He reins in his later disillusion to recount his memories of events which he knew at the time would shape his life, and which he now knows, looking down the perspective of time, would shape two continents. The Spanish who stood looking across the waters that autumn day in 1519 were mostly born between 1480 and 1500, and comprised the first generation of common people to read for pleasure. Chivalric tales were popular, often old ballads and books as fanciful as Arthurian legends, unreal in detail, but potent with symbols and meaning. The most successful book of their era was *Amadís of Gaul*, published in 1508, but much older. It was famous enough to be parodied by Cervantes in *Don Quixote*. It was *Amadís* which came to old Díaz's mind when he reached for legends, to help him describe what he now saw arrayed before him on the earth.

'And when we saw all those cities and villages built in the water, and other great towns on dry land, and that straight and level causeway leading to Mexico, we were astounded. These great towns and temples and buildings rising from the water, all made of stone, seemed like an enchanted vision from the tale of *Amadís*. Indeed some of our soldiers asked whether it was not all a dream. It is not surprising therefore that I should write in this vein. It was all so wonderful that I do not know how to describe this first glimpse of things never heard of, seen or dreamed of before. And when we entered the city of Iztapalapa, the sight of the palaces in which they lodged us! They were very spacious and well-built, of magnificent stone, cedar wood, and the wood of other sweet-smelling trees, with great rooms and courts, which were a wonderful sight, and all covered with awnings of woven cotton.

'When we had taken a good look at all this, we went to the orchard and garden, which was a marvellous place both to see and walk in. I was never tired of noticing the diversity of trees and the various scents given off by each, and the paths choked with roses and other flowers, and the many local fruit trees and rose-bushes, and the pond of fresh water. Another remarkable thing was that large canoes could come into the garden from the lake, through a channel they had cut. Everything was shining with lime, and decorated with different kinds of stonework and paintings which were a marvel to gaze on. Then there were birds of many breeds and varieties which came to the pond. I say again that I stood looking at it and thought that no land like it would ever be discovered in the whole world, because at that time Peru was neither known nor thought of. But today, all that I then saw is overthrown and destroyed; nothing is left standing.'

Now, the lake itself is gone, filled in, built on.

Leaving Iztapalapa, the Spanish ventured on to the causeway. It was eight yards wide, but so many ordinary Aztec people had crowded on to it to watch the strangers pass that the Spanish could barely move. Again and again, their allies had warned the Spanish that the city was a trap from which they would never escape. Yet they marched on. Díaz marvelled at his own youthful courage. 'Let the interested reader consider whether there is not much to ponder in this narrative of mine. What men in the world have shown such daring?' The resplendent Lords of Texcoco, Tacuba and Coyoacan, all nephews of Moctezuma, greeted Cortés, then went on ahead to escort Moctezuma to him. The Argentine scholar Jorge-Luis Borges, a master of story, has said there are only really two stories: a man leaves town, and a stranger enters town. They are the bookends of the same story. This is the moment when the second part begins.

Moctezuma and Cortés met on the causeway at a place called Huitzillan, now on the modern Avenida San Antonio Abad, at the metro station of the same name: an avenue as straight as an arrow because it follows the line of the Aztec causeway. The Native account compiled by Sahagún has a primary Nahuatl text, sometimes more candid, and a secondary Spanish version of the material. For the key exchanges between Cortés and Moctezuma I have used the Nahuatl version because they understood how it looked from the other side. It describes Moctezuma dressing in finery and ensuring the correct display of flowers and gifts were ready for a state occasion. Moctezuma would have used *tecpillahtolli,* the highly formal speech of court. Before Cortés arrived, Malinche had not mixed in this high-flown company, with its diplomatic corps dialect. As a woman, her mere presence would add tension to the situation, as she would be speaking in a forum where no women ever spoke. She is pictured in codices staring him in the eye as she speaks. This would have been doubly insolent. We do not know how well she coped with the flowery speech, in which it was polite not to say what you meant, or you might even say the contrary, in a kind of irony of manners. A repetitive style was considered the only proper way to communicate formally. Aztec poetry used the same convention.

Moctezuma arrived with a retinue of two hundred lords, and

descended to the ground under a canopy of green feathers the lords held aloft for him. They swept his path and laid down cloaks for him to walk on. Sahagún's Native version says: 'Moctezuma himself put a necklace of gold and fine stones on Captain Don Hernán Cortés, and gave flowers and garlands to all the other captains. Don Hernán Cortés asked Moctezuma, "Is it not you?" Moctezuma said, "Yes, it is me." At which he stood up straight, he stood up with their faces meeting. He bowed down deeply to Cortés. Moctezuma said "O our lord, be doubly welcomed on your arrival in this land; you have come to satisfy your curiosity, about your estate in Mexico, you have come to sit on your seat of authority, which I have kept for a while for you, where I have been in charge for you.

"For I am not just dreaming, not just sleepwalking, not just seeing it in my sleep. I am not just dreaming that I have seen you, have looked upon your face. For a time I have been concerned, looking towards the mysterious place from which you have come, among clouds and mist. The rulers said on departing that you would come in order to acquaint yourself with your estate, and sit upon your seat of authority. And now it has come true, you have come. Be doubly welcomed, enter the land, go to enjoy your palace; rest your body. May our Lords be arrived in the land."'

Cortés thanked him in what the Nahuatl scribes called 'his babbling tongue', and said, 'Let Moctezuma be at ease, let him not be afraid, for we greatly esteem him. Now we are truly satisfied to see him in person and hear him, for until now we have greatly desired to see him and look upon his face. Bit by bit he will hear what we have to say.'

The Aztecs observed wonderful details: 'Thereupon the Spaniards took Moctezuma by the hand. They came along with him, stroking his hair to show their good feeling. And the Spaniards looked at him, each of them giving him a close look. They would start along walking, then mount, then dismount again in order to see him.' With these strangers, great meanings may reside in the smallest thing. In his second letter to Charles V, Cortés wrote an account of two welcome speeches made by Moctezuma. Professor John Elliott at Oxford describes them as 'founded more on fantasy than facts'.

Academic verdicts do not come much more damning than that. In his account, Cortés begins plausibly, as good liars do, and records his own gaffe: attempting to embrace Moctezuma in brotherly fashion, a breach of etiquette forestalled by the swift intervention of Aztec nobles. Cortés's Moctezuma confesses: 'For a long time we have known from the writings of our ancestors that neither I nor any of those who dwell in this land, are natives of it, but foreigners who come from very distant parts.' It continues elaborately; describing a chieftain who brought them here, then departed, promising to return and rule by right. 'Because of the place from which you come, and the things you tell us of the great king who sent you here' – in fact Cortés has barely spoken at this stage – 'we believe and are certain that he is our natural lord, especially as you say he has known of us for some time. So be assured that we shall obey you and hold you as our Lord in place of that great sovereign of which you speak. In all the land that lies in my domain, you may command as you will, for you shall be obeyed and all that we own is for you to dispose of as you choose. You are in your own country and your own house.'

After this first meeting, Cortés pretends that Moctezuma, who like the US President, is both head of state and commander-in-chief, has abdicated and handed both offices to a foreigner from an unknown land. Cortés wrote this letter nearly a year later in October 1520, when he was regrouping, and conquest was still highly uncertain. The great political value of his fiction is that sovereignty has been conceded. Any resistance which follows is therefore not the lawful protection of a sovereign state, but rebellion and treason.

Useful as this is, Cortés seems too much of a showman to know when to stop. Earlier he has given Moctezuma the words: 'We give thanks to our gods that our time which was long expected has come to pass.' The quote eerily echoes the passage in the gospel of St Luke 2:29-32, known as the *nunc dimittis*, which is the story of the old man Simeon, who has been told he will live until he sees the Christ. When Jesus was brought to the temple for circumcision, Simeon picked him up, and recognising the Christ, asked to be released from life, with the words, 'Lord, now lettest thy servant depart in peace, according to thy word.' Cortés is using a literary model from the Bible to portray himself as Christ and Moctezuma as Simeon. Moctezuma continues, in Cortés's script, to point out he is human and does not live in halls of gold. 'Then he raised his clothes and showed me his body, saying as he grasped his arms and trunk with his hands, "See that I am of flesh and blood like you and all other men, and I am mortal and substantial."' This mirrors the description of Jesus's resurrection in Luke 24:39, when he appears to his disciples, in Jerusalem: 'A spirit hath not flesh and bones as you see me have.'

None of this appears in Díaz or the Native version, and Cortés's own version clearly acknowledges Moctezuma saying he is made 'of flesh and blood *like you* and all other men'. This is not something Moctezuma would say to a being he thought was a returning god. The massacre committed by Cortés at Cholula, a holy city dedicated to Quetzalcóatl, had dispelled any lingering notion that Cortés was a deity.

The versions of Cortés and the Aztecs agree that Cortés closed with soothing words. 'Tell Moctezuma that we are his friends. There is nothing to fear, we love him well and our hearts are content.'

They marched into the heart of the famed metropolis, escorted by dignitaries as exotic as figures from Babylon. The dust towered into the air, iridescent plumes danced on bodies whose copper skins were lit by the glister of gold, the sheen of silver. Díaz was still in a rhapsody fifty years later. 'It was a wonderful sight and, as I write, it all comes before my eyes as if it had happened only yesterday.' Round-eyed locals crowded onto flat roofs or brought their canoes to the edge of the causeway to gawp at the strangers. As the causeway reached the main island, the Spanish would have seen warrens of narrow streets running away on either side. Those who were mounted may have glimpsed the tops of the temples across the low roofs. In time they would see the street ahead shining brighter, promising open spaces. Then they passed into the civic centre, and the plazas and palaces were spread before them. Nearly all the Spanish came from villages and small towns. Most would have seen Seville, if only as they left Spain. Those who had years of service as soldiers knew Italy and its Renaissance cities, and one man had gazed on Constantinople. They told their companions they had seen nothing to equal this.

Aztec priests would have considered what the stars had in store. The day was 1-Wind, a day signifying Quetzalcóatl's role as Ehecatl, the wind-god. Astrologically, it was a day of special opportunity for thieves.

29

Time Falters

The following signs were witnessed, warning Moctezuma of the tragedy to come:

1. The night sky lit up from midnight to dawn.
2. The Temple of Huitzilopotchli burnt to the ground; water brought to extinguish it only fanned the flames.
3. Xiuhtecuhtli's temple was struck by lightning though there was no thunder.
4. A three-headed comet crossed the sky from west to east.
5. On a day without wind, the surface of the lake boiled, demolishing houses.
6. A female voice trailed the streets at night wailing, 'My children, we must flee the city.'
7. A crane was found with a mirror, pierced in the middle, on the crown of its head.
8. Men, including one with two heads, were found wandering the city; they vanished when Moctezuma looked at them.

One could start to look for rationalisations for the individual prophecies. The comet arrived several years before the Spanish, but has been made to do duty as prophecy. The stucco on the temple would be rich in nitrates from the lake, which, once they reach a certain temperature, create a fire so hot, water only fuels it. In a volcanically active region, lakes can be agitated by seismic movements. But there is a more general explanation: these prophecies were a later attempt to rationalise the unforeseen catastrophe which had destroyed not just Tenochtitlán, but their entire notion of time and history.

The eight prophecies appear in only one Native account, that collected by Sahagún, and Nahuatl expert James Lockhart believes the section recounting the prophecies contrasts starkly in style with the rest of the document, and it was filleted in long after the conquest. Furthermore, the number eight was potent in Nahuatl thought. It was used the way Christians would find groups of three to match the trinity, or twelve to parallel the apostles. It is prophecy in retrospect. Cultural theorist Tzvetan Todorov has written: 'The whole history of the Aztecs, as it is narrated in their own chronicles, consists of anterior prophecies, as if the event could not occur unless it has been previously announced.' With these prophecies we see the evidence.

The Spanish had entered the heart of empire with tension high on both sides, but they were now lodged peaceably in a palace which had belonged to Moctezuma's father, Axayácatl. So what disaster was being foretold?

My hotel was in a tranquil suburb a few minutes' walk from Chapultépec, where the Mexica had first arrived on the lake shore, and seen the promised sign: the eagle alighted on a prickly pear. I took the Metro to the centre. Women bundled in layers of clothing against the chill of the early mornings sweated up and down hot, stuffy trains selling snacks, or cigarette lighters, pens, religious tracts, school books and whatever else could be bought cheaply and carried lightly. Trade was steady. Buskers came and went; few people gave. A young man came on and stood at my shoulder. At the height of my ears, his backpack was splitting apart under the weight of a ghetto-blaster playing the CD he was selling. The passenger opposite me winced as the brass instruments came in for the chorus, 'Listen! Each in his favourite key!' He opened his bag and unfolded panels of cloth cut for a suit. 'I embroider them by machine and now I am taking them to the tailor who sews them together. They are for a mariachi group: white for the boys, black for men.'

Because this trip had twice been postponed by illness, I had read about Tenochtitlán for seven years. It was hard to believe I could now just walk out and see it. Five minutes later, heart pounding with excitement, I was striding up the steps to emerge in blinding sunlight onto one of the largest city squares on earth. In front of me was the cliff-like facade of the Metropolitan Cathedral. Under my feet, wherever I walked this morning, was the heart of Tenochtitlán.

The Zócalo is the original of all the squares with the same name across Mexico. Only in Mexico does it mean square. The reason is that in the nineteenth century this plaza was to be restyled around a new monument to the Revolution. A great plinth was built. The monument was never created. Popular irony named the square Zócalo, which means plinth.

A Christmas funfair filled it, including toboggan rides down an artificial snow slope. It triggered a memory of spending time at Christmas fifteen years before in the house of the mayor of the world's most southerly town, Puerto Williams on the Beagle Channel in Tierra del Fuego. In the warm kitchen, we listened to the storm outside and watched the television news where children in Mexico City were looking up open-mouthed to catch snowflakes on their tongues. I stood there in hot sun, but I could feel the same starry tingle.

It was hard to orientate myself properly because the only constants between the two cities are the lines of the Aztec causeways that became the principal avenues of the Spanish city. The new city overlies the rest of the old as carelessly as a frank on a postage stamp. I faced the cathedral, looking north. The current building was begun in the 1570s, enveloping the church erected on Cortes's orders in the 1520s, and using the stone from the Templo Mayor, which stood near to it, on my right. Soon the temple's exact location was forgotten, and remained the subject of speculation for centuries. Visitors were told it was under the cathedral. Behind me, still on my right, was Moctezuma's palace, which was torn down to build a fortified mansion for Cortés. The Government's National Palace now stands there, forming the east side of the Zócalo. The metro exit had brought me up through the end of the Iztapalapa causeway, by which the Spanish entered. But, apart from those causeways, the centre of Tenochtitlán did not have streets. The temples and palaces occupied open plazas crossed and bounded by narrow canals of sparkling water brought from the hills by two aqueducts running along the causeways. A dozen or more principal structures were laid out in formal symmetry. Sahagún recorded seventy-eight religious structures in this precinct alone.

The cathedral and National Palace were flying the national flag, at whose centre is the Aztec symbol of the eagle on a prickly pear. The ground beneath the cathedral was part of the plaza in front of the Templo Mayor, and its footprint at the rear right crosses the site of the Temple to Ehécatl, and at its rear left, stands over a large ball court. Farther to my left, the Late Colonial buildings facing the Zócalo stand on the site of the palace of Axayácatl, where the Spanish were lodged. I spent the morning off-duty, enjoying being a tourist, visiting the cathedral, and walking the streets, and drinking coffee in Colonial courtyards whose foundations delved into the rubble of Tenochtitlán, and whose facades were often cracked, as the rubble continues to settle into the soft mud on which both cities were founded. The islands of the lake must barely have risen above water level, because almost no variation in relief was discernible as I walked around the city centre.

I saved the highlight for the following day.

In the early hours of 21 February 1978, electricity company workers were digging up the street on the east side of the cathedral to lay a cable. The district was nicknamed the Isle of Dogs, because when it rained heavily, street dogs gathered there, discerning (as I had not) that this area was slightly elevated. The digging was halted by a stone, a big one: eight-and-a-half tons. It seemed to be carved with a woman's body and severed limbs. The archaeologists were called. The centre of the stone was revealed as a woman's torso, naked except for a belt, with the rest of her body in pieces. The stone was a disc depicting Coyolxauhqui. She was the daughter of the earth goddess Coatlicue, and when she discovered her mother was pregnant with the boy who would become the war god Huitzilopochtli, she led her 400 sisters and brothers to kill her. Huitzilopochtli emerged from the womb, stepped straight into a suit of armour and routed them, dismembering Coyolxauhqui. He cut off her head and, showing his tender side, placed it in the sky, where the moon would always be a solace to their mother. There is a photo of the archaeological team, in telltale 1970s wing-collars, standing in the pit around the eleven-foot wide circular stone. Their beaming smiles show more than the usual pleasure of uncovering an exceptional find; the disc was the key to locating the Templo Mayor, for the chronicles specify it lay at the foot of the temple steps, and it was here that the dismembered bodies of sacrificial victims landed when they were thrown down the 113 steps of the pyramid, in re-enactment of Huitzilopochtli's victory over his sister. The location of the Templo Mayor was now pinpointed. It makes sense that it was found alongside, not under the cathedral, for the pyramid was used as a quarry to build it. But if it was to be excavated, a whole city block of early Colonial houses in a smart residential area had to be demolished. In just weeks, President Portillo bit the bullet and authorised it. The appropriately named Eduardo Matos Moctezuma began the longest and most expensive dig ever undertaken in all the Americas.

The excavations clearly show how earlier temples were nested inside it like Russian dolls. The first was the timber and stucco one erected at the time of settlement, while the last was built by Moctezuma, after a major rebuild under the previous ruler, Ahuitzotl, who died in 1502. The traditional accounts of its inauguration ceremony still attract controversy. Chronicler Diego Durán said 80,400 captives were sacrificed, and even describes how they counted them. It was said to have taken four days to kill them all. Human sacrifice is common, but this single record has been the basis for portraying the Aztecs as practising it on a scale vastly greater than any other culture. However, the most curious thing about this figure is that nothing about it adds up. Eighty thousand people is four times more numerous the size of a large army of the time, and they would be ungovernable. They would simply walk off. Assuming it would only be possible to work in daylight, it would mean relays of priests killing someone every nine seconds without pause. Given that human sacrifice was a religious practice intended to secure the stability of the universe, and that it was only the end of a very complicated set of rituals sometimes lasting months, killing at this speed would reduce a profound act to meaningless butchery. It would also create 80,400 corpses to dispose of in a hot climate. They would form a charnel house of flesh 100 feet square and 50 feet high. There is no mention in any literature of how these bodies might have been disposed of; bodies are very difficult to burn. Modern crematoria have to grind the residue in the furnace to completely reduce it to ashes. Disease, very likely epidemics, would have been inevitable. There is no word of this in the record. The actual numbers can only be guessed at.

Sacrifice was part of the ordinary cycle of ritual, but much of it involved animals and birds, especially quail. When humans were killed, the skulls of victims would be threaded onto racks of poles by knocking holes in their temples, and there are equally dubious accounts of how large these racks were. There are no great bone dumps in the archaeology to suggest more than a few dozen were sacrificed on important occasions. A major win in battle, or the inauguration of a temple, might have seen that rise to hundreds. In Peru, we know the Incas sacrificed hundreds of adults and children when a new ruler was enthroned.

There is no doubt that the public sacrifices were, like public hangings (carried out in Britain up to 1868), intended in part to keep the population docile. For nearly a century, sacrificial victims were chosen from captives seized in wars of conquest, or in the suppression of rebellions. The heads of tributary states were even invited along to watch their own people being sacrificed; to refuse would have been a declaration of war. But a little over half a century before the arrival of the Spanish, a new and sinister institution was brought in by the power behind the throne of three rulers: a fixer called Tlacaelel. He said the gods should not have to wait for sacrifices until there was a pretext for war, there should be a more reliable supply. Nor should they have to attack distant races whose barbarian flesh would not be to the gods' taste. It was better that certain nearby states should expect to fight a war at recognised times, and have their young men harvested as captives. These false wars to gather victims were known, in grim euphemism, as flower wars.

Discussing the flower wars, the Tlaxcalan historian Ixtlilxochitl described a style of warfare that was more like a blood sport. 'A field should be marked out where regular battles would take place, and those captured and made prisoners in these wars would be sacrificed to their gods. In addition to this, it would be an occasion for the sons of the lords to practise [fighting] so that they would emerge from there as famous captains, and it was understood not to exceed the limits of the field laid out for the purpose, and not to attempt to gain land or chiefdoms.'

Inga Clendinnen is the greatest scholar of what it meant to be an Aztec. She examines their actions, rather than their words, especially in ritual. I summarise her conclusions on the Aztecs: we may manage to imagine the lure of the Roman Circus, but the civic cruelty of Mexico, so matter of fact, is hard to relate to either as function or fantasy. It is emotionally near the territory of the camps and gulags, challenging our sense of a shared common humanity. We cannot acquiesce in such sacrifices without surrendering something of ourselves that we value.

The Aztecs did not even attempt to keep prisoners docile by ignorance, as the Nazis did with Jews. They were greeted at city gates by priests describing their fate. The men were tied together by passing a rope through the pierced septums of their noses. The boundless anger generated by this terrible policy may explain what happened in the final days of Tenochtitlán, when the Spanish soldiers stayed their hands through pity, but their allies, the Aztecs' longtime victims, did not.

Today, visitors to the Templo Mayor are mostly kept to the periphery of the nest of stub walls, each marking a phase in its enlargement. But one walkway crosses the centre of the site, where the top of an earlier temple is still visible. The temple was, like that at Tula, the centre of the universe, and on a platform in the centre of the pyramid, a chac mool sacrificial stone still reclines, starved of blood for five hundred years. For me it is emotive archaeology; seeing it in the dense shade under the protective canopy I felt a chill run over my skin. The Spanish thought they were looking at a demon who had bewitched the people into devil-worship. They

293

would have experienced a deep revulsion and scalding anger. Modern Christian societies usually have a very benign view of God and his intentions. This view is unusual. Rudolph Otto, the first great twentieth-century investigator of comparative religion, writing his masterpiece *The Sacred* in 1917, argued that to a true believer God was not an idea; he was instead a terrible power, manifested in wrath. That was how the Aztecs saw their gods and the world they created in their image. A temple, in any higher civilisation, is a microcosm of that world. It is not a tame space.

Each temple is a point that creates an axis in space linking the underworld, the earth and the heavens. This is the place where these normally separate worlds have been joined, and a breakthrough from one world to another is possible, and repeatable. If we thought of it in scientific terms, we would call it a port in the space-time continuum. The underworld is represented by the ball court, through the legend of the twins descending to play with the gods of the underworld. Sure enough, in Tenochtitlán there was a large ball court next to the Temple of Ehécatl. The historian of religions, Mircea Eliade, sees religious rites as being a way to enter sacred

Sacrificial stone or chac mool from Tula.

time safely, to enter into its eternal present. 'Sacred time is infinitely recoverable, infinitely repeatable. From one point of view it could be said that it does not "pass" at all.' This is not an eccentric view: the Greek philosopher Parmenides, who influenced Plato, saw time as enduring, not passing.

When I left the site in the afternoon, the falling sun silhouetted the bulk of the cathedral. It was a cluster of stacks beaten about by time's sea and the gale of the passing years. Inside, devotees kneeled to perform the stations of the cross; thin old ladies lowered bony knees to the stone floor, and entered the timeless time of worship. Christ fell for the third time, Christ is always falling for the third time. Christ was stripped of his garments, Christ is always being stripped of his garments. Christ was nailed to the Cross, Christ is always being nailed to the Cross.

The cosmos was brought into secular time by the construction of a temple, centring the world. It sacralised the space in which they lived, and made it more real. The temple was a microcosm of the universe and thus, the dwelling place of the gods. It represents the world and continually sanctifies it. It fulfils the desire, said Eliade, 'to live in a pure and holy cosmos, as it was in the beginning, when it came fresh from the Creator's hands.' The desire to live in the divine presence, in sacred time, is a hankering after Eden. It has dangers; it risks man being paralysed by the thought that there is no progression; we all walk time's treadmill. Removing it leaves the opposite problem, the unrolling of a never-ending spool of formless, meaningless linear time – in other words, a modern, Western atheist's time.

It is quite new in the history of the world, that large numbers of people seek to live wholly in secular space and time. Such people, people like me, feel that some places and times have special meaning. But we see those as personal or historical associations, not a profound truth intrinsic to the world. And the world can still seem a terrifying place when we stop and look unguardedly at the place of one human life in it.

Time spoke to the Aztecs. It might first appear that immersing yourself in the still centre of the world, as their priests and their rulers did, is a kind of retreat from reality. But at that centre, outside time and space, they found an absolute reality, which transcends this world and makes it real. A human life reaches its potential to the degree that it is religious, and that it participates in the true reality. Religious people invest more in reality, not less. To live in sacred reality is to acquire power. Nor is it an easy option. Investing belief in ritual time brings enormous burdens. You take on responsibility for the orderly conduct of the universe. When it falls, so do you.

The lands that remained outside religious structures comprised profane space: less real. Any attack on the Aztec state and its religious duties threatened a return to chaos. Enemies of the state were therefore demons. A victory over such people was sacred in itself, for it re-enacted the gods' first victory against the dragon of chaos, who presided over a formless universe. We may seem a long way from such ideas now, but the headlines in US newspapers after the destruction of the Twin Towers did not focus on words like death and destruction, but on the threat to order and civilisation. The two commonest words in the headlines were 'chaos' and 'pandemonium'. In Milton's *Paradise Lost*, Pandæmonium was the capital of Hell, the meeting place of the evil spirits. The Aztecs would have understood America's fears.

Like the Incas, the Aztecs headed an explosive empire. It was founded by Acamapichtli in 1375, and did not become extensive until the rule of an earlier Moctezuma, who died in 1469. Its heyday was little more than half a century, while Queen Elizabeth II alone has been on the British throne for over sixty years. An empire's power is often paraded ostentatiously precisely because it is illusory. The glue binding its parts is fear. Fear is exercised through the civil displays of power through architecture and ceremony, and displays of wealth, but also through violence in war, the criminal code, and sacrifice. Conquest does not confer contentment on defeated peoples, it incites bitter resentment. Those tensions can be exploited to spring it apart.

In 1519, the square pyramid of the Templo Mayor was topped by twin temples to Tlaloc, the ancient rain god of the valley, and

Huitzilopochtli, the war god the Aztecs brought with them. Facing it was a four-tiered circular temple dedicated to the wind god Ehécatl. On the top platform was a large, round room, whose roof was a truncated cone. The entrance was so low the priest who entered every dusk had to stoop. At sunset, wrote the chronicler José de Acosta, he beat a 'drum so large that its harsh sound could be heard all over city, and when the people heard it they fell so silent that it seemed not a soul was there; the markets emptied, and the people went indoors, so that everything was left in great quiet and peace.' It could be heard across the sprawling city and six miles into the countryside. Did the men from Trujillo think of their home town and the seven city gates slamming shut each night, closing up the Moorish walls, the noise rumbling over the darkening plains to mingle with the thuds from the portals of Medellín, Mérida, Cáceres, and Badajoz?

Darkness falls on the eyes, and seeps into the mind, bringing its special perturbances. There are even two words for anxieties triggered by dusk: achluophobia, fear of what might happen as darkness descends, and lygophobia, the fear of twilight, bringing fantasies of what might happen in the night. The palace in which the Spanish were lodged had a view over the temple of Ehécatl to the twin shrines on the Templo Mayor. They knew what went on there. Those that stayed awake, the guards, the worriers, would know that unless they achieved a bloodless coup, some of their number would be captured; some would take that long walk up the cruelly steep stairs.

The next noise from the city was the priests' fanfare of conch shells, followed by drumbeats greeting the rising sun, and calling the city to labour. Food and water arrived, also fodder for the horses, and meat for the mastiffs. Cortés went to Moctezuma's palace with four of his captains, and five soldiers, including Díaz. They were given presents, and so acute had been the observations of the Aztec emissaries travelling with the Spanish, the gifts accurately reflected the rank and status of each recipient. Moctezuma said he had organised a tour of the city, and would join them later.

Bernal Díaz took leisure to give us an intimate portrait of their host. 'Moctezuma was about forty years old, of good height, well-proportioned, spare and slight, and not very dark, though of the usual Indian complexion. He did not wear his hair long but just over his ears, and he had a short black beard, well shaped and thin. His face was rather long and cheerful; he had fine eyes, and in his appearance and manner could express geniality or, when necessary, a serious composure. He was very neat and clean, and took a bath every afternoon. He had many women as his mistresses; he was quite free from sodomy.'

The tour of the city was designed to explain and impress, and took in Tlatelolco, conquered by Tenochtitlán in the 1470s, and the home of the greatest trading market not just in the Aztec empire, but in the whole of Mesoamerica.

I took the metro to the northern suburbs and emerged at street level at the an intersection of a large dual carriageway and a much bigger dual carriageway with a tramway down the central reservation. I stood with my map in the palm of my hands, slowly rotating it, with an increasingly furrowed brow. A young couple took pity on me and indicated the way. The ruins of the central temple complex of Tlatelolco are surrounded by widely spaced tower blocks separated by acres of shapeless spaces. The Aztecs made a last stand here, after the fall of Tenochtitlán. So colossal was the destruction that the ruins now sit yards below the surrounding land. A church overlooks the site from the high ground. There is a quote cut into a commemorative stone: *It was not a triumph or a defeat, it was the sad birth of the Mestizo people who make the Mexico of today*. It is a wise man who draws optimism out of such events, and this sense of sad hope is the touchstone of Mexican sentiment about the erosion of their indigenous foundations.

In 1968, Tlatelolco hit the world's news over a second battle. Mexico City was completing preparations for the Olympics, and, as would become common in the television age, domestic protesters knew demonstrations would attract a world audience, and punch well above their weight. Ten thousand people gathered on the nearby Plaza de Tres Culturas to protest peacefully about Government attacks on independent trade unions. Students were joined by locals and onlookers. As night fell, government helicopters flew over the demonstration and dropped flares. Shots rang out from the residential tower blocks, then security forces on the ground opened fire on the demonstrators. Three hundred people died. The government blamed provocateurs among the demonstrators for opening fire on the police.

Thirty years later something unthinkable happened: the corrupt machine of the ruling PRI party lost an election. This was the first win by the opposition since 1910. The incoming president, Vicente Fox, ordered an inquiry into the Tlatelolco massacre, which showed the government of Gustavo Díaz Ordaz had set paramilitaries in the apartment blocks, and snipers had incited the attack by firing on police. The Interior Minister in charge of this had been Luis Echeverría. Ordaz had nominated him as successor, and he had assumed the presidency two years later.

When Cortés and his captains surveyed the marketplace, they again had to admit it dwarfed the largest equivalents they knew in Spain, but the sights that most impressed Díaz were the aviaries and the zoo. The zoo was on the spot half a dozen blocks west of the Zócalo where the Church of the Monastery of San Francisco now stands. The monastery ruins have been built into the modern church, and fragments of old arches and columns are lodged in its plaster like fossils. Its friars ran a small estate, much larger than the present site, with a stream and orchards. Díaz saw a temple here, with carnivores, including 'tigers, and two sorts of lion, and beasts rather like wolves. They were fed on deer, fowls, little dogs, and other creatures which they hunt and also on the bodies of the Indians they sacrificed, as I was told. As for the horrible noise when the lions and tigers roared, and the jackals and foxes howled, and the serpents hissed, it was so appalling that one seemed to be in hell.'

Díaz describes metal workers, naming three whose art he thinks would equal Michelangelo, as well as dancers, jugglers, stilt-walkers, seamstresses, feather workers and all the paraphernalia surrounding a sumptuous and showy court. Trying to describe the riches of Tlatelolco market he exclaims 'But why waste so many words on the goods in their great market? If I describe everything in great detail I shall never be done.'

As the Spanish tour of Tenochtitlán climaxed at the Templo Mayor, Moctezuma joined them, to lead them past the stone of the goddess Coyolxauhqui being dismembered to the foot of twin staircases of 113 steps, which they climbed. The steps were high, and the forty-five degree angle would have made the walk feel precarious. The slope and step size are designed so a human body will keep rolling to the bottom. I walked up similar steps in the Maya city of Tikal in the jungles of Guatemala, and at Cobá in the Mexican Yucatán. It is hard work and a little frightening. Cortés would probably have been wearing armour to make a display. At the top Moctezuma courteously said, 'You must be tired.'

'We Spanish never tire,' Cortés replied. His complexion probably suggested otherwise.

Díaz describes seeing the causeways coming across the lake from three directions, pierced with bridges to permit the lake commerce to come and go. At intervals throughout their length there were fortress towers. From the temple heights they could catch the hubbub of the market, on the edge of the city. Moctezuma may well have been showing them, as historian Hugh Thomas puts it, that although his diplomatic speeches might end with the equivalent of 'Your humble servant', he was far from being either. The view should have inspired admiration, respect and even fear, but these were not Cortesian traits. The smell coming from an alcove with a sacrificial altar turned his mind in another direction. 'The stench here too was like a slaughterhouse, and we could scarcely stay in the place.' Against his friar's advice, Cortés chose this moment, in the most sacred space in the city, to make his usual speech about the evils of Native religion. Moctezuma took his religion so seriously that he once proposed moving the whole pyramid a dozen feet to one side to achieve a more accurate astronomical alignment. The temple priests were furious at Cortes's remarks, and Moctezuma did not hide his own anger. 'Lord Cortés, if I had known you were going to utter these insults I should not have shown you my gods. We hold them to be very good. They give us health and rain and crops and weather, and all the victories we desire. So we are bound to worship them, and sacrifice to them, and I beg you to say nothing more against them.'

Cortés backed off, and Moctezuma excused himself, saying he had to remain to pray and make sacrifices to atone for his guest's insults to the gods. Cortés almost did the rarest of things: apologise, but he changed his line of attack and asked permission to build a chapel in his lodgings. This was granted, but the fact of having to ask betrays that Cortés knew perfectly well he was a house-guest, and, contrary to his account of the leaders' first meeting, he had not been granted any right to assume rule. The carpenter called in to work on the chapel was Alonso Yánez, a native of Córdoba. His professional eye observed that a door had recently been sealed up in one of the adjacent walls, and there was a concealed void in the building with no door into it. Cortés ordered him to break through a wall, and they experienced a Tutankhamun moment as the dust settled and light shone into a room of gold and fine featherwork. Díaz gives the best account. 'Cortés went in first with certain captains. When they saw the quantity of golden objects, jewels and plates and ingots which lay in that chamber, they were quite transported. They did not know what to think of such riches. The news soon spread to the other captains and soldiers, and very secretly we all went in to see. The sight of all that wealth dumbfounded me. Being only a youth at the time and never having seen such riches before, I felt certain there could not be a store like it in the whole world.' They sealed it up; the black opening grew smaller as each stone was reset. They could not close up the thoughts in their heads.

That is the Spanish version. The Native accounts tell of them 'quickly going in everywhere, as though covetous and greedy,' taking Moctezuma's personal property. It was so shocking, the Aztecs would no longer bring them provisions.

Cortés wrote lyrically to Charles V about the quality of the goldsmithing, but most of it would arrive home melted into ingots. For the moment, he had other things to worry about. A delegation of captains arrived. The group included the five who had climbed the pyramid: two cronies of Velázquez, Cortés's close allies Diego de Ordaz and Gustavo de Sandoval, and the loose cannon he needed to keep on side, Pedro de Alvarado. The view from the top had impressed on them, as it was surely intended to, their vulnerability, especially the ease with which the causeways could be closed, trapping them in their palace. All the roofs were flat and movement through the narrow streets could be made insufferable by missiles safely thrown from above, while canoes could be deployed to harass movement on the causeways. That view of causeways radiating out from the small island lodged in their minds. Several Spanish wrote of feeling trapped like flies in a spider's web. They were supposed to be an occupying force; it felt more like luxurious house-arrest.

Bernal Díaz expressed their anxiety graphically: 'We pointed out that all the gold Moctezuma had given us, and all that we had seen in the treasury of his father, was turning to poison in our bodies, for we could not sleep by night or day.' The captains urged Cortés to seize Moctezuma, and while considering this he looked south from the roof of their palace saw two bridges on the causeway by which they had entered had been lifted. He began to wonder how a coup could be effected and justified, given, in his mind, that Moctezuma was now a vassal of the King of Spain, and any seizure would be an affront to Charles V.

The threat posed by their seclusion in the palace, the huge army at Moctezuma's command, and the ease with which they could be isolated from help, wormed into them. The suspicion that Moctezuma could not be trusted became a conviction he was about to attack them, then a compelling reason to act swiftly against his person. If you first paint yourself as a victim, any outrage is justified.

'All night we prayed to God,' wrote Díaz, 'to direct events in the interest of his holy service.' Back at the coast, their Cempoalan allies had received a demand from Moctezuma's regional governor Qualpopoca for the half-yearly tribute. The commander at Villa Rica fort, Juan Escalante was a reliable lieutenant. It was an important post, because they expected a second force to come out from Cuba to challenge Cortés. Escalante guaranteed the Fat Chief he need not pay, and rode out with a Spanish force backed by Cempoalans to demand gold from Qualpopoca. He refused. Jamie Cortés Hernández, the government heritage officer I had met in Veracruz, described to me what happened next. 'Battle commenced, but the Cempoalans deserted the field, and the Spanish were left isolated and exposed. They were forced to withdraw, losing a plump man from León called Juan de Argüello in the retreat. He was sacrificed, and his curly-haired head was delivered to Moctezuma. Escalante made it back to the fort, but he and seven others died of their wounds. When I excavated Villa Rica we found a burial of eleven men. The lab later showed they were all Spanish. The pattern of cavities on the inside of the skull is different to Native ones, I can't tell the difference, but experts can. There was a distinct group of eight among them, and that rang a bell. I think our eight bodies were Escalante and his men.'

'Could you see wounds on the bones?' I asked.

'The skeletons were too incomplete. But there were no other groups of men who died at the same time.'

It was the first Spanish defeat in the New World. If Cortés had a pretext to seize Moctezuma, he had also had a severe warning.

Cortés obtained a meeting with Moctezuma on 14 November, six days after they had arrived. He went with a large group, all armed. The Spanish wore arms all the time, so this would not have aroused suspicion. He took senior captains and about thirty men. Moctezuma was in relaxed mood, and made gifts of jewels, which were accepted, and young women. He offered his own daughter to Cortés. The wives were refused on the grounds that the Spanish could not marry non-Christians. This was a purely political pose, as Cortés had never been averse to adultery. Then Cortés got down to business. 'Lord Moctezuma, I am greatly astonished that you, a valiant prince who has declared yourself our friend, should have ordered your captains to take up arms against my Spaniards.' He coldly compared the provocation to that at Cholula, making Moctezuma recall the massacre that followed. He accused Moctezuma's generals of plotting to kill the Spanish and concluded, 'Everything will be forgiven provide you come quietly with us to our quarters, and make no protest. But if you cry out or make any commotion, you will immediately be killed by these captains of mine, whom I have brought for this sole purpose.'

In scorn and shock, Moctezuma responded, 'I am not a person to whom such orders can be given,' he said. Different accounts claim that they argued for between half an hour and all day. It was long enough for Juan Velázquez de León, a broad-shouldered man with a harsh, stuttering voice to say angrily to Cortés, 'What is the use of all these roads? Either we take him or we knife him. If we do not look after ourselves now, we are dead men.'

Moctezuma sensed matters were coming to a head, and anxiously asked Malinche what was going on. For the only time in her life, we have a record of words she said for herself, not as the mouthpiece for someone else, and they shaped the future of Mexico. 'Lord Moctezuma, I advise you to accompany them immediately to their quarters and make no protest. I know they will treat you very honourably as the great prince you are, but if you stay here you will be a dead man. In their quarters the truth will be discovered.'

Moctezuma begged that his children be taken as hostages in his place, not out of cowardice, but because of the shame to his office. Cortés refused: this was a power-play, not diplomacy. Moctezuma, desperate, agreed. Relieved, the Spanish apologised, said it was all necessary, and required Moctezuma to tell the princes and his guards that he was going on the advice of his priests. He went to the Spanish quarters with his servants, his women, twenty lords, and his captains and counsellors.

Cortés played a psychological battle against Moctezuma, and won. When the ruler's chief lords asked why he was a prisoner, Moctezuma dutifully assured them that he was a free man acting on advice from priests who had consulted Huitzilopochtli. He continued to receive ambassadors and conduct court business as usual. He even summoned the men who had attacked the men of Villa Rica, and let them report to Cortés privately. It is hard to tell why he did so, for under no duress, said Díaz, they admitted the attack was carried out on Moctezuma's orders. Cortés told Moctezuma that in Christian eyes Moctezuma was guilty of murder, but he would forgive him. This is the pattern of behaviour in an abusive relationship; the victim is made to feel at fault, and the bully poses as long-suffering.

Cortés now had sufficient autonomy to order the Aztec captains who attacked Escalante to be burned alive on the plaza in front of the palace. He placed a furious Moctezuma in chains, and forced him to watch the executions, just as Moctezuma had forced his subject rulers to watch their citizens sacrificed. The populace watched in silence. They had seen men die before. They had never seen their leader chained and in distress, watching helplessly. He was damaged goods.

Afterwards Cortés tenderly removed the chains and offered Moctezuma freedom. Moctezuma had tears in his eyes as he said it was best for him to stay, because if he were at liberty he would be pressed to attack the Spanish. He had hostage syndrome: he was identifying his needs with the wishes of his captors. Cortés slyly mirrored his victim's predicament, having Malinche confide to Moctezuma that although Cortés might wish to release him, the Spanish captains would never permit it. Hugh Thomas sees this as the moment when Cortés grasps his final strategem; Moctezuma will continue to govern Mexico, but Cortés will govern Moctezuma.

The question staring us in the face is why a powerful ruler, in the heart of his own empire, permitted himself to be used as a stooge. Very significantly, the suspect passage of Sahagún that contains the eight retrospective prophecies is the main source of evidence for that other great myth of the conquest: that Moctezuma was a weak and prevaricating leader, even though his conduct until 1519 had been everything that a bellicose society expected of a leader. Cultural historian Tzvetan Todorov is one of the most articulate proponents of the argument that the Aztecs were culturally disposed to fail, and that Moctezuma displayed fatally flawed behaviour because he was trapped in ineffective ways of treating with the world. Critics suggest his great scholarship finally just shows a new route to the tired conclusion that the West is a superior civilisation, destined to triumph. I think the critics are right, for nearly all the other Aztec leaders acted effectively, but Todorov puts his finger on something that accounts for Moctezuma's poor leadership from the moment of meeting Cortés onwards. In typical Todorovian language, which falls like an eclipse between the reader and understanding, he suggests that when faced with a crisis, Moctezuma had a tendency to ask epistemological questions, while the Spanish asked praxeological questions. More plainly, while Moctezuma gazed heavenwards and wondered, 'How are we to know?', Cortés poked a problem and asked, 'What is to be done?' After Moctezuma died, more pragmatic minds squared up and focused on action, uninhibited by their supposed cultural paralysis.

Moctezuma might have died with honour in ordinary times, having done what had always worked. But just as the decent and principled Neville Chamberlain, British Prime Minister in 1939, failed to step outside past experience when faced with Hitler's Big Lie, Moctezuma was not the man to adapt politically, as his armies had in battle, to aliens with new versions of the truth. This religious man may simply have clung to his priest's hat when he need his general's helmet. Seen from that perspective, even initiative may have seemed fatal. Mircea Eliade says of religious man: '[W]hat men do on their own initiative, what they do without a mythical model, belongs to the sphere of the profane; hence it is a vain and illusory activity.' Nobel-prize winning Mexican poet Octavio Paz more pithily called Moctezuma's fascination with the meaning of Cortés 'a sacred vertigo'.

Moctezuma was the ruler, but he was one man. Most of the Aztec nobles thought him wrong and refused to visit him. The mood of the city changed. It is worth quoting Sahagún's Native history from the expressive Nahuatl version, instead of the Europeanised Spanish text usually cited. The citizens looked at the palace where this drama was being performed behind closed doors. 'But the Aztecs no longer at all dared to go there. They were greatly afraid; they were limp with fear; they were taken aback. Fear greatly prevailed; it spread about. No one dared come out. It was as though a wild beast were loose, as though it were the deep of night. Yet there was not, for that reason, a halt or hesitation in delivering everything the Spanish needed, but they delivered it fearfully, they went in fear, they ran in fear as they went to deliver it. And when they had spilled it on the ground, everyone came running back in a flash, panting and trembling.'

Inside the palace, the plot of the drama was not what they thought. Moctezuma and the Spanish coexisted amicably, the usual court entertainments continued, and two instances of rude behaviour by Spaniards guarding Moctezuma were smartly punished. Weeks passed in this directionless way, but before the month was out, Cortés ordered four small brigantines, forty feet long, to be built, giving them freedom to evacuate the city, if the need arose. They told Moctezuma they were pleasure boats, and received help from Aztec carpenters. Men were sent to the coast to strip fittings and gear from the grounded ships. Small expeditions reconnoitred for gold and new harbours. Diego de Ordaz even set himself up as a farmer.

But by the end of 1519, the disaffection of many Aztec nobles was moving towards resistance. Suspicious Spaniards, probably without a good translator to hand, misunderstood the despatch of a messenger to the court of the Texcoco king Cacama, who was Moctezuma's nephew. One of Cacama's sons was seized in the mistaken belief that an ambush was being set up. Cortés condemned him to be hanged, and only Moctezuma's weeping intervention saved him. Cacama was infuriated at both the high-handedness of the Spanish, and the Aztec ruler's craven begging. Cacama began seeking allies for a blockade of Tenochtitlán, but was betrayed and handed over to Cortés. He tried to buy his way out of custody by ordering his stewards to hand over gold. Pedro de Alvarado, the captain Cortés could neither trust nor depose, was sent to escort a shackled Cacama to his palace to fetch more. Neither returned. A delegation despatched to see why, found Cacama tied to a stake and Alvarado burning him with red-hot irons, believing there was more gold than Cacama had produced.

Moctezuma convened a meeting of the principal lords of the states around. According to Spanish accounts, he said he had accepted becoming a vassal of the King of Spain, and, weeping, commended them to do the same. Weeping is not the emotion expected during a voluntary oath of allegiance. The other lords were said to accept vassalage. Those associated with Cacama were in chains, and had little choice. The rest could see the way the wind was blowing. From now on, resistance to Cortés would not be self-defence, but rebellion. The barrack-room lawyer that whispered in the ear of Cortés and every Spanish administrator was satisfied. They began rounding up treasure as tribute to Mexico's new overlord. They kept the gold, they sent the jade to their Tlaxcalan allies, for whom it was much more valuable than gold. Then Cortés carried out an act of great symbolic importance. He climbed the Templo Mayor and vandalised the idols, which were so bloated by sacrifices, that congealed blood lay inches thick on them. A few days later, several hundred priests arrived and lowered their idols down the steep steps where thousands of people had died in their honour. The Spanish never saw them again, and no bribe or threat would make anyone say where they had been taken.

On 14 February the new Aztec calendar year changed from 1-Reed, regarded as ill-omened for kings, to 2-Flint. It was a good year for their war-god Huitzilopochtli. Moctezuma, under pressure from nobles who thought he should move against the Spanish, or be moved out of the way, decided the Spanish must leave. The past months had been quiet on the Aztec side, but not idle. Vassals had been conscripted. One of the lords who answered the call was a young cousin of Moctezuma called Cuauhtémoc. He would become the lynchpin of resistance to the conquest.

Cortés received the Aztec request to leave with a smile. Of course they would leave. Unfortunately they had no ships fit to sail the sea. Would Moctezuma help? Naturally. This display of diplomatic lying was rudely pre-empted by news from the coast. A Spanish fleet had appeared, and it did not look like help.

30

Dancing to Other Music

In Mexico night is falling,
war rages on all sides.
Oh Giver of Life!
war comes near ...

AZTEC SONG

The fleet of nineteen ships was under the command of Pánfilo de Narváez, a tall man with red-blond hair, executing orders from Velázquez in Cuba. The governor had received charters from Spain to colonise the mainland, something Cortés was doing without permission. Narváez was to take over in Mexico.

A stowaway in one of these vessels would do more to weaken Native resistance than any soldier or captain: the smallpox virus. In 1519, in the sandy-banked river port of Sanlúcar de Barrameda near Cádiz, and in the neighbouring towns, there had been an epidemic. Many Spanish had resistance to it, and did not see the disease as any more virulent than measles. Someone, perhaps the black slave Francisco Erguía, brought it to Hispaniola, where the Natives had no resistance, and were already suffering every kind of deprivation, from genocide, to slavery and the wiping out of everything they held dear. Most died. As Cortés was entering Tenochtitlán, smallpox was invading Cuba.

The replacement commandant at Villa Rica was Gustavo de Sandoval, a loyal friend of Cortés, from Medellín. He was built for riding, with a barrel chest and bow legs, and his horse, Motilla, a dark bay with a white star on his forehead, was reckoned the best in the New World. A deputation from Narváez came ashore, led by a Friar Guevara, who recommended that Sandoval surrender his duties to Narváez, and asked a lawyer, Vergara, to read out the relevant papers. Sandoval told Vergara he would get a hundred lashes if he tried, and said the only reason Guevara was not getting a beating for his insolence was respect for the cloth. The threats may have sounded a little comical, as Sandoval had a pronounced lisp, but his actions were deadly serious. He arrested the delegation, put them in packing cases and had Native porters carry them to Tenochtitlán, where Cortés feigned regret that his captain had treated them so poorly. He entertained them lavishly, and the delighted delegation blabbed all they knew about Narváez's expedition. It was stronger than Cortés's force, they said, but many men were disaffected. Cortés sent the delegates back with friendly messages and a horse weighed down with gold, to tell the new troops how much they would benefit from marching with him rather than against him. They also carried a letter from Cortés to Narváez, along the lines of: 'Rather surprised to see you here when all hunky-dory.' Unsurprisingly, Narváez made no reply, but set up camp in the town of Cempoala, and befriended the Fat Chief. Tlacochcalcatl probably sided with Narváez simply because he was on his doorstep, and led a larger force than Cortés. Cortés held a council to endorse a decision already made: 'Death to Narváez and anyone who argues about the matter.'

Leaving 120 troops in Tenochtitlán under Pedro de Alvarado, a necessary gamble given his limited forces, Cortés set off with 350 men to meet up with Sandoval's 60 or so at Villa Rica. Estimates of Narváez's forces range from around 750 to over double that. Cortés spurned all offers of help from Native warriors, possibly because he did not want to show them how to attack Spanish troops. En route to the coast, he learned Narváez had been exchanging pleasantries and gifts with Moctezuma. Cortés's anger hardened his resolution, and changed the way he regarded the ruler. The Spanish genuinely seemed to have liked the man, and found him good and cheerful company, but Moctezuma's dealings with Narváez reminded them he was an active enemy.

Cortés approached Cempoala down the lush green valley of the

Alcopan River, sending ahead his friend Friar Olmedo as an envoy. Holy orders did not prevent Olmedo spreading bribes and promises among Narváez's captains, most of whom were more concerned with maximising their profit than enforcing Velázquez's paper claims. Cortés put a bounty on Narváez. Narváez thought Cortés would never attack his superior forces, and sat around making jokes. One of his captains proposed they cut off Cortés's ears and eat one.

That night it rained heavily and the noise smothered the sound of Cortés's advance. A sentry was captured and had his neck squeezed by Cortés until he felt inclined to discuss the disposition of Narváez's men. They were scattered and ill prepared. Cortés attacked. Narváez was soon retreating into a thatched shrine on top of the main pyramid, which still stands to a height of about fifty feet. He had left his right eye on the end of a pike belonging to Pedro Gutiérrez.

In ordinary times, Narváez's voice, Díaz remembered, sounded 'hollow, as if coming from a vault'. Now it was. When they torched the roof, and falling straw set his feet on fire, he surrendered.

They were still recuperating from the battle when news came that in Tenochtitlán all hell had broken loose. Cortés hastened back to see what folly Alvarado had committed this time. As they approached Tenochtitlán the land was deserted, and Cortés admitted it 'aroused in me a terrible suspicion that the Spaniards in the city were dead and all the Natives had gathered waiting to surprise me'.

The calendar had brought the feast of Toxcatl, in which a young man who had been treated as the god Tezcatlipoca, and pampered for a year, was sacrificed at the height of an elaborate ceremony. To test the Spanish, Moctezuma had asked permission to hold the ceremony. Alvarado agreed, but stipulated there must be no sacrifice. Moctezuma countered by stopping deliveries of food. The Spanish had to buy in the markets. The nervous Tlaxcalans drip-fed stories of past sacrifices of their own people at this festival. The Spanish saw an effigy of Huitzilopochtli being prepared, in which a figure was moulded around a frame using seeds glued together with fresh human blood. Alvarado later testified he had seen girls and young men dressed for sacrifice, and ropes brought to raise the

311

effigy to the top of the pyramid to replace the painting of the Virgin, something Alvarado had also forbidden.

That day in mid-May, the dancers included four hundred of the flower of Aztec nobility, though not Moctezuma or his entourage. The nobles assembled in the closed square in front of the Templo Mayor. Their finery included deer and ocelot skin furs hung with golden bells, jade, shell, and iridescent feathers, and patterns of brilliant parrot feathers. The driving instruments of the dance were large wooden drums. The steps had to be performed perfectly; even in the paroxysmal climax a false step would be punished by a beating or death.

The Spanish, fully armed, were unexpected guests at the feast. Alvarado was a man of animal courage. Back in Spain, when there was scaffolding on top of the tower of Seville Cathedral, he had walked out on a single plank high above the square, turned round and strode back. He was now thirty-five years old, well built and handsome, with red-gold hair that had earned him the Indian name *Tonatiuh*: the Sun. He was always smiling.

The gates of the courtyard were closed, the heavy drums began to beat. The dancers began to turn in their finery, stepping the holy patterns on the ground. Spanish soldiers moved to the gates. Alvarado's order was simple: *'¡Mueran!' Let them die!'*

The Nahuatl account couples unsparing detail with a dry, factual style. They had assembled to watch a ceremony in which human sacrifice was embedded. When the massacre began, they described what they saw as if it were a new dance. 'They surrounded those who were dancing, going among the cylindrical drums. They struck a drummer's arms; both of his hands were severed. Then they struck his neck; his head landed far away. Then they stabbed everyone with iron lances, and struck them with iron swords. They struck some in the belly, and their entrails came spilling out. They split open the heads of some; they cut their skulls to pieces, into little bits. And some they hit on the shoulders; their bodies broke open and ripped. Some they hacked on the calves, some on the thighs, some on their bellies, and then their entrails would spill out. And if someone still tried to run, it was useless; he just dragged his intestines along.

There was a stench as if of sulphur. The blood of the warriors ran like water; the ground was almost slippery with blood, and the stench of it.' All this happened on the site where Mexico City cathedral now stands.

The Spanish killed every person they could get their hands on. Tenochtitlán's lords sent the alarm out through the city, summoning the Aztec warriors. By dusk the city was smokey with fires burning the dead. Afterwards, Natives were seen re-enacting the massacre in dance, as if trying to understand this new ritual, to re-establish control over these monstrous events. Moctezuma appeared in irons on the terrace of the royal palace. Itzquauhtzin, the Lord of Tlatelolco, was his spokesman. 'Cease fighting and lay down your weapons, because these men are stronger than us. If you do not stop making war on them, the whole people will be greatly harmed.'

The people below were furious at this surrender, and turned on them both: 'What does this faggot Moctezuma say? And you are a rogue along with him. We will not halt the war.' The Spanish had to use their shields to protect them from a volley of missiles. Alvarado was no longer smiling.

In the next forty-eight hours, the causeway bridges were lifted, and the four brigantines built to give the Spanish an escape route were burned by the Aztecs. The public markets were shut, and anyone trying to bring food to the Spanish was killed. Three weeks later, Cortés returned at the head of a thousand Spaniards. The people of Tenochtitlán snubbed him, remaining indoors, but did not bar his entry, as, in eerie silence, he went to his palace. Moctezuma welcomed him, but Cortés, as yet undecided as to who had caused the collapse in relations, refused to speak to him. Moctezuma was isolated and frightened. There is no doubt that from this time he was a liability to his people. They knew it, and told him so. He was still the ruler, but he was despised, and there was a power vacuum being filled by popular rage against both the Spanish, and Moctezuma's passive collaboration. No one stepped forward to assume the throne. Deposing a ruler was an almost unthinkable step, and many of those with the authority to do it had been butchered at the dance.

313

Alvarado told Cortés he had information that the Aztecs planned to attack the Spanish as soon as the dance finished; he had got his retaliation in first. Cortés told him it was a great mistake. He was furious but, as ever, did not punish Alvarado. By the end of June, the situation deteriorated into day after day of assaults on the palace where the Spanish were lodged. Cortés asked Moctezuma to order the markets to reopen, and provide food. Moctezuma said he would not be obeyed, and asked his brother Cuitláhuac to be released to arrange it. Cortés agreed, but when Cuitláhuac returned, it was to stand alongside the new, young ruler of Tlatelolco, Cuauhtémoc, and help direct the attacks. A shattered Moctezuma now said he only wanted to die, but he was conducted to the palace terrace to ask the nobles to call off the assault. Spanish soldiers stood round him, shields ready. There was a moment's silence as he appeared on the balcony, then a hail of missiles knocked him down. In three days he was dead. An Aztec poet wrote that in the age of giants, they greeted each other thus: 'Do not fall down, for whoever falls, falls for ever.' A giant had fallen. The Nahuatl phrase for the death of ruler was: 'Now the sun is overturned.'

Native accounts casually mention that Moctezuma has died, as though it no longer mattered. The leader they needed had died some time before. His funeral took place with ceremony, but without love or respect. His people looked back and complained that he had punished the common people for trifles, then failed to protect the nation. The aged lord of Tlatelolco died around the same time and was buried with tenderness and grief.

Moctezuma had been attended by a retinue of twenty or thirty of the greatest lords in his realm, men who would now need to be guarded at a time when the Spanish needed every single soldier to be available for combat. Cortés killed the lords and threw their bodies outside the palace. The translator Aguilar watched from above as the men's wives and sisters and daughters came looking among the corpses for their loved ones. He said to his companion, 'Have you seen the hell and the lament down there?' He knew a backlash would come. 'Never in the whole war, did I have such fear as when I heard that terrible lament.'

31

The End of the Island

And what strength I have's my own, Which is most faint:

Recovery is slower than anyone tells you. Over a year has gone by since I felt the first symptoms. Slowly I have come back to the world. I have come off the morphine patches, so sleep is elusive. I worry about the small things in life, and if the same dream recycles my anxieties in a neurotic loop I play the World Service to move my thoughts on. I later wake with different and very specific concerns such as the success of new initiatives in crop spraying in Lesotho.

On the last day of March the clocks go forward to British Summer Time and it is like a rebirth, cold to warm, dark to light.

I still sleep in the spare room, in a single bed, an island I can defend. I can wade back to the mainland, talk about my voyage. But no journal will tell you how it really was. It was another world, a flying island that is moving away from me as I look back: Jonathan Swift's Laputa – in Spanish, it means the slut. Only a client knows. My body is stripped of its accessories. The tube in my stomach is taken out, not during an operation, just pulled out under local anaesthetic. It remains today as a sunken scar hole; it would pass for a bullet wound, and will, when I talk to small children misbehaving. The drugs tube and port come out of my chest. I have lost so much weight the line of the vein, distended by its plastic lining, stands proud of my skin. Nearly two years after treatment finished, I cannot eat more than a snack of real food; the rest of my calories come from nutritional drinks that taste like cheap milkshakes. I can't eat in front of anyone but Celia, because at intervals the food trapped in the mucous over the wound will come

315

back into my mouth and needs to be spat out. Celia blanks me, and carries on with her meal. But I always cook for her, because I want to have some contact with real food.

I am not the person I was before. I'll remain, not an island, but a peninsula. Somedays, that neck of land will be wide and high. Other days, the tide sweeps in. But I'm alive to watch it. As the Macmillan cancer care leaflet on Docetaxel warned, I have noticed changes in the way my heart works, but there has not been an increase in the production of tears.

I saw Dennis Potter at Hay-on-Wye Festival in 1994 when he was dying of liver and pancreatic cancers. He described the plum tree in blossom below his study window in Ross-on-Wye. His senses were heightened by knowing it was the last spring he would see, and he not just saw, but felt, that it was 'the whitest, frothiest, blossomest blossom that there ever could be.'

With luck I shall join the squirrels and the pigeons for a few seasons more. As Ariel says:

Merrily, merrily shall I live now, Under the blossom that hangs on the bough.

32

Time Fails

'The thing that hath been, is that which shall be;
and that which is done is that which shall be done;
and there is no new thing under the sun.'
ECCLESIASTES 1:9

The remainder of the story must be telescoped. Cortés's captains told him they must abandon the city. He argued, but bowed to either their arguments or their resolve. Believing the Aztecs were loath to fight at night, they planned a midnight flight. When the hour arrived, troops began to creep out along the western causeway, carrying beams torn out of the palace to replace the missing bridges. A solitary woman, up late to draw water, saw them, and raised the alarm. Aztec forces fell on them, turning the evacuation into chaos. Horses laden with gold and silver fell into the lake waters and the treasure was never again seen by Spanish eyes. Chaos became a massacre. Command broke down, some panicked, the war mastiffs went berserk, and at the second breach in the causeway the temporary bridge failed, and crossing it only became practical after dead bodies had filled it up. The Aztecs thought the Spanish dead looked 'like white reed shoots'. The Native warriors no longer fought to capture, but to kill. Many of these Spanish skulls were stoved in at the back, the special blow used to execute criminals.

It was 2 July 1520. Cortés led a shattered remnant of his forces to the lake shore, then began a clockwise loop around the north of the lake, harried by the Aztecs. The Spanish found safety back in the territory of the Tlaxcalans. Antonio de Benavides, who would later run the smelters that melted down the loot, testified that without the Tlaxcalans 'no Spaniard would have escaped the Aztecs because there was nowhere else to go'. Half the Spanish died, maybe more. The evacuation was so poorly organised that up to half may never have received orders to leave. They were besieged, taken prisoner and led up the steps of the temple, to the rhythm of the familiar drumbeats. This shambles of a retreat is still known as the *noche triste*, the sad night.

Bernardino de Sahagún had no doubt about who won that night. 'The Great Devil, and captain of all demons, called Satan, who reigned supreme in this New Spain with all his pleasure and will, was greatly vexed when the Spaniards came to this land, because our Lord God had decided to take from him those kingdoms over which he ruled. Therefore Satan was overjoyed when he won that victory against the Spaniards.'

It was a year before Cortés was ready to mount his next assault on Tenochtitlán. He regrouped, and took over the province around Tepeaca, east of Cholula, to block the Aztec route to the coast, and block trade. With the earlier exception of his massacre at Cholula, designed to shock the Aztec army standing by, he had usually treated the Natives with restraint. This restraint began to slip away from him. At Tepeaca, he sent Cristóbal de Olid to the neighbouring town where he secured the surrender of the male population and led them to Cortés, who took them into the fields and butchered them all. Four thousand women and children were sold into slavery. These were the tactics of terror: displaced vengeance for the *noche triste*.

Cortés built a fleet on the lake shore. The young Cuauhtémoc was now ruler. Moctezuma's brother Cuitláhuac had inherited first, but immediately died at the hands of Cortés's most powerful ally: smallpox, which, three months after the Spanish flight, began ravaging Tenochtitlán. It had already made estates in Cuba unworkable through lack of labour. The Natives of Hispaniola, modern Haiti and the Dominican Republic once numbered around 60,000. By 1520, they were almost extinct.

1492 was not just Columbus's year and the defeat of the last Moorish state in Spain; it was the year the Jewish population was expelled. Prior to 1492, the three most reliable medical writers in

318

Spain were three Jewish doctors. One, Alonso de Chirino, advised for plague: '[F]irst pray, then flee.' But for smallpox he advised neither, because mortality was low. Diseases mutate through time, and smallpox was not then so virulent as later, and because it was endemic in Spain, most Spaniards had good resistance to it. In Chirino's time, three widespread smallpox epidemics did not dent the national economy at all. One medical book classified it, along with chickenpox and measles, as a childhood disease. But the Natives had suffered no exposure to it.

The Franciscan Motolinía, who was one of the so-called Twelve Apostles who arrived in 1524, saw that 'because they all fell ill at a stroke, they could not nurse one another, nor was there anyone to make bread, and in many parts it happened that all the residents of a house died, and in others almost no one was left.' Nursing care is vital. During the US smallpox epidemic of 1898-99 Hopi Indians accepting nursing care suffered 6 percent mortality, while those who refused it suffered 74 percent.

The Spanish broke the city aqueducts, and on 1 June 1521 attacked Tenochtitlán on all four main causeways at once. They had the support of thirteen brigantines built on the lake shore, using as a model a ship from the coast broken down to its parts and carried up. In terms of numbers, it was a civil war between the Aztecs and an alliance of states from its disintegrating empire, including Tlaxcala, Cholula, Texcoco, Huexotzinco, Xochimilco, and Otomí. These allies fielded a combined army of over 20,000 Natives: larger than the remaining forces of the Mexica. The Spanish directed the war, but brought only 900 soldiers to the fray. The so-called Spanish conquest can just as easily be seen as the continuance of a long series of Native wars, with some involvement by Spanish mercenaries paid with booty and land.

They made slow progress, despite resistance being greatly weakened by the epidemic. Vázquez de Tapia, a soldier at the siege of Tenochtitlán, wrote: 'The pestilence was so severe and cruel that more than one-fourth of the Indian people in all the land died. This loss had the effect of hastening the end of the fighting, because a great quantity of men died, and warriors and many lords and captains and valiant men against whom we would have had to fight and deal with as enemies. Miraculously Our Lord killed them and removed them from before us.' Theirs was an Old Testament God.

The Aztecs were prepared, disciplined, and were led by the strong and charismatic Cuauhtémoc. He was handsome, with steadfast grey eyes. The Spanish would make so little progress each day on the causeway that they failed to reach the next defensible position, and had to retreat to the same place each night. Ten days later they were still stuck on the causeways.

When Spanish men or horses were captured, they were taken to the Templo Mayor, where the Spanish could hear the drumbeats start, and see the prisoners taken up the pyramid to be slit open and hurled down the steps. Their skulls were added to the racks. The Aztecs fought with fearless fury, and if they died, their wives were now picking up arms. To Cortés's shock, they were determined never to surrender. Treasure was being taken out of the city and hidden. They realised they would never reclaim more than a fraction of the loot they had lost on the *noche triste*. They launched a drive for the city's core on 10 June, and reached the central plazas, but as night fell they were driven back to where they had begun. The same happened on 15 June. The Aztecs were running out of food, and drinking dirty water. Dysentery was rampant. But the ferocity of the defence did not abate. At one point Cortés became isolated and was seized by Aztec hands. They were obsessed with capturing him to sacrifice, and did not even injure him. Spanish with swords arrived, upon which the Aztec hands fell to the floor. To retain any advances, they had to demolish everything as they went, denying the defenders the buildings from which to throw stones and missiles. They torched the palace they had lodged in, and the house of birds which had enchanted Diaz. They blocked the canals to keep the roads open without bridges. There was so much rubble in the streets they could hardly set the cannons to fire them. Each day was a return to brutal hand-to-hand fighting. Destruction which had been intended to inflict terror and dismay merely stiffened Aztec resolve with anger. When counsellors suggested to Cuauhtémoc that he might negotiate, he executed them. Miguel León-Portilla is the greatest cultural historian of the Aztecs. He concluded, 'The Mexica will to power developed into a mystical warlike world view.' To the elite, they were not just fighting for their world: fighting was their world.

The awful truth began to dawn on the Spanish officers and soldiers alike, that to take the city they had to destroy it. Those citizens who did not die would flee. They would inherit ruins walked by ghosts and skeletons.

Díaz had first looked on the cities of the lake and said they 'seemed like an enchanted vision from the tale of Amadís. Indeed some of our soldiers asked whether it was not all a dream.' The dream became one depicted by their contemporary, Albrecht Dürer: *The Four Horsemen of the Apocalypse*.

For the whole of June they fought, and on into July. The defenders were eating straw and grass. For want of physical strength, resistance weakened. Had they ever enjoyed eating human flesh, as the Spanish always alleged, they would have turned to the corpses. None did. Cortés was sickened by the relentless bloodshed. On 24 June, after over seven weeks' fighting, the Spanish on the west causeway entered and secured part of the city. 'We again entered the city and found the streets full of starving women and children.' An old man asked a soldier, 'Why do you not kill us and end our suffering?' Cuauhtémoc's palace was torched, but he had retired to his base in Tlatelolco, a mile to the north. One day Alvarado took his cavalry and broke through Aztec lines so weak they could hardly raise their arms. The Tlaxcalans followed without pity. For generations their young men had been harvested for sacrifice in Tenochtitlán. The Spanish tried with no success to stop the Tlaxcalans' indiscriminate killing of men, women and children, but this was not war, this was a final punishment, breaking the political body of Tenochtitlán for ever. In a famous phrase, Cortés wrote, 'No race has ever practised such fierce and unnatural cruelty.'

Still, Cuauhtémoc did not surrender. Cortés did not secure the last district of the city until 13 August, the seventy-fifth day of fighting. So much for the inevitable triumph of the more advanced civilisation. They saw privation which was 'beyond our

321

understanding of how they could endure it'. The ordinary people, half-dead, still tried to flee, many drowning in the lake. The Tlaxcalans were still killing. Cortés: 'There was not one man among us whose heart did not bleed at these killings.' That day a grand boat was seen leaving across the lake. The captain of one of the brigantines, García Holguín, pursued it, and captured Cuauhtémoc. The day was the feast of St Hippolytus, the patron saint of prison guards.

Cuauhtémoc means Descending Eagle. This unquenchable spirit was brought before Cortés, and defiantly said he had done no more than try to protect his people. He asked Cortés to take the dagger at his belt and stab him. But he was led to jail.

Dusk was silent; the priests did not sound the conches to mark the sunset. The night brought heavy rain. Thunder shook the emaciated survivors hiding in the dark wreckage of their city. The life they knew was over. A new time would start up, but these were the terrifying days between. They shivered at the end of the world, looking back on the ruins of time.

A Native poet wrote, 'This is how the Mexica, the Tlaltelolca, perished. He abandoned his city. There in Amaxac we all waited. And we had no more shields, we had no more weapons, we had nothing to eat, and so ate nothing. And all night long the rain was falling on us.'

We have a Native account of the night, probably composed by Netzahualcóyotl, the poet and Lord of Texcoco. All accounts say he led a blameless life, apart from a David and Bathsheba moment. The girl he fell in love with was betrothed to a noble. Netzahualcóyotl sent him into the most dangerous part of a battle, where he died. Of the fall of Tenochtitlán Netzahualcóyotl wrote:

We mourned for ourselves, our lot.
Broken spears lie in the bye-ways,
we have torn out our hair by the roots.

Palaces stand roofless, blood-red walls.
Maggots swarm the squares and huts.
Our city walls are stained with shattered brains.

Water flows red, as if someone had dyed it,
and if we drink, it tastes of sulphur.

In grief we beat our fists
against the walls of our mud houses,
a net of holes our only heritage.

Our strength was in our shields,
but shields could not resist this desolation.
They have abandoned the capital already.
Smoke rises, the mist is spreading.

Weep my friends,
and know that by these deeds
we have forever lost our heritage.
Our despair is woven to a precious thing.

If I never died, if I were never to vanish ...
I should go where there is no death,
where we could win some victory.
If I never died, if I were never to vanish ...

For this is the inevitable outcome of all powers, empires, and
    domains;
They are transitory and unstable.
The time of life is borrowed,
In an instant it must be left behind.

Ixtlilxóchitl's *Historical Works*

33

To Begin Again, At The End

In the opening pages, I described watching frigate birds from the balcony of my room at Rio Lagartos. I withheld something from you. Since books, like time, may be circular, the opportunity to tell it comes round again.

I opened my iPad, and went online. Swift shadows told me that frigate birds, those great sea wanderers whose bones are lighter than their feathers, were framing their pteradon silhouettes against the sky. In the far distance, beyond the band of mangrove on the seaward side of the lagoon, lay the open sea, where, Aztec scholars taught, the waters of the ocean merged with heaven at the horizon.

I browsed the Welsh newspapers, and found that my friend, the poet, activist, and much else, Nigel Jenkins, had died, aged 64. When we travel, we do not step outside life. It goes on regardless. I had been pondering how the last week of the trip would be wound up. Now it already was. Home was here already, and death, and resignation. I had had no idea he was ill, but nor (emailing soon established) had other mutual friends.

When I had told a few people about my cancer, he was the one who came straight back and said, 'When you are well enough, come to Mumbles to convalesce.' I went in August. By the Swansea seaside he cooked the few things I could eat, including sewin, Welsh sea trout, and watched me have a beer when it was an alcohol-free day on his diet. We walked along the cliffs of the Gower peninsula, which he was writing about, and he regaled me with the memories of his own life, his family's farm, and the biographies of the villages and the ruins, and the oldest burial in Western Europe in Goat's Hole Cave at Paviland, a 33,000 year-old skeleton buried with red ochre, talking us back to geological memories constructed from the contortions of the rocks. He took the lid off the landscapes and we peered into history's well. In the evenings, we swam before supper. I smiled at my skeletal figure beside his beefy frame, and hoped I still floated. My cancer had been treated, but it was too early to know if it had gone. Neither of us knew he had pancreatic cancer. You learn the status of the different cancers' horror. Ones on the pancreas create few symptoms until you are nearly dead. At first he had good news, that it was treatable. Further scans showed it had spread to the liver, and was not treatable. Diagnosed in the run-up to Christmas, he died before January was out. My first meeting with friends back in Britain would be his funeral in the family grave in the heart of the Gower peninsula, on a breezy, showery day. He chose the music himself, entering the church to Breton pipes, leaving to a Bach partita. The end of music leads us back to silence.

My former wife, Cath, died of her cancers four days after Nigel's funeral, on Valentine's Day. It was also her mother's birthday. That is all I know of it.

I could not come to terms with the fact that the strong man who had cared for me had, in reality, himself been near death, and I was still here. Not survivor guilt, but a deep strangeness. My blissful mood on the hotel terrace was swept aside by a deep, indigo sadness. Now, writing after an interval of half a year, this association has returned with new meaning. Nigel was a fighter. The Aztecs believed that everyone who died in battle transformed into magnificent birds and became a follower of the Sun, escorting him from sunrise to the zenith at midday. When I think of that day on the Gower, of Nigel and his writing and his principled life, I think of the frigate birds. I remember their jagged beauty and power of flight. They flew on another wind.

34

The Heart Of The Maya

I headed east, closing the circle. In Oaxaca, where the Monte Albán's calendar was crafted, the bus timetable slowly admitted that all journeys east required overnighting at places without interest for me. I lunched on a local dish, a bowl of grasshoppers, and considered options, when I wasn't considering how much they looked like cockroach parts. There was a night bus, but everyone said don't travel at night. That is when the drug traffickers and paramilitaries go to work. And the hold-up gangs. One bus went to within a few hours of Palenque's Mayan ruins, but it detoured 200 miles west first, doubling the journey to around 700 miles. I took the front seat looking down the highway ahead. Dusk filtered a tea-dark wash over the pastel colours of Oaxaca as we left the city and began to lick up cat's eyes. Nearing ten o'clock we skirted Puebla and turned back east into the mountains. On a pass, at half-past midnight, roadworks made single-file traffic. A fire burned in the lee of a gravel heap. Tea-sellers, their faces shining red or white in the glow of the car lights, sold brews to the waiting drivers until the flagmen changed the flow, and we growled through the gears and began the long roll into the next valley.

A name went past: Miahuatlán, already behind in the night. At four-fifteen I woke in a street lined with dust-grey buildings: a town re-imagined as a multi-storey car park. Nothing moved: no cat, drunk, policeman or pigeon. A single bicycle was parked beneath a lamp. I woke again as we entered a yard, and changed drivers. A sign: Yolís. Was it a village, or just a truck-stop? I sleepwalked into a white-lit dining room. Everyone stared at the gringo. I ordered black tea, but the thin youth whose shirt hung on him like washing on an airless day, barked '*¿Mande?*' – 'What?' I didn't know how loudly I was speaking, the mountains had wrecked my ears. I asked again and everyone stared. He repeated '*¿Mande?*' I was whispering, hearing everything through my jawbone. I spoke louder. My ears popped, and the world was back, I winced as chairs scraped over the concrete floor, and I found I was shouting.

When the sun came up, we were near the coast, and Coatzacoalcos. The driver cleared the coach to take on more fuel, handing the wheel to our third driver. Rainstorms broke as we came into Villahermosa, a crested caracara racing past the window for cover with deep, surging wingbeats. I found a minibus service to Palenque, and eighteen hours after leaving Oaxaca, stepped down into the pocket-sized bus station and, to stretch my legs, walked three miles to my jungle hotel.

Beginning two hundred years before Christ, Palenque flourished for a thousand years, then there was a readjustment in Maya life. Coastal settlements flourished, suggesting sea trade was becoming more important in a land where the only pack animals were men. The overall population remained much the same, and despite the claims of populist narrators like Jared Diamond, there was no collapse, but, in a region of city states, power moved from one to another, particularly from the south and east of Yucatán towards the north. While Palenque, Calakmul – 150 miles north-east, Tikal In northern Guatemala, Copán in western Honduras all declined, Chichén Itzá prospered until around 1250 AD, and was still inhabited, though without a rich, powerful elite, when the Spanish arrived. Expensive palaces, temples and public buildings were no longer erected, but the vast bulk of ordinary people had never enjoyed comfortable stone buildings. They went on living as they always had, and merchants continued to bring trade goods not available locally. One way of looking at this change is not as collapse, but reform; ordinary people no longer had to support the leeches at the top. I rested in a hammock overlooking a pond where gallinules paddled past motionless green herons, while a belted kingfisher, a stumpy street fighter a foot high, gripped a dead branch and glared down at the effontery of fish which remained uneaten. Next morning I flagged down a *colectivo* driven by a man in his

327

seventies, with a military moustache, a little English, and no ability to listen.

'One year, I guided a jungle tour, and Carol Thatcher was in the group, you know who she is?'

'Yes.'

'Well I'll tell you. She's Mrs Thatcher's daughter, and a photographer.'

'A journalist.'

'No, she had a big camera and couldn't relax. Spent the whole time asking about snakes.'

'Are there many?'

'Haven't seen one in five years.'

He charged four times the going rate, and stuck to it. It was tourist town.

As I waited at the entrance, drink sellers set up their stalls, hammering ice from slabs, the flying splinters sparking in the low sun. I walked through the last rags of morning mist into green plazas ringing with low visceral growls, answered by other roars from the trees across the plaza. Unseen howler monkeys made their way through the canopy. I was on the border of the range of the the mantled howler monkey and the Mexican black howler, whose calls are the same.

Below them was a city that prospered in Europe's Dark Ages, when the Beowulf poet sat out sunless winter days and spun rush-lit horror to pass the evenings. In his culture, a lord's status was signalled by fancy fire-irons, fine horse-harness and carved beam-ends on his mead hall. In Palenque, it was a square mile of gleaming palaces covered in complex bas-reliefs, civic buildings, temples raked from ground to top by staircases, and lined with brilliantly coloured frescoes. The European lords are forgotten and their halls survive only as post-holes in the earth. At Palenque we have a list of the rulers for 400 years, and their towering structures stand high above the forest of cedar, mahogany and *sapodilla*, bleached bones above a chlorophyll flood.

Palenque was found by the Spanish in 1773, but became a sensation after the arrival in 1840 of American adventurer and

Pakal ruled Palenque (also featured on cover photograph) from 615-683 AD.

author John L. Stephens, with London artist and architect Frederick Catherwood. Catherwood carried a camera lucida, a contrivance of mirrors and lenses which makes the object being depicted appear over the paper on which it will be drawn. It helped him organise the fantastically complex carvings correctly on the page. The public fell for the romance of unknown cities emerging from the sprawling jungle. The images are a metaphor for life. We struggle, carve out a corner for a while. When we stand back to admire it, it is already disappearing. Pomp is pierced by roots, hubris overgrown with vines, a tree splits the palace wall. Yet there is something admirable about our human determination to continue striving. At worst, Ozymandias lying ruined in the sand is better than an empty desert: worth a poem.

I emerged onto a green plaza with the mass of the Great Palace ahead, and the Temple of the Inscriptions rising over eighty feet high on my right. In 1952, after four years' work, excavations cleared staircases leading from the summit, down through the temple, to a burial chamber below ground level. At the bottom, on a fifteen-ton stone sarcophagus, lay a five-ton slab. In it, beneath a jade mask, was the face of K'inich Janaab' Pakal, King War-Shield, whose reign over Palenque lasted longer than any other monarch in the history of the Western hemisphere. Born in 603 AD, he took the throne aged twelve and ruled for sixty-eight years, beginning in the aftermath of Calakmul's conquest of Palenque. He may have been an outsider, perhaps a puppet installed by Calakmul, who took over the theatre. The sarcophagus was too large to have been brought down the tunnels: the pyramid had been built over him, and his chamber still supports those 50,000 tons of masonry.

I walked Palenque for four hours, then found the river Otolum, which flows through the middle of the site and into woodland, where it falls through cascades so artlessly picturesque you suspect a landscape gardener has been here. I snacked in the reviving shade and continued for three more hours, but I was still too tired to see one entire district. At night I sat in the modern town's square and read the local newspaper as the grackles swarmed rowdily above. A twenty-eight-year-old man had been found practising sexual self-suffocation in the public park three days before, and been driven out by disgusted citizens. Someone had found him there again and cut his throat then decapitated him. The assassin had struck before, and had been nicknamed *El Diablo*. I was leaving town anyway.

There was still full darkness just before six as I boarded the minibus. The full title of Mexico is the United States of Mexico, and I was in the most volatile of them: Chiapas. A third of the population is indigenous, divided between twelve ethnicities, and disaffection has been deep. In 1994 the Mexican President Carlos Salinas signed the North American Free Trade Agreement with the USA and Canada. The agreement would boost Mexican exports, but allow US firms to outsource factories to the north of Mexico, and benefit from lower wages and laxer regulation. Looking at this from the southern end of the country, Chiapas did not see it as relevant to their needs, and rose in armed rebellion, quelled by a mix of violence and diplomacy, followed by the government breaking the ceasefire. Tensions still simmer.

We followed the Usumacinta Valley. Most houses were traditional Maya huts, but they were walled with roughly-sawn hardwood boards. The way people stood and moved was different, standing as though there might be no need to move until the forest enclosed them, walking languidly as if the journey were uncertain, and might not be completed by the end of the day, or the end of another day. At roadblocks, torches approached through the rain, and police quizzed the driver about his destination and his passengers. A mounted machine gun stood behind a pile of car tyres. The police waited in barricaded command stations, or behind sandbagged walls, for the inevitable arrival of drug men who will be armed like commandoes, and may be dressed as policeman. At dawn we pulled over to breakfast at a thatched roadside café called Yax-Lum. Rags of mist washed the hills; this was the start of the highlands. The roads become rough, dry and dusty. They also grew narrower, and the jungle pressed closely in on us. At ten o'clock a row of huts came into view, standing in small yards, aspiring to be a village. Pale pink pigs with grey and brown mottles rooted and sniffed self-importantly. One concrete building, behind a wall topped with railings, was the emigration post for passengers crossing the River Usumacinta to the far bank, and Guatemala. Our pirogue took us downstream, over swiftly gliding green waters. Rising in Guatemala, it is Mexico's second largest river, after the Río Grande. Huge crocodiles lay on the riparian sandbanks. Ordinary males reach sixteen feet and weigh nearly half a ton. Birds were curiously rare, and mostly vultures and egrets: black and white. Gigantic dead trees were lodged in the banks, their roots stripped of earth: tangles of white ropework. Ten miles downriver the Usumacinta began a meander that has almost become an oxbow lake, enclosing a raised boss of jungle two miles in diameter. The spectacular location was one reason for wanting to visit Yaxchilan; the other was that the British Museum has fine panels from the site. When I returned, there would be a little bit of the Yucatán two miles from my home where I could bolster sentiments, and revive memory.

The grandest Maya sites mostly stand in landscapes manicured with lawns and gravel paths. Yaxchilan is still embedded in the forest. The site is so remote there are no fences, just a jungle trail, which soon showed signs of being a restored Maya path. A yellow and black bird like an oriole flashed in the corner of my eye. A stomachy roar came from ahead, and grew louder.

From the feature known as the Acropolis, I could see across the ravine the telltale signs of branches sagging as a troop of Mexican black howler monkeys fed on fruit and leaves. They were three times as far away as I had guessed from the power of the roar, and were only half the size. Adults weigh only ten to fifteen pounds, but they sound like miniature gorillas. It was a fitting place to watch them, the river's name, Usumacinta, means howler monkey. The main site is reached through corridors in windowless buildings where my torch lit up insect monsters the size of my hand, which gave me the same sense of unease as a tarantula. I emerged into a rectangular jungle clearing with ruins more dilapidated than others I had seen, but more emotive for the extent of their entwinement with the jungle. A central American agouti, a rodent the size of a middling dog, trotted across the clearing without concern. A pale-fronted thrush turned one eye to the sky as light rain tapped on the leaves.

On the return canoe trip, there were even larger crocodiles: big specimens approaching a ton in weight. They picked their feet up almost vertically, in a mechanical motion, like trainee robots. I found myself reading the river for hazards. This would not have been a good time to capsize. A final drive took us to Bonampak, home of the greatest Maya frescoes. My local guide, heavy-jawed, with epicanthic eyes, and wearing a traditional native white smock admitted 'They are losing the intensity of their colour, but the preservation is still remarkable: brilliant blues and chestnuts. One details dispels any idea of a tolerant Eden before the Spanish arrived. The year, the glyphs tell us, is 790 AD, and King Chan Muan is stabbing his spear through the face of a captive chieftain. Around the dying man are his nobles and generals, their fingers bleeding from having their fingernails torn out.' I climbed back in the minibus. For three seconds I watched the dreaming face of a young girl, leaning on a wicker gate, unselfconscious, thoughts passing like faint clouds across her face, never disturbing her beauty. Then the door slid shut and she passed into the shadow of memory. It was nearly midnight when I fell into bed. A dog howled like all purgatory perishing.

I returned to Campeche, and next day moved back into the interior of the Yucatán, and the Mayan ruins of Uxmal, which flowered as one of the finest cities of the eighth and ninth centuries. The first structure has a speculative modern name that suits it entirely: the Temple of the Magician. It breaks, like a submarine's conning tower, above the green forest sea, and its sides rise at angles of nearly fifty degrees, to a height of 130 feet. Broadly pyramidal in shape, the corners are smoothly rounded, giving it the air of a castle keep. Maya legend says an old childless woman cosseted an egg, and when it hatched, a boy dwarf crawled out. She told him he was destined to be king of Uxmal. The reigning king gave him three impossible tasks, the final one of which was to build a structure bigger than any other; in one night he built the Temple of the Magician.

Fifty-four steps lead to the entrance of the temple, whose doorway is the jaws of the cosmic monster. The architectural details are even finer than Palenque, and the air before them is graced by swallows which nest in the ruins of a courtyard as fine as any Oxbridge quadrangle. The first impression made on John L. Stephens in the 1840s was that they were the equal of Thebes. Uxmal boasts the longest carved panels of any Maya architecture, and those of the Governor's Palace are almost intact. The dominant motif is that of Chac the rain-god, a vital deity in a limestone plain where water is fugitive. His trunk-like nose fuelled early speculation that the ancestors of the hut-dwelling Maya the Spanish met could not have built these marvels; the Hindus, or perhaps the ancient Chaldeans had been here.

I went on, to Chichén Itzá, and Cobá and finally Ek' Balam where, as my journey was drawing to an end, I decided to treated myself to a special night. Ek' Balam is little known outside the Yucatán, and many visitors will drive past it to spend a full day at Chichén Itzá. I toured with Juan Tomás, who from the top of the pyramid pointed out his home village of Huauk. 'I didn't learn Spanish until I went to school, at home we spoke Yucatec Maya. I always loved the ruins. You can see the double wall enclosing the centre, it's one-and-a-half kilometres long, with fifty-two structures in it. Around it are about

The Temple of the Magician rising above the jungle at Uxmal.

six thousand platforms that used to be houses, so we estimate 24,000 to 30,000 people lived here.' Occasionally the top stone of a wall moved to better catch the sun, then the eye and mind blinked, and it became an iguana. Now, not a house is visible; the small villages lie below the level of the forest canopy. The pyramid on which we sat has a terrace midway up, and its doorway is a gaping mouth of a feline monster. I was suspicious of the crisp plaster detailing. It showed superb quality but appeared heavily rebuilt. 'Not at all,' said Juan. 'Ninety per cent was intact, we have done restoration, but no reconstruction.' In my last week, I was still being surprised.

Over a mile down a narrow track was a cenote, a collapsed cavern in the limestone whose bottom lies below the water table. In a land with almost no lakes and few rivers, they were invaluable sources of water in the dry season. Rough wooden steps had been built to climb down the fifty feet to the water. Cenotes often form neat circles, and the walls are lined with tree roots and lianas hanging the full length to suckle below. I stripped off and dived in among the lazy fish, while northern rough-winged swallows drank on the wing. Some cenotes are part of cave systems; one has been explored for a distance of sixty-two miles. I tried to quell the B-feature scenarios forming in my head of some plug being blown out and my beginning the underground roller-coaster ride to die for.

Nearby there was a café, where women's voices speaking Maya quietly mingled with chinking plates. Woodsmoke scented the air. At five o'clock they left, leaving me alone. I pitched my tent under the trees and lay in a hammock, reading as the sun set. Bird calls faded and died. I went again to the cenote and sat with my feet in the water. The swallows had been replaced by bats. A moon one night past full rose behind the curtain of trees in front of me; fish brushed their lips along my feet.

I walked to my tent, but I was not alone. All over the leaf litter, almost on top of each other, spiders' eyes reflected my lamp; the forest floor a jeweller's tray under the sweep of a burglar's torch.

35

Envoi

When Spain shall be in America hid
and Mexico shall prove a Madrid.
Then think strange things are come to light,
whereof but few have had a foresight.
A PROPHECY SENT TO SIR THOMAS BROWNE
FOR INTERPRETATION. *COLLECTED WORKS* 1684

My mind goes back to Gonzalo Guerrero, the shipwrecked sailor who refused the pleas of his companion Aguilar to return to the Spanish world. He had become the son-in-law of Na Chan Can, Lord of Chactemal. Guerrero: his name means warrior, and he fought for his Maya masters. He knew the Spanish and the Maya, and he chose the Maya. When Spanish ships arrived, he was under no illusions as to what the countrymen of his birth would do. Negotiation was useless, he advised. The Maya must kill and kill again. Guerrero led them in that fight for nineteen years. In the end, on 13 August 1536, he was killed by something he could not fight: a lead ball fired from an arquebus. His body was found floating in the sea, still suspended between two worlds: the salt cool below, the quivering air above.

When Odysseus, that sufferer of the sea, met Tiresias in the underworld, the seer predicted: 'When you get home you will take your revenge on these suitors; and after you have killed them, you must take a well-made oar and carry it until you come to a country where the people have never heard of the sea and do not even mix salt with their food, nor do they know anything about ships. A wayfarer will meet you and will say it must be a winnowing shovel

336

that you have got upon your shoulder.' There Odysseus must fix the oar in the ground, and sacrifice to the gods. Before you can rid yourself of the sea, penance must be performed. Did Guerrero march with an oar that had saved him from drowning, going inland until he could let go of the past?

His fellow captive Aguilar chose the other route, returning to the Spanish fold, and playing a key role in the victory as a translator. After the conquest, he was rewarded with a gift of land and several *encomiendas*, which granted the use of Natives as tied serfs. He later fell out with Cortés, and gave evidence against him in proceedings in 1529.

When Aguilar was first freed, he had been questioned about his religion during the time with heathens, and he had assured them his faith had never been deflected, and pointed to the battered prayer book he still kept by him. But a feeling lingered, as he told stories of Maya temples, idols, and sacrifices, that he must have been contaminated. The Spanish came from a homeland only recently freed from Islam. After 1492 Moors and Jews had to convert or be expelled. When they had gone, the appetite for persecution had been whetted, but the only remaining targets were Protestants abroad and the converts at home. Were the *conversos* sincere, or was it done out of convenience? Did they practise their old religion in secret? Guilt fuelled suspicion, for we never forgive our victims. The spirit of the witch-hunt haunted the rest of Aguilar's life, but his faith seemed strong, and he became a canon of Mexico City Cathedral in the 1520s, with well-known friends. But when the light falls on him for the final time, he dies of buboes 'poor and in want', aged about fifty-seven, perhaps when he was living in a house in Calle Moneda opposite the side entrance to the modern Government Palace on Mexico's main square. It later housed the first printing press in the New World, linking the translator again with communication. He left little, but we all inherit something.

When I return home, I will visit my father. The clutch between the current time and memory fails to engage. He asks 'When are you going? It's lunchtime; they'll be bringing my food.'

'I've just spoken to the carer. Lunch isn't for an hour.'

337

'Isn't it?'

'No, another hour. We can talk.'

'Oh! That's good. And when do you have to go?'

'In an hour.'

'That's awkward because lunch will be here any minute.'

My father's time is cyclic, and the loop is a noose whose knot is slipping tighter.

My mother suffered a decline like this over two years. I was not upset when she died. Not because it was a blessing, but because I had been saying goodbye to little pieces of her for years: to her ability to go for walks along the cliffs, to shop, to leave the flat alone, to leave it at all except for treatment. She had said farewell to conversations, to continence, to recognising the face of her husband of sixty years. I said hello to introducing myself to her each time we met.

I have this gene on both sides.

Now I am saying goodbye to my father in small sad ways. The goodbyes are nearly finished. But when I move towards the door, his face animates in a big smile, 'Thank you so much for coming, it was such a lovely surprise.' His eyes are dry, mine moist. We hug carefully, gently, both bony thin. And so the generations pass.

There is an anonymous Aztec poem.

It is not true, it is not true
That we come to this earth to live.
We come only to sleep, only to dream.
Our body is a flower.
As grass becomes green in the springtime,
So our hearts will open, and give forth buds,
And then they wither.

The industrial expansion of Seville westward has engulfed the village of Castilleja de la Cuesta. Cortés, came to the house he owned here in 1547, aged sixty-two years, my age as I finish this manuscript, and had survived everything the New World had thrown at him. He had been a Nimrod, the Biblical Hunter, stalking Moctezuma. His imagination drove him to dare, to conquer, then, as he understood how he had done it, through butchery, terror, disease and starvation, his purpose withered, until only a dark, formless ambition drove him on. He was lured forwards by the receding horizon of conquest, following it to spiritual and political wastes, the Hell of Honduras, hunting down his former lieutenant Cristóbal de Olid, who had briefly carved himself a kingdom there. On the way out they passed through Malinche's old village. Cortés summoned the chiefs. Malinche's mother, and the half-brother Lazaro for whose preferment she had been sold, came trembling, expecting revenge. Díaz reported Malinche looked very like her mother. When she saw their tears, Malinche forgave them. She gave them gold and clothes.

Cortés fathered a terrible entropy. He dragged Cuauhtémoc, the last ruler of Tenochtitlán, along with them in chains. Cuauhtémoc was never cowed, and held on to his contempt until the last. When he and another chief were tortured to try to extract more treasure, he disdained the other victim's cries: 'Do you think I am lying on a bed of flowers?' His feet were being burned in a fire at the time. On the way Cortés accused Cuauhtémoc of conspiring with local tribes to attack the Spanish. Cuauhtémoc was tortured and hanged. The execution was an act of pointless, vicious violence symbolic of the whole expedition. Mexican historian Salvador de Madariaga expresses the national melancholy bound up with these losses: 'Every day, within the soul of every Mexican, Moctezuma dies and Cuauhtémoc is hanged.' Cortés reached Honduras after extraordinary hardships to find that Olid had been disembowelled by two friends of Cortés even before Cortés had left Mexico City. He was visibly aged and began wearing a black Dominican gown. Cortés divested himself of Malinche, marrying her to Juan Jaramillo. She gave birth to Jaramillo's baby on the terrible journey home.

Returning to Mexico he found it becoming a land of administrators; the days of autocratic military governance were gone. He was sidelined. Carlos Fuentes has written that Cortés was stifled with estates and titles, when ambition and movement were his life. He returned to Spain expecting to lead a massive naval attack on Algiers for which he was qualified only by hubris. He was incredulous to see it led by Andrea Doria, a military man experienced enough to believe the venture was folly, but loyal enough to still do his best. It was a disaster.

Cortés had spent heavily on campaigns, lost his best jewels in a shipwreck, and needed cash. His daughter could marry the son of a marquis if Cortés could find 60,000 ducats for a dowry. He spent three years in Madrid, seeking preferment at court, or just a pay-off. Cortés then picked up an old man's vice: litigation. He was forever petitioning, and claiming to be impoverished (he was not). The court had stopped listening; he could defeat generals but not courtiers. Obsessed by his legacy, he worried that his line would die out. Cortés's last letter to the Emperor Charles V ventured, 'If daughters succeed, memory is lost.' In 1629, Pedro Cortés, the Fourth Marquis de la Valle, died. This grandson was his last male heir. The vast palace on the square in Cuernavaca would, after a generation, be shut up, unusable. It became an ironworks, then a tannery, a barracks and a jail.

Cortés gave up and determined to return to Mexico, but he had contracted dysentery, and was unwell. He reached his house in Castilleja de la Cuesta and took to his bed. An orange tree outside the window still bore the last of its fruit. There he died.

Nimrod had conspired with another giant, Antaeus, to build the Tower of Babel, and so had brought upon mankind the confusion of many languages, while Nimrod himself was condemned to speak the old language, which no one else understood any more.

The monarch Cortés served during the conquest was the Emperor Charles V. As well as being Holy Roman Emperor, he was king, archduke, duke, margrave or count of twenty-two territories. This was achieved by his family, the Habsburgs, marrying and remarrying in a small pool of European aristocrats. The price was paid in infirmity and deformity. Charles ate in private because his large and twisted jaw made chewing difficult, and caused poor digestion. He developed crippling gout. His son Philip II would marry Queen Mary Tudor and become King of England, but die a vile death as his body rotted, but he lived on for fifty-three days before succumbing to fever, dropsy, and a gout which erupted in open wounds all over his body.

The last Habsburg, Charles the Bewitched, would die in Madrid in 1700, five days before his thirty-ninth birthday. The physician who conducted the post mortem recorded that the body 'did not contain a single drop of blood; his heart was the size of a peppercorn; his lungs corroded; his intestines rotten and gangrenous; he had a single testicle, black as coal, and his head was full of water.'

Bernal Díaz died soon after completing his decades-long history. In his prologue he had written 'What I myself saw'. It is a simple phrase of great weight. As we grow older, and describe the time behind us to younger people whose time lies mostly ahead, we insist on the value of witness, or else why did we live, endure?

Malinche, in a fashion paralleling the way Aztec gods acquire new associations and meanings, became a complex symbol, which has changed over time. The Aztecs saw her as an enemy not a traitor. She owed nothing to them. In the nineteenth century, white Hispanic nationalists like the writer Ignacio Ramírez recast her. She had to fill one of the limited number of roles male history grants women. She was rewritten as a collaborator. All Indians were alike, so she had betrayed her own, she was the Eve who helped exile Mexicans from Eden.

Because of the mores, or lack of them, of the men she was taken by, Malinche was never the exclusive partner of any man she was with, but she was a strong personality who throughout her short life coped with extremes of fortune without faltering. She would pray with the deposed emperor Cuauhtémoc in Nahuatl when he was about to die, and later marry a former theologian at the Sorbonne, who had been personal confessor to the Emperor Charles V of Spain.

She was not more than twenty-nine at the time of her own death. The last document to refer to her concerned a grant of land for a sheep-run in the city, 'beside the wall of Chapultépec'. Her burial place is unknown. The son she bore Cortés was ignored by his father, who called him Martín, then also named his next son, born to a Spanish mother, Martín, as though the Mestizo did not exist. Malinche's son went to Spain, became a page to Queen Isabela until her death in childbirth, and then served King Philip II: a long journey for a slave's son.

341

His Hispanic half-brother may have met him in England when Philip II married Mary Tudor there in the summer of 1554. Hispanic Martín was definitely there in December of that year, as we have a fascinating window on him among the English aristocrats. A rare book of chivalry, William Segar's *Honor Military and Civill* of 1602 says that a tournament was held in Westminster yard, lasting from midday until five o'clock and those jousting for their ladies' honour included Sir Thomas Percy, Sir George Howard, Prince Philip and Martín Cortés.

This Martín was of course made heir to the titles and estates of Hernán Cortés, and he became obsessed with status. But he valued his father's money more than his achievements. It is always nice when a contemporary who knew him well can sum him up. A third half-brother, Luis, called him *cargadito,* the little shit.

After death, she took on another persona for the indigenous people, which spread to the Mestizos. It derived from the Aztec goddess Coatlicue, or serpent skirt, who was Huitzilopochtli's mother. A nine-foot tall statue of her, dug out from the Zócalo in 1790, is one of the most terrifying objects in Mexican art. She stands on massive taloned feet, which protrude from a skirt of live rattlesnakes, held up by a belt whose buckle is a human skull. Her breasts are covered by a necklace of severed hands and hearts. She is pictured at the moment which brings both her death and the birth of her avenging son, Huitzilopochtli. She holds out the bleeding stumps of her arms, demanding vengeance, and from the socket in her neck spring the heads of two snakes which turn to face each other, creating a new reptilian head. The image was terrifying to the Spanish, but when the statue was exhumed and went on display Native people began placing flowers round her and kneeling to pray. It was reburied, and when the polymath Alexander von Humboldt came to Mexico City in 1803 wishing to make a drawing of it, he had to have it dug up once more. Such was its potency to the Natives, it was afterwards committed to the ground yet again.

If you were awake at night and heard the howls of a woman, that was Coatilcue, wailing for the children murdered by her son to save her. Her cries foretold impending disaster. They was heard before the Spanish came. She morphed into Malinche, wailing for lost Mexico. She had a house just north of Mexico City's Zócalo at 96 Calle Cuba. It is now a school, where sleepless children hear her crying at night. She is La Llorona, the Weeping Woman.

There is a picture in the Florentine Codex of Malinche on top of a low tower with Cortés, but her head is turned over her left shoulder talking to a Native in the street below. After the fashion of Native codices, the words she addresses are drawn as a flight of glyphs, motifs like bird chicks, taking wing unsurely, fluttering to the man below. Like La Llorona, Malinche's own words, her true self, were carried far on the wind, and never fell to the page.

The country they conquered is today so big that Tijuana in north-west Mexico is nearer to Juneau Alaska than it is to Cancun in the Yucatán. Old Native Mexico has not gone away. It has remerged in forms more palatable to the Mestizo culture which forms mainstream Mexico. Widespread exposure to the bland non-culture of international consumerism, especially from its hugely powerful neighbour, the United States, has confirmed in many minds how important it is to be Mexican first. Look in a hotel mirror and the world seems much like any other Latin country. Look in a Native obsidian mirror; panther-dark figures are behind you in the room.

36

Final Diagnosis

I walked through the streets of Paddington to St Mary's Hospital for the results of the whole body scan, taken a few days before. For an hour I had been left in a small room and told not to read or listen to music. Such pleasures stimulate parts of the brain to show up as false hot spots on the scan, like cancers. After an hour, in which the parts of the brain dedicated to boredom and anxiety had been stimulated to the full, I had been laid carefully in position in the sarcophagus tube of the scanner, and wedged still. The narrow platform on which I lay moved in and out of the scanner's eye. Then I went home to wait.

After months of focusing on the business of treatment, and blanking out the unknowable question, *Is it working?*, I would now find out if I had a lucky lottery ticket. Spin a dial with ten numbers on it. Nine are good. What's yours? A 10 percent chance of dying. But as my neighbour Tony had put it so simply: if it's you, you're 100 percent dead.

The consultant started to ask how I was, flicking through files on screen. Celia realised before I did.

'We haven't had the result of the scan yet.'

'Haven't you?'

Imaginary responses filled my head, none of them helpful to a constructive long-term relationship with the doctor.

'No.'

'It's ... ' He brought up the report on the screen.

What he says now is not just good news or bad, but my life, do I have one or not? ' ... excellent. I haven't seen it myself but the radiographer's report is excellent.' Celia and I hugged, not ecstatically, the delivery had been too anticlimactic. But I had a future. I would plant seeds and bulbs on our patio and see them come up next autumn and spring.

He loaded up the scan on his computer and took me through it, showing slices of my body starting at the feet. The throat was fine, the Christmas tree lights which had lit up most of my chest were almost all gone: they were secondary irritations, sarcoid growths, not cancers.

I saw a small but very bright hot spot in my neck. 'What about that?' 'The report doesn't mention that.' He leaned forward, perplexed. 'Where is it on my body?'

He turned and reached out with a finger, touching me on the neck. Just before the scan, on that exact spot, a gland had swollen then subsided in a few days, leaving me terrified in the interim. I had shown it to Tony, who pointed out it was soft not hard, and it soon vanished of its own accord. 'An infection,' I said.

'Was it?' he asked, a mild frown disturbing his ski-tan.

I asked about Doctor Basak, the kind and patient young registrar who had done all the day-to-day management of my case. 'Moved on, but she mentioned your name. Wants to do a paper on your case.'

'What aspect?' I felt vaguely flattered that some incidental benefit would come out of this, something to help others, to give me a small footnote in medical history.

'Sort of warning to others really.'

Some lifestyle choice others should not follow?

'Not to give up. I didn't say before, but when we saw the initial body scan and all those lights in your chest, I nearly cancelled all treatment as useless. It was an image I'll never forget: so many lights. In the end I thought we'd treat what we knew, the cancer in the neck, and leave alone what we couldn't, hoping they were benign.'

When I managed to speak I moved on. 'So I don't need any more treatment, it hasn't come back?'

He looked surprised at my comment. 'If this comes back it's very serious indeed. You have had all the radiation we could ever give you, a lifetime's supply. No, you don't want this back.' I went out holding Celia's hand tightly, into a cool afternoon, feeling the fragility of all life. This all-clear was not a key to immortality, just the start of the rest of the lease we all have, short and insecure. After a bitterly cold spring the trees were bolting into leaf and straight into flower so as not to waste any of this sudden warmth. Between Victorian terraces we walked, into the shapeless spaces between tower blocks. I stopped every fifty yards to embrace and pull Celia's soft body against my washboard ribs. Pressed close, we could feel our slowly dilating lungs, and hear anxious loving hearts.

Explanatory Notes

Accents

Spanish uses the acute accent on vowels to mark where the stress falls in irregular words. It does not alter the pronunciation.

Aztec

Aztec is a wrong word that has stuck, through being popularised by W. H. Prescott's masterly nineteenth-century narrative history *The Conquest of Mexico*. I use it because there are so many unfamiliar Spanish names and wholly exotic Native words that the general reader deserves not to have the few familiar handles like Aztec changed to something strange. The people were known as the Mexica, and their country, so far as they thought of themselves as having a country beyond the city-state of Tenochtitlán, was Mexico.

Indian

Natives of the Americas were called Indians through Columbus's insistence that he had reached India and China, and not a new continent. In the USA it can cause offence to use the term now. In the region I am writing about it does not, and is often embraced as a distinction from the Hispanic peoples and the Mestizos, mixed Indian and Hispanic peoples.

Nahuatl

Nahuatl is the language spoken by the Aztecs and some neighbouring groups. Their language was Nahuatl, with the stress on the first syllable. Where Native words have *tl* in them, the *l* is hardly pronounced, so it sounds as if one had started to say 'Atlantic' but stopped abruptly after the L; there is no syllable after it, of the kind English has in 'rattle'.

Quotes

I have altered some quotes from old chronicles to make them clearer, replacing, for instance, a pronoun with a person's name.

Spelling

Place names in particular may vary when European spelling is applied to Native words. The letters z, x and j may appear for each other. I have used the version I saw most used in the place itself.

Tenochtitlán – Mexico City – Mexico

The Aztec capital was a very different place before and after the conquest, and I call it Tenochtitlán before and Mexico City afterwards, although the Hispanic city sits right on top of the Aztec one. Mexicans, confusingly for the new arrival, simply call their capital Mexico. I don't employ that usage without saying so.

X in Native words

X in a Native word is usually pronounced sh: Texcoco is *Teshcoco*.

List of Maps

Acknowledgements

Sources

A full bibliography will appear on my website:
www.cloudroad.co.uk.

Hugh Thomas's magisterial *The Conquest of Mexico,* Random House 1993, provided the spine of the historical narrative, while pocket portraits of the Spanish usually come from his invaluable *Who's Who of the Conquistadors*. Any book by Inga Clendinnen is an informative treat to read. I studied *Ambivalent Conquests, Maya and Spaniard in Yucatan, 1517-1570*, CUP 1987, and *Aztecs*, CUP, 1991. The article I refer to on Monte Albán and the calendar is *Sun Above Sun Below: Astronomy, Calendar and Architecture at Monte Albán and Teotihuacán*, Arqueología Oaxaqueña Serie Popular 2, by Damon E Peeler and Marcus Winter published by CONACULTA-INAH 2010. Matthew Restall's *Seven Myths of the Spanish Conquest* OUP 2003 provided ideas and guidance on re-writing the narrative of the conquest. Patricia A. McAnany and Norman Yoffee's *Questioning Collapse* deserves wide readership for debunking simplistic analyses of cultural change to serve modern needs.

Thanks to Allen J. Christenson, for quotations from *Popol Vuh: The Sacred Book of the Maya*, Winchester Books 2003. Most Cortés quotes are from Anthony Pagden's scholarly edition of *Letters From Mexico Hernán Cortés*, Yale UP edition 1986, and I am indebted in my discussions of the early descriptions of the New World to Pagden's books *The Fall of Natural Man* and *European Encounters with the New World*. Stephen Greenblatt's *Marvellous Possessions* covers similar territory with equal aplomb, and I am indebted to Greenblatt's *The Swerve: How the Renaissance Began,* for my summaries of Lucretius.

The quotes of Bernal Díaz come from J. M. Cohen's Folio Society edition of 1974: *The Conquest of New Spain*, and those of Francisco López de Gómara's *Cortés, The Life of the Conqueror,* from Lesley Byrd Simpson's University of California Press edition of 1964. José de Acosta's *Natural and Moral History of the Indies* I read in the translation of Frances López-Morillas, edited by Jane E Mangan, 2002 Duke University. When quoting Diego Durán's *The History of the Indies of New Spain*, I am grateful for the Orion Press translation of 1964 by Doris Heyden and Fernando Horcasitas. Quotes from Bernadino de Sahagún's *History of the Things of the New World* come from both James Lockhart's version, *We People Here: Nahuatl Accounts of the Conquest of Mexico*, Wipf and Stock 1993, and the 1989 University of Utah Press edition of H.F. and S.L. Cline. Burgos R S Thomas with kind permission of Orion Books. Day of the Dead endpapers with kind permission of Nicole Deleon Design.

Quotes from Dante's *Divine Comedy* are courtesy of the Everyman edition translated by Allen Mandelbaum.

People

I must first embarrass my partner Celia for being everything I could want from a partner in good times and bad, and being my first editor when I read each day's work to her. I owe a real debt to Francesca Rhydderch, my wise and painstaking editor.

Special thanks to all the professional people in Mexico who gave me their time and knowledge, especially Areli López Carmona, tourism director at Ixtacamaxtitlàn, the archaeologists Jamie Cortés Hernández and Arlette Soloveichik, and Alejandro Negroe of INEGI.

Thanks also to the Mexican Embassy, Elizabeth Baquedano of UCL, Elizabeth Graham of UCL and to Richard Mawdslay of the British Mexican Society for their invaluable advice.

I would like to thank the Welsh Books Council and Parthian for the initial commission to write and research this book.

Because of my illness, and loss of earnings, I am especially grateful to Arts Council England for a grant to assist with travel costs, and the award by the Society of Authors under the Authors' Foundation and K. Blundell scheme of a grant to buy time to write on my return.

A short version of some of the cancer material was published first in the *New Welsh Review* Spring 2014, republished here with kind permission of editor Gwen Davies.

All photographs and illustrations are by, and copyright of, John Harrison, except the cover photographs of the author which are the copyright of Celia Ansdell. Portrait of Moctezuma courtesy of Museo degli Argenti Florence.

My greatest thank you is to all the ordinary people all over Mexico who took time to guide a stranger, explain things, cook invalid food for me, and let me walk a mile with them.

CYNGOR LLYFRAU CYMRU
WELSH BOOKS COUNCIL

Supported using public funding by
ARTS COUNCIL
ENGLAND

JOHN HARRISON

Winner of the **BRITISH GUILD OF TRAVEL WRITERS'**
BEST NARRATIVE BOOK AWARD

THE FAR-SOUTH TRILOGY

'His approach is thorough and his excitement contagious...'
The Independent on Sunday